Born Again

Born Again
A Biblical and Theological Study
of Regeneration

Peter Toon

BAKER BOOK HOUSE
Grand Rapids, Michigan 49516

Copyright 1987 by
Baker Book House Company

ISBN: 0–8010–8885–2

Library of Congress Catalog Card Number: 86–72755

Printed in the United States of America

To my good friend
Jim Douglas,
editor of fine reference books
and a kind, witty, and caring brother

Contents

Preface

The expression "born again" became increasingly common in North America in the 1970s—much to the amazement of us Europeans, for whom personal religion is a more private affair. We noticed articles in prestigious magazines (e.g., *Time,* 27 Sept. 1976) and concluded that America must be a very religious country since there are so many twice-born people in it! We realized that "born again" was taken from the old translation of John 3:3, and, rightly or wrongly, many of us tended to attribute the modern-day emphasis on the new birth to the evangelistic activity of Billy Graham. We pictured him always preaching on "Ye must be born again."

In the late 1980s, it is still perhaps true that many in Europe think of "born again" as a peculiarly American expression pointing to some kind of conversion experience followed by religious activism. As a minister of the Church of England, I am better informed than most of my fellow Europeans as to the "born again" phenomenon because I have had the time and taken the opportunity to study the theology of the new birth. This book is the result of my study of both the sacred Scriptures and the teaching of the church throughout history.

I see the book as primarily for those who preach or who teach in colleges and seminaries. However, I hope that it is written in such a way that the person who is not schooled in theology will be able, with a little extra effort, to understand it. To help such a person and any who are slow starters in theological thinking, I begin the book with a simple chapter paraphrasing the famous conversation between Jesus and Nicodemus which is recorded in John 3. This easy-to-read chapter sets the scene for the rest of Part One, a study of the biblical evidence concerning what is called personal regeneration. In Part Two I present a chronological study of the most important approaches to and explanations of regeneration. Theologians from the patristic period up to Billy Graham are represented. Finally, in the Epilogue I offer a summary of what I see as the doctrine of new birth.

My work is not definitive; rather it is explorative. Others will certainly write better books on this theme. My purpose is to stimulate interest and further study by Christian leaders, preachers and teachers.

I owe a debt to my friend Walter Elwell of Wheaton Graduate School for linking me to Baker Book House and to their kind editor Allan Fisher. I am also most grateful to the trustees of the Billy Graham Center at Wheaton for making it possible for me to travel to and work in their archives and library. Other friends have given me help—of these I particularly wish to mention Steve Motyer, Albert Freundt, Joel Carpenter, and Wesley Wilkie.

Peter Toon

April 1986
The County of Suffolk
England

PART ONE

The Biblical Evidence

1

Jesus and Nicodemus

By no means the only, but certainly the most familiar biblical source on the topic of new birth or spiritual regeneration is John 3:1–15. This is the record of the conversation between Jesus and Nicodemus. We shall begin with a dramatized paraphrase of what passed between them. It will prepare us to study in subsequent chapters the theme of birth from above.

Narrator: In Jerusalem for the purpose of observing the Jewish Passover, Jesus has dramatically cleared the temple of those who were not treating it with due reverence. He has also performed certain notable miracles which have given him an immediate following. One of those who are attracted to Jesus is Nicodemus, a member of the supreme Jewish council and lawcourt, called the Sanhedrin. He belongs to the Pharisees, a religious sect devoted to the law of Moses, to the "tradition of the elders," which is a strict oral interpretation of that law, and to the hope that the Messiah will liberate the Israelite people from Roman rule. The Pharisees also believe that when the Messiah eventually comes, there will be a resurrection of the dead.

Nicodemus comes to Jesus by night, partly because rabbis tend to teach late into the night and partly because he wants to talk to Jesus alone, free from the interruptions of others.

Nicodemus: Some of my colleagues and I know that you are a teacher sent from God. We acknowledge that God is with you; else you could never perform the miracles that you have been performing in Jerusalem and in Cana of Galilee. I would like to know more of your teaching, especially how and when the kingdom of God will come.

Jesus: This is not the time for abstract discussion but for plain speaking! I tell you solemnly and truthfully that unless a man is begotten from above, he cannot in fact see the kingdom of God. To see and recognize the kingdom of heaven requires spiritual eyes, and only those who are born from above, who have a new life which originates in heaven, possess such eyes. It is necessary to be born of God in order to inherit eternal life.

Narrator: Nicodemus is startled by this direct but somewhat mysterious speech. He is obviously not familiar with this kind of religious talk, especially the idea of being born all over again.

Nicodemus: How can a man be born all over again when he is old like me? How can I shrink to enter again my mother's womb? It is impossible for me an old man to put aside what I have become through the course of more than fifty years and begin all over again. You do not seem to be speaking of real possibilities.

Jesus: I solemnly and truthfully tell you that unless a man is born of both water and the Spirit, he is totally unable to enter the kingdom of God. The birth from above is caused by the Holy Spirit; the birth in water is the act of baptism, which is, first, an outward and visible sign of both inner washing and renewal, and, second, a commitment to God in repentance and faith. John the Baptist offered the sign of baptism and so do my disciples and I, but the begetting by God is the work of the Holy Spirit alone.

Consider the birth of a human baby. The child is begotten by the father, whose sperm causes the baby to be formed in the womb where he or she develops until born. When born the baby is of the same human nature and flesh as the parents. Consider now being begotten by God or birth from above. This is the work of the Holy Spirit, and thus what is created is new spiritual life in the soul, a nonphysical, nonfleshy reality.

In the light of this, you should not be surprised, Nicodemus, that I insist that you and your colleagues, in fact all Jews, must be begotten or born again if you are to see and to enter the kingdom of God. The wind is invisible but its effects can be seen; in a similar way, the Spirit is invisible but his effects on human lives—repentance, faith, and faithfulness—can be seen. Remember the prophecy of Ezekiel [ch. 37] concerning the valley of dry bones, how God's breath caused them to become living people!

Narrator: Nicodemus still looks puzzled even though he appears to be grasping the drift of what Jesus is telling him.

Nicodemus: How can a person be begotten from above, born of the Spirit that comes from heaven? Where and when does such a thing happen, and what has to be done to cause it to happen?

Jesus: Surely as a professional teacher of the sacred Scriptures, which record God's Word for us, you must have read in the Prophets of the new covenant, the new communion with God, the outpouring of the Spirit, the dwelling of the Spirit in human hearts, and the rich spiritual blessings of the new age. John the Baptist, my disciples, and I have been speaking of these promised gifts from heaven. For us the idea of being born from above is not strange but biblically based. Nicodemus, I have used simple earthly illustrations of birth and wind to communicate what I proclaim and teach from God. But you along with the Jewish people have not received my teaching in your hearts. How will you believe if I now go on to speak of further heavenly teaching? You see, I came into this world from heaven and so I do truly speak of heavenly things. I know what I am talking about, and that is why you must receive what I say. There will come a time when I shall be lifted up (just as, you will recall, the serpent on the pole was lifted up by Moses in the wilderness centuries ago). The purpose of my being lifted up will be to give people an opportunity to believe in me and, being born from above, to receive eternal life.

Narrator: Here we leave the conversation (which continues as only a monologue as Jesus explains more of his position as God's Son and the Light of the world). Only later will Nicodemus come to realize what it means to be born of the Spirit and for Jesus to be lifted up, via the cross, to heaven in resurrection and ascension. In fact, Nicodemus will accompany Joseph of Arimathea to ask Pilate, the Roman governor, for the body of Jesus in order to give it a proper burial.

2

Jesus and the Spirit

However we may define the new birth, it clearly occurs in the human soul through the action of the Spirit of the living God, who has been called, since the resurrection of Jesus, the "Spirit of Christ." Further, the new birth is dependent upon the saving work of Jesus' life, death, and resurrection (as John 3:14–15 shows). He was, and is, the Christ-Messiah, that is, the One anointed with the Spirit of God. Indeed, his public ministry began when he was uniquely anointed as he came up out of the river Jordan following his baptism.

With this in mind, it is appropriate that before we turn to examine what may be called personal inward regeneration, we briefly look at the relation of Jesus to the Holy Spirit. Obviously the Spirit who regenerates the individual and who creates the new people of God is the same Spirit who came upon (and remains upon) Jesus the Messiah. We shall, therefore, better appreciate the action of God in bringing new life to the human soul if we set that work against the background of the action of God the Holy Spirit in, upon, and through Jesus, who is the new Israel.[1]

Ezekiel had prophesied the rebirth of Israel by the action of the breath of God the Spirit. In the well-known prophecy of the valley of dry bones the Lord says, "I will put my Spirit in you and you will live, and I

---

1. A useful study of the person and work of the Spirit is Alasdair I. C. Heron, *The Holy Spirit*.

will settle you in your own land. Then you will know that I the LORD have spoken, and I have done it" (Ezek. 37:14). Jesus as the Messiah is the new Israel: in and through him alone can the rebirth and renewal of Israel occur. (In John 2 this work of Jesus is foreshadowed by the making of water into wine and by the cleansing of the temple.) The Messiah had the double calling of causing both the whole Jewish people and each individual member to be reborn by the Spirit who was in and with him.

We shall now look briefly at the information available in the synoptic Gospels, John's Gospel, and the Acts. This done, we shall attempt to understand the meaning of the baptism of Jesus, since it provides light by which to appreciate the meaning of the rite of baptism in the apostolic church. This task is necessary because there is in the apostolic teaching a close relation between the gift of the Spirit and baptism.

Biblical Material on the Relationship Between Jesus and the Spirit

The Synoptic Gospels

In the synoptic Gospels there is not an abundance of material on the relationship between Jesus and the Spirit because the center of attention is Jesus and his proclamation of the arrival of the kingdom of God—the age of fulfilment of the prophecies. However, that information which is provided is highly significant when it is read against the background of the prophecies concerning the Spirit's anointing the Messiah (e.g., Isa. 11:1–5; 42:1–4; 61:1).[2]

1. The conception of Jesus is presented as occurring by the action of the Holy Spirit, the Life-Giver, in the womb of Mary the virgin (Matt. 1:18–20; Luke 1:35). With the conception and birth of Jesus, God had begun his new creation. It is important to observe how much Luke, especially, in his first two chapters emphasizes the presence and work of the Spirit in the events connected with the birth and early days of Jesus (see, e.g., 1:15, 35, 41, 67; 2:25–27).

2. The baptism of Jesus was the occasion for the descent upon him of the Holy Spirit in the form of a dove (Matt. 3:16; Mark 1:10; Luke 3:22). Though sinless, Jesus identified himself with a baptism for the sinful in order to become the Savior of the sinful through his role as the Messiah anointed with the Spirit.

3. The testing of Jesus occurred immediately after his baptism when he was led into the wilderness by the Holy Spirit (Matt. 4:1; Mark 1:12;

---

2. For the Holy Spirit as presented in the Gospels see J. D. G. Dunn, *Jesus and the Spirit,* and C. K. Barrett, *The Holy Spirit and the Gospel Tradition.*

Luke 4:1). There Jesus began his fight against Satan and demonic power. He also faced the temptations which ancient Israel had faced in the wilderness centuries before, and where they had failed he triumphed as he was empowered by the Spirit. He was steadfast in his worship of, trust in, and obedience to God and so left the wilderness as he entered it, led by the Spirit (Luke 4:14).

4. Throughout his ministry Jesus continued his conflict with demonic forces as he, in the power of the Holy Spirit, challenged and overcame the might of Satan, the fallen angel (Matt. 12:24–32; Mark 3:20–30; Luke 11:14–23). Jesus released the power of the Spirit as he proclaimed the kingdom of God, and evil spirits were forced to acknowledge his true identity and flee from his presence.

5. Jesus promised his disciples that after his departure the Holy Spirit would be with them (Matt. 10:20; Mark 13:11; Luke 12:12; see also Luke 11:13; 24:49). This corroborates the basic promise made by John the Baptist that, in the new era of grace, the Messiah would baptize his people with the Holy Spirit (Matt. 3:11; Mark 1:8; Luke 3:16). How this actually occurred is told in the Acts of the Apostles and explained in the Epistles.

The synoptic Gospels present Jesus, the Messiah, as the One who fulfils the prophecies concerning the special anointing of the Spirit. The Holy Spirit of promise rests upon him and works through his ministry in anticipation of the fullness of the kingdom of God to be realized in the age to come. Furthermore, the Synoptics present Jesus as promising that once he has completed his work on earth, he will give the same Spirit to his faithful disciples so that his own work will continue through their work.

The Gospel of John

Most of what is said in the Synoptics concerning the relationship of the Messiah and the Spirit is said in greater detail in John's Gospel. Here Jesus calls the Spirit, whom he promises to send to his disciples when he leaves the earth, by the name of *Paraclete* (the One who comes alongside to serve as our Comforter, Counselor, and Friend). In fact, Jesus insists that it is necessary for him to go away so that he can come again, universalizing his presence in and through the Holy Spirit. Thus he can be with and in his disciples wherever they may be.

What is said in the Gospel of John concerning the relationship between Jesus and the Spirit can be summarized as follows:

1. The Spirit descended upon Jesus (1:32–33). While there is no specific mention of the baptism of Jesus, we are told by John that the Spirit descended like a dove and *remained* upon Jesus. That is to say, he came permanently.

2. The Spirit was given to Jesus not only permanently, but also without limit (3:34–35), because the Father loves the Son and willingly places everything in his hands.

3. The Spirit who remained in and upon Jesus is the same Spirit who will bring new birth and eternal life to believers (3:5–8; 6:63).

4. The Spirit will be given to the people of the new covenant after Jesus has been glorified (7:37–39). When Jesus has been raised from the dead, then, at his request, the Father will send the Spirit to his people so that they can be baptized in and by the Holy Spirit (1:33).

5. The Spirit will be the counterpart of Christ, the other Paraclete (14:16). The Spirit, inhering in and flowing from the exalted Christ, will come to the disciples in order to bring them the presence and mind of Christ (14:16–18, 25–26; 15:26; 16:12–15).

6. The Spirit will also work through the disciples upon the people of the world to bring them to faith in the Messiah (16:7–11).

7. After his resurrection from the dead, Jesus breathed on his disciples in order to impart to them the Holy Spirit (20:22). This action recalls God's breathing life into Adam (Gen. 2:7; cf. Ezek. 37:9). It is not easy to square this account of the giving of the Spirit with that provided by Luke in Acts 2. Possibly what Jesus did on the day of resurrection was a symbolic act preparing the way for the pouring out of the Spirit fifty days later at the Feast of Pentecost. He may on the earlier occasion have been constituting his disciples as "the body of Christ," the "temple of the Holy Spirit."

John's Gospel, then, emphasizes the relationship between Jesus and the Spirit, and between the Spirit and the disciples, more strongly than do the Synoptics. Further, it is very clear from John that the Spirit who comes to indwell and guide the disciples bears the name, virtues, and characteristics of Jesus, the exalted Messiah.

The Acts of the Apostles

At the end of his Gospel, Luke records the resurrected Jesus' promise of the gift of the Holy Spirit: "I am going to send you what my Father has promised; but stay in the city until you have been clothed with power from on high" (24:49). From the Father in heaven the Holy Spirit will come to the apostles and disciples. We find in the second volume from Luke's pen that Jesus again is recorded as saying, "Do not leave Jerusalem, but wait for the gift my Father promised, which you have heard me speak about. For John baptized with water, but in a few days you will be baptized with the Holy Spirit" (Acts 1:4–5). Interestingly, though Luke mentions the Holy Spirit more than do the other two synoptic Gospels, it is John who records in greatest detail Jesus' promise to send the Spirit (especially in John 14–16).

Acts 1 describes the ascension of Jesus into the cloud of glory. Then, in the second chapter, Luke proceeds to report the glorious arrival of the Holy Spirit at the Jewish Feast of Pentecost.[3] On that occasion all the followers of Jesus were filled with the Holy Spirit and enabled to speak in languages which they had never learned. When a crowd gathered, Peter proclaimed to them that the day of the Lord and the pouring out of the Spirit which the prophet Joel had foretold had arrived. The prophecy could now be fulfilled because Jesus the Messiah had been raised from the dead and exalted to the right hand of the Father: "God has raised this Jesus to life, and we are all witnesses of the fact. Exalted to the right hand of God, he has received from the Father the promised Holy Spirit and has poured out what you now see and hear" (2:32–33). This is an extraordinary claim from the apostle Peter. He is saying that the Spirit of the Lord has come at the direction of the exalted Jesus and with his characteristics and virtues. No longer is the Spirit "naked deity," but he is clothed with the personality and character of Jesus. Even as Jesus has always done the Father's will in glad obedience, from now on the Holy Spirit will be the Spirit of Christ, doing his will and representing him and his cause (as the teaching in John 14–16 makes abundantly clear).

Joel had prophesied that God would pour out his Spirit on all people and that this heavenly baptism would be accompanied by great signs (Joel 2:28–32, cited in Acts 2). This prophecy began to be fulfilled when the Spirit fell upon each and every one of the Jewish apostles and disciples who were gathered in a house in Jerusalem on Pentecost. It was further fulfilled when the Spirit fell upon each and every disciple in Samaria (Acts 8:14–17) and then upon all the Gentiles who heard the gospel message in the home of Cornelius (10:44). Jews, Samaritans, and Gentiles all received the heavenly Spirit in a manner that can only be described as remarkable.

Further, this Spirit who had rested upon, filled, and guided Jesus worked in a similar manner with his apostles, evangelists, prophets, and disciples. Luke delights to tell of how they were filled and led by the Spirit of Jesus. However, since Luke's account in Acts is of a historical nature, he tells us more of what we may call the observable and identifiable external activity of God and its results than of the secret internal activity of God as the Regenerator of souls. When, we may ask, was Saul of Tarsus born from above? We know of the externals in his case. That is, we know when he saw the vision of the exalted Jesus, when he was baptized and filled with the Spirit, and when he began to preach, but Luke does not tell us of Paul's internal regeneration. Take also the case of

3. For the Holy Spirit as presented in Acts see J. H. E. Hull, *The Holy Spirit in the Acts of the Apostles*.

Lydia (16:14b): Luke reports merely that the Lord opened her heart to respond to Paul's presentation of the gospel.

Even after a careful reading and study of Acts, it is difficult to come to a clear judgment as to whether Luke believed that each and every believer was the recipient of, or ought to have been the recipient of, the kind of outpouring of the Spirit experienced by the first Jewish, Samaritan, and Gentile disciples. He certainly does not mention such a baptism with the Spirit in his accounts of the conversions of Lydia and the jailor in Philippi (16:31–34), to name but two examples. On the other hand, he presumes that all conversions occur because the Spirit is working both through the preacher and within the listener's heart. In other words, Acts presumes that all who are truly converted have in some sense or another also received the Holy Spirit in their souls. Whether the promise made by Peter in 2:38–39 concerning the gift of the Spirit to all who repent and are baptized refers to (a) an extraordinary baptism with or outpouring of the Spirit or to (b) the indwelling of the Spirit (as Ezekiel [36:27; 37:14] had prophesied) is, then, a difficult question to answer. The evidence of Acts seems to be that in some, but not all cases, the Lord Jesus Christ actually pours out his Spirit in remarkable ways upon his disciples. The choice of who will receive this extraordinary gift rests in the sovereignty of Jesus as Lord and King.

The Significance of the Baptism of Jesus

There can be no doubt that the baptism of Jesus is important because of what it meant personally to Jesus and what it indicated concerning his ministry as the Messiah. For our purposes it is also important because of what it implies about the gift of the Spirit, in particular the relation of the Spirit and baptism in water, for those who believe in Jesus the Messiah.[4]

We read that "Jesus came from Nazareth in Galilee and was baptized by John in the Jordan. As Jesus was coming up out of the water, he saw heaven being torn open and the Spirit descending on him like a dove. And a voice came from heaven: 'You are my Son, whom I love; with you I am well pleased'" (Mark 1:9–11; cf. Matt. 3:13–17; Luke 3:21–22). Jesus deliberately identified himself with the people who were going out to the Jordan to be baptized by John as a sign of repentance and cleansing in preparation for the coming of the Messiah. Though without sin, Jesus identified with sinners and was baptized as if he were a sinner repenting

---

4. On the relationship between the baptism of Jesus and Christian baptism see W. F. Flemington, *The New Testament Doctrine of Baptism,* and G. W. H. Lampe, *The Seal of the Spirit.*

of his sins. This was to fulfil his calling as the Suffering Servant, who in fulfilling all righteousness (Matt. 3:15) would make many righteous (Isa. 53:11).

Jesus' baptism in water, followed by the descent of the Spirit, recalls the association of water and the Spirit found in such prophecies as Ezekiel 36:25–27 (cf. Ezek. 47:1–12; Zech. 13:1). The actual descent of the Spirit from heaven to remain upon Jesus recalls the prophecies and foreshadowings of the unction upon the Messiah which are found in Isaiah 11:2; 61:1; 63:11–12; 1 Samuel 16:13; and Psalm 89:20–21. And the words from heaven which affirm that Jesus is uniquely the Son of the Father recall such texts as Psalm 2:7 and Isaiah 42:1. Thus we have the close association here of water, the gift of the Spirit, and sonship. Likewise, as we shall see, in Christian baptism there is the same triad of water, the gift of the Spirit, and adoption as children of God.

When Jesus left the Jordan, the Spirit remained upon and with him; he was conscious of his unique relationship of fellowship and love with the Father, and he knew that he was the Messiah who must fulfil the prophecies concerning the Suffering Servant of the Lord. His mission was to establish the new covenant and bring in the kingdom of God. Further, he knew that his baptism was highly symbolic, pointing to his suffering on behalf of the many and his death at Calvary. In fact, he would later use the term *baptism* to refer to his approaching crucifixion (Mark 10:38; Luke 12:50). It is also noteworthy that the Gospel of John, which has no account of the sharing in the cup of the covenant in Christ's blood at the Last Supper, has instead the account of the washing of the feet of the disciples—a kind of real-life parable signifying the washing, the cleansing, the "baptism" associated with his atoning death. It was after the baptism of his death had been completed, after God had raised him from the dead, and after he had ascended that Jesus poured out the Holy Spirit from the Father, that is, sent and gave the Spirit to the believing community. We are reminded that it was after Jesus' baptism and during his ascent from the water that the Spirit descended on him. On this point, it is perhaps significant that the verb used in Mark 1:10 to describe Jesus' arising from the water is *anabainō,* the very verb used in John 3:13; 6:62; 20:17; and Ephesians 4:8–10 to refer to the ascension of Jesus. Thus there is probably an allusion to the ascension of Jesus in his coming up out of the river. And, of course, following this ascent there was the descent (*katabainō*) of the Spirit upon him.

Converts to Christianity were baptized in the name of Jesus, the Messiah and Lord; and their baptism corresponded in important respects to his. They were baptized in water, signifying that they had died and risen with him; and as he had received the Spirit, so they too were given the indwelling Spirit so that they could know God as Father and live as his adopted sons and daughters. By being baptized, the converts came to belong to Christ; and through participation in him, the Anointed One, they received a share in his anointing, the gift of the Spirit.

On the day of Pentecost, when the Holy Spirit was poured upon the waiting disciples by their exalted Lord, Peter declared to the bewildered crowd that had gathered, "Repent and be baptized, every one of you . . ."; thus far he could have been following the example of John the Baptist. But he did not stop there; he continued, "Be baptized . . . in the name of Jesus Christ for the forgiveness of your sins. And you will receive the gift of the Holy Spirit" (Acts 2:38). The rite of baptism had been given new content! Jesus himself had undergone baptism in water and then baptism in death, which led to his resurrection. At the time of his baptism in the Jordan he had received the Spirit, and now, having ascended to the right hand of the Father, he bestowed the Spirit from heaven. Baptism in water into the name of the Lord Jesus is therefore the external sign and symbol of the inward baptism with the Holy Spirit of which John the Baptist spoke.

To claim that baptism in or with water is the external sign of baptism with the Holy Spirit may seem to be setting aside an occasion recorded in Acts when the Spirit is first given to believers through the laying on of hands. In 8:17 Peter and John lay hands on the Samaritan believers, who then receive the Spirit. Although these Samaritans had earlier been baptized in the name of the Lord Jesus (8:16), they had not received the gift of the Spirit at that time. Perhaps a clue is to be found in the ancient rivalry and division between the Jews and Samaritans. Peter and John's coming to Samaria signified that, with the introduction of the new covenant, the division was now healed. The gift of the Spirit may have been withheld by the exalted Lord until the two apostles arrived to formally mend the rift.

3

Born of God

The concept of birth from God or rebirth is more prominent in the Johannine literature of the New Testament than in any other biblical source. It will be our task in this chapter to look at various passages in which this image occurs. We will look first at the Gospel and then at the First Epistle of John.

The Concept of Rebirth in the Gospel of John

He came to that which was his own, but his own did not receive him. Yet to all who received him, to those who believed in his name, he gave the right to become children of God—children born not of natural descent, nor of human decision or a husband's will, but born of God. [John 1:11–13]

The first passage to be examined occurs in the prologue to the Gospel of John (1:1–18), the subject of which is the Word or Logos of God, the eternal Son of the Father, who became incarnate as a Jew, Jesus of Nazareth.[1] He came to that which was his own—the land of Israel and

---

1. For the material on the Gospel of John, I am indebted to C. K. Barrett, *The Gospel According to St. John;* Raymond E. Brown, *The Gospel According to John;* and Leon Morris, *The Gospel According to John.* Karl Heinrich Ringwald's article on "Birth" in Colin Brown, ed., *The New International Dictionary of New Testament Theology,* vol. 1, pp. 176–80, is valuable.

the city of Jerusalem—but his own people did not, as a whole, receive him as their Messiah; instead, they rejected and crucified him. Nevertheless, there were some who did receive him as Messiah and believe in his name (the name *Jesus* means "salvation from God"). To such people he gave the right or authority to become the children of God, a status which means that they were begotten of God and thus placed in a special relationship with him.

It is important to remember that the male was looked upon as the principal agent in generation, while the female's role was merely to be fertilized by the male and carry the embryo until birth. Thus God is here being presented as the sole cause of the origin of life, the expression "born of God" meaning "begotten of God." Further, it is important to notice that the word used by John for "children" is *tekna*. This word is related to the verb *tiktein,* "to beget," and thus here conveys the idea of being begotten by God himself. In contrast, the word *huios,* "son," is never used by John in conjunction with the genitive form "of God" except to designate Jesus as the incarnate Son. Paul, however, who insists that believers are sons (children) of God by adoption, does use the phrase "sons [*huioi*] of God" for believers (e.g., Rom. 8:14), for he sees them as sons *in Christ—filii in Filio.* We become *tekna* by regeneration and *huioi* by adoption.

In order to make it absolutely clear that being begotten by God is the only way to become a child of God, John adds various negatives. This being begotten by God can never be equated with being begotten by, literally, *bloods* (the fusion of the blood of mother and father in generation), *the will of the flesh* (human planning or determination), or *the will of an adult male* (the desire of the father). John would hardly have produced these elaborate negatives if all that he wanted to say was that one cannot become a child of God through the process of human reproduction. He probably had a second meaning in mind—a comparison with the virginal conception of Jesus himself. The conception and subsequent birth of Jesus were not the result of normal procreation, human planning, or the will of the husband, but they were the creative work of God himself acting through the Holy Spirit. Thus the conception of Jesus provides a pattern of the rebirth of believers in his name (i.e., those who wholeheartedly believe that he is the Messiah and thus their Savior).

As we ponder this passage, we note certain ideas and themes which recur in later passages and which have been variously interpreted over the centuries. The first is the relationship between believing in Jesus' name and being born of God. It is often asked, "Which of these occurs first?" C. K. Barrett asserts that "the birth is conditional upon receiving

Christ and believing on his name."[2] However, William Hendriksen points out that the verbs *elabon* ("received") and *edōken* ("gave"), both being in the aorist tense, are simultaneous. As we receive Christ, we are given the right to become children of God; that is to say, at that very moment we are also born of God.[3] Now if John 1:12 is judged to refer only to the time of the itinerant earthly ministry of Jesus in Palestine, then Barrett must be right, for while many believed in the name of Jesus the Messiah, they did not actually receive the permanent presence of the Holy Spirit until after Jesus' resurrection. However, if the text is seen as referring to the period after the outpouring of the Spirit, then Hendriksen's point has more weight, since the work of the Spirit, as the Paraclete of Jesus, is to convince the world of sin, righteousness, and judgment (John 16:8–11), and thus bring people to belief.

Another theme is being born of God and being a child of God. Already we have commented upon the words *tekna* and *huios* and the different emphases in the Johannine and Pauline material. Being born suggests entry into a family; being a child suggests having brothers and sisters all of whom have been begotten by the one heavenly Father. What is implied in having the authority to become children of God is not realized immediately, but is, as we shall see in 1 John, to be fully attained only in the life of the age to come.

> Now there was a man of the Pharisees named Nicodemus, a member of the Jewish ruling council. He came to Jesus at night and said, "Rabbi, we know you are a teacher who has come from God. For no one could perform the miraculous signs you are doing if God were not with him."
> In reply Jesus declared, "I tell you the truth, no one can see the kingdom of God unless he is born again."
> "How can a man be born when he is old?" Nicodemus asked. "Surely he cannot enter a second time into his mother's womb to be born!"
> Jesus answered, "I tell you the truth, no one can enter the kingdom of God unless he is born of water and the Spirit. Flesh gives birth to flesh, but the Spirit gives birth to spirit. You should not be surprised at my saying, 'You must be born again.' The wind blows wherever it pleases. You hear its sound, but you cannot tell where it comes from or where it is going. So it is with everyone born of the Spirit." [John 3:1–8]

An extended paraphrase of John 3:1–15 has already been provided in chapter 1. We will limit our considerations here to the first eight verses, where the references to regeneration occur. We will look particularly at verses 3, 5, and 7.

---

2. Barrett, *Gospel According to St. John,* p. 137.
3. William Hendriksen, *The Gospel of John,* p. 81.

Verse 3: *"No one can see the kingdom of God unless he is born again* [margin, *born from above*]*."* The expression "the kingdom of God" occurs only twice in this Gospel, here and once again in verse 5. The kingdom of God properly belongs to the age to come when the new creation will be totally in harmony with the will and purpose of God. However, Jesus announced that the kingdom of God was at hand; he was referring to both his words and deeds. In and through Jesus the future kingdom has become a present reality; he, as it were, is the kingdom in microcosm, and thus vital contact with him is contact with the kingdom of God. And vital contact with the kingdom means that we as trusting servants come under the gracious, saving, and fatherly rule of God. To see the kingdom in this age it is necessary to have spiritual eyes which can discern its presence in the person and work of Jesus the Messiah. Here in verse 3 Jesus insists that to see, that is, to experience and participate in, the kingdom, a person has to be born again (or from above). Since all pious Jews were looking for the arrival of the kingdom, Jesus is making a most important statement not only to Nicodemus but to all religious Jews like him.

The crucial verb in this sentence is the passive of *gennan* and can mean either "to be born" (of a woman) or "to be begotten" (by a man). Further, the Greek word *anōthen* can be rendered "again" or "from above." Thus it is possible to have the following translations: to be born again, to be born from above, to be begotten again, and to be begotten from above. Since the word *begotten* is little used in modern English, there is a natural bias in favor of the verb "to be born." And Jesus may well have been seeking to make Nicodemus think in terms of "being born again"—which at the literal level refers to physical birth but could be a veiled reference to a new kind of birth, a spiritual birth. Or he may have been seeking to make Nicodemus think in terms of "being born from above," thereby providing a strong hint to Nicodemus that he was speaking of a special kind of birth. Nevertheless, we may presume that the exact meaning within Jesus' own mind is best conveyed in English by the expression "begotten from above." This assumption is based upon the fact that the ancients put the greater stress on the male's role in generation: he begets by placing his semen within the female where it joins one of her eggs to form an embryo. God himself through the Spirit directly causes the beginning of new life in the human soul; this action is at the center of regeneration. A person in whom this creative work has occurred can then see the kingdom of God centered upon Jesus.

Verse 5: *"No one can enter the kingdom of God unless he is born of water and the Spirit."* There is probably no basic difference in meaning between "seeing" and "entering" the kingdom of God. As far as the

individual believer in Jesus is concerned, seeing or entering the kingdom occurs through new birth, and the attendant blessings will continue as one enjoys the gift of eternal life. Though, as we noted, John has
only two references to the kingdom of God, he has many references to the
gift of eternal life, that is, life of superabundant quality that is everlasting in nature, life that begins at the moment of new birth and will grow
in intensity and quality in the age to come.

The verb "is born" is the same one which is used in verse 3, and so it
also can be translated "is begotten." That "water" and "Spirit" are governed by a single preposition suggests a close relationship between the
two. Throughout the history of the church, "water" has usually been
taken to refer to baptism as the outward sign and symbol of internal
change in direction and in one's relationship with God. "Water" and
"Spirit," then, are a double emphasis on the necessity of spiritual birth.
Jesus could have had in mind either the baptism of John or the baptism
which he himself and his disciples performed. There is, however, another
possible meaning of "water." Hugo Odeberg suggested some sixty years
ago that "water" in verse 5 could refer to procreation, since rabbinic
sources use "water" to refer to semen.[4] If he is right, Jesus is saying,
"Unless a man is begotten of man and the Spirit . . . ," that is, Jesus is
pointing to the necessity of both physical and spiritual birth. We should
be on guard here, however, lest our horror of crude doctrines of baptismal
regeneration too easily induce us to interpret "water" as something
other than baptism.

Verse 7: *"You must be born again."* The word *you* is in the plural, and
so it is not only Nicodemus but all Jews who are being addressed by
Jesus. A literal translation of the Greek would read: "It behooves [or, it is
necessary for] you to be born again [or, from above]." The word *dei,*
meaning "it behooves" or "it is necessary," is used by Jesus at other
points in his ministry—of the necessity of his crucifixion, for example
(John 3:14; 12:34). There is no question here of Jesus' telling people that
they must go ahead and do something in their own power and by their
own volition. Rather, the opposite is being stated: there is no way other
than rebirth from heaven through the direct action of the Holy Spirit.
That which people are commanded by God to do is to repent of their sins
and to believe the Good News of the kingdom of God, which centers on
Jesus, the incarnate Son. Jesus wanted the *rebirth* of Israel as a whole.

Having now looked at these three references to the new birth, we
must face the question of whether John imported the image of rebirth
and divine begetting from Hellenistic religion and placed it on the lips of
Jesus. In answering we must, first of all, acknowledge that the image is

---

4. Hugo Odeberg, *The Fourth Gospel,* p. 48.

found not only in Gnosticism (e.g., in tractate 13 of the Hermetic writings), but also in various writings by Philo, the Alexandrian Jewish philosopher. However, in the second place, we must point out that, since birth is a universal human experience, it is highly probable that the image naturally appealed to Jesus, who we know, from the synoptic Gospels, spoke of the need to become like children. Further, Jesus was well aware of Psalm 2:7 (repeated in Heb. 1:5; 5:5), where God is portrayed as saying to the Davidic king: "You are my Son; today I have become your Father [margin, begotten you]." This important text could have been the source of Jesus' use of the image of being begotten or born from above. It is true that official Judaism rigidly avoided language of this kind in order to preserve the distinction between this present evil age and the future glorious age of the kingdom of God. To speak of birth from God compromised this distinction by bringing into this age what was believed to apply only to the future age. However, for Jesus as for John, there was no such obstacle since they knew that the kingdom of God of the age to come had already begun to make its presence and power known in the present age.[5]

Recognizing that this talk of new birth is authentic teaching from Jesus himself, let us review some of the basic relationships which are implied in John 3. There is the relationship of new birth, entry into the kingdom of God, and eternal life. There is the connection between being born of water and of the Spirit, which, in church history, has been interpreted as the connection between baptism and regeneration. There is the connection between believing in Jesus and being born of the Spirit. Then, also, there is the important fact that regeneration can never be treated in isolation from other aspects of the work of God in behalf of sinners. In John 3, which speaks of regeneration, there is also teaching concerning the love of God for the whole world, the incarnation of the eternal Son, the lifting up of the incarnate Son on the cross and in exaltation to heaven, and the work of the Holy Spirit in human lives. This reminds us that there can be no personal regeneration unless the almighty God, who is Father, Son, and Holy Spirit, moves towards sinners in mercy and grace.

Related Concepts in the Gospel of John

Before leaving the Gospel of John, it will be helpful to note (1) its teachings on the work of the Holy Spirit in the world as he acts upon sinners in the name of the Lord Jesus; (2) its teachings on the gift of

5. See Barrett, *Gospel According to St. John,* pp. 172–73.

eternal life which comes as a result of being begotten by God and born of his Spirit; and (3) other images which point to momentous change.

The Work of the Spirit

In his address to the disciples at the Last Supper, Jesus spoke of the Holy Spirit's role in the world, that is, in the sphere where God is not worshiped, trusted, and obeyed:

> But I tell you the truth: It is for your good that I am going away. Unless I go away, the Counselor [Paraclete] will not come to you; but if I go, I will send him to you. When he comes, he will convict the world of guilt in regard to sin and righteousness and judgment: in regard to sin, because men do not believe in me; in regard to righteousness, because I am going to the Father, where you can see me no longer; and in regard to judgment, because the prince of this world now stands condemned. [John 16:7–11]

Jesus is looking forward to his ascension into heaven from where he will send the Holy Spirit to the community of disciples to be their Paraclete, that is, to be alongside them as a trusted friend to assist and guide them as their Counselor, Comforter, and Advocate. In John 14–16 Jesus has much to say about the ministry of the Holy Spirit to and within the disciples themselves, but in this passage he speaks of how the Spirit will help them in their evangelism by his work upon the hearts and minds of those who actually hear the evangel, the Good News of the risen Lord Jesus.

What will the Holy Spirit do as the evangel is proclaimed? First, he will convince people that their judgment of Jesus is wrong. It is not true that Jesus was crucified because he was a sinner; rather, he died in place of sinners. Further, it is not true that human achievement, however righteous it may appear to be, will satisfy God and merit eternal life; rather, only the righteousness of the exalted Jesus will satisfy God. And it is not true that Jesus was judged by God at the cross; rather, Satan was judged and defeated in the crucial battle of the cross. In the second place, the Spirit will convince those who hear the gospel that the sin of all sins is to reject Jesus as God's Messiah, that their only hope is to be included within the righteousness of the Messiah through faith in him, and that at the final day of reckoning the judgment which occurred at the cross will be fully executed as God then judges Satan and those who serve him.

Obviously Jesus' words here have reference to the future apostolic preaching to those who are Jews or proselytes from the Gentile world. The principles set forth do, however, apply to the work of the Spirit in connection with all genuine evangelism. The Spirit secretly works in the human mind, heart, and will to help sinners recognize their sin and see in Jesus the Savior of the world and their own Savior. The creation of sincere faith and real repentance happens only through the ministry of the Spirit. Note, however, that the precise point at which the divine begetting and new birth occur is not specified.

Eternal Life

In the prologue John tells his readers, "In [the Word] was life, and that life was the light of men" (1:4). The Son possesses life (*zōē*) and serves as the Light (*phōs*) of men by revealing deity to them. The Son is the Life (11:25; 14:6), the Bread of Life (6:35, 48), the Light of Life (8:12), and he alone gives the water of life (4:10–14; 7:37–38). Thus his words are spirit and life (6:63); they are, in fact, words of eternal life (6:68).

When we receive the incarnate Son and believe in him, God bestows on us revelation and eternal life. It is not without significance that eternal life is first mentioned in this Gospel (3:15–16) immediately after the sole references to the kingdom of God (3:3, 5). Thus the gift of eternal life, received now in anticipation of its fullness in the age to come, is identified with, or at least related to (as in the synoptic Gospels), entry into the kingdom of God.

The function of the adjective *eternal* (*aiōnios,* which literally means "pertaining to an age") is to give what we might call a quantitative dimension to the qualitative life received from God in the new birth. Eternal life begins at the birth of the new age of the kingdom of God (the age to come after the last judgment); it is life of quality and without end and is the gift of God through his Son. The Father has life in himself (5:26) and he has granted the same life to the Son (5:26); and, by divine grace, those who are born from above are brought into and given this life in this age in anticipation of what shall be in the age to come. Those who are born from above and possess the gift are those who know God, that is, they have spiritual communion and fellowship with God as Father and with Jesus Christ as Lord (John 17). They participate in the love which is of God as they grow deeper in their union with the exalted Lord through the Spirit.

Related Images

We have just noted that by revealing deity to humans Jesus serves as the Light of the World. Therefore, the experience of those who, illuminated by the light which he shines upon them via the gospel, receive and believe in him, is well described as passing from darkness to light. It is a movement from a state where the soul is filled with darkness to a state where it is filled with living knowledge of God. Jesus said, "I am the light of the world. Whoever follows me will never walk in darkness, but will have the light of life" (8:12; see also 12:35, 46). The light of life begins, from the human side, with the new birth.

In the darkness of the world there is spiritual death—no communion and fellowship with the living God. The divine begetting causes new life. What happens to the believer is an inner resurrection in anticipation of the bodily resurrection that will occur at the parousia. It is a passing from death to life. Jesus said, "Whoever hears my word and believes him who sent me has eternal life and will not be condemned; he has crossed over from death to life" (5:24; see also 8:51). That this new life is from God through the work of the Son and the Spirit is made clear in John 5:21 and 6:63, where the apostle uses the verb *zōopoiein,* which means "to give life" or "to make alive."

In the world and in the human heart are falsehood and ignorance; the divine begetting begins the process of the victory of God's living Truth (the incarnate Son) over falsehood and ignorance. Jesus said, "If you hold to my teaching, you are really my disciples. Then you will know the truth, and the truth will set you free" (8:31–32; see also 17:19 [KJV], "sanctified through the truth"). To be free is to be free from the bondage of sin in order to enter into God's salvation and serve him.

Finally, not only is there the victory of truth, there is also the victory of love, the love of God revealed in the Son and imparted to the believer in and by the Holy Spirit. The divine begetting imparts the love of God to the believer (14:21). Thus Jesus can command that his disciples love one another even as the Father loves him and he loves them (13:34; 14:15; 15:9–10; 17:23).

We have seen that the new birth is portrayed in the Gospel of John as birth into light, life, truth, and love. It is the beginning of a new order of existence whose quality is guaranteed by the character of God himself. Further, the life that is placed in the soul by the indwelling Spirit is like a fountain vigorously leaping up and abounding in energy (4:14; 7:38). It is ever seeking to beget new and abundant life in others (10:10).

The Concept of Rebirth in the First Letter of John

We shall look at six passages from the First Epistle of John which make mention of the new birth. Though we recognize that this letter was written partly to combat false views and doctrines, we shall emphasize its positive teaching. The reader who wishes to fill in the background should consult a commentary.[6]

---

6. E.g., John R. W. Stott, *The Epistles of John;* Kenneth Grayston, *The Johannine Epistles;* and Raymond E. Brown, *The Epistles of John.*

And now, dear children, continue in him, so that when he appears we may be confident and unashamed before him at his coming. If you know that he is righteous, you know that everyone who does what is right has been born of him. [1 John 2:28–29]

John addresses the church members affectionately as *teknia,* "little children," because he writes as both an old man and faithful pastor. He looks forward to the second coming of Jesus and desires that the readers be ready to meet their Lord, Savior, and Judge in confidence and without any shame. They certainly know that the God and Father of the Lord Jesus is righteous, and thus they also know that everyone who practices a similar righteousness has been begotten by God and born of the Holy Spirit. The evidence that church members have been truly begotten of God is their practice of righteousness, which shows that they have a proper relationship with God and with fellow human beings. The new birth results in a family trait: being righteous and doing righteousness. Those who show this trait will joyfully welcome the Lord Jesus in his parousia.

Dear friends, now we are children of God, and what we will be has not yet been made known. But we know that when he appears, we shall be like him, for we shall see him as he is. Everyone who has this hope in him purifies himself, just as he is pure. [1 John 3:2–3]

This time John affectionately addresses the church members as *agapētoi,* "beloved friends," before speaking of their common privilege as the *tekna,* "children," of God. *Tekna* is related to the verb *tiktein,* "to beget"; thus, to be a child of God means to have been begotten by God. This spiritual birth is but the beginning since the children of God look forward to an enlargement of their experience of being members of God's family. In the life of the age to come, when the second coming of Christ occurs, believers will be clothed in immortal resurrection bodies for their new life of seeing God as he is and serving in his kingdom. Those who have this expectation will make use of all the help God provides to purify themselves so that they will be without the stain of sin when he appears. Those who are born of God seek to be pure, even as the God who begot them is pure.

Dear children, do not let anyone lead you astray. He who does what is right is righteous, just as he is righteous. He who does what is sinful is of the devil, because the devil has been sinning from the beginning. The reason the Son of God appeared was to destroy the devil's work. No one who is born of God will continue to sin, because God's seed remains in him; he cannot go on sinning, because he has been born of God. This is how we know who the children of God are and who the children of the devil are: Anyone who does not do what is right is not a child of God; neither is anyone who does not love his brother. [*1 John 3:7–10*]

Again John affectionately addresses the church members as *teknia,* "little children," as he warns them of false teachers eager to persuade them to leave the narrow way of Christ which leads to eternal life. From a theological perspective human beings can be divided into two types— those who do what is right in terms of God's commands and those who do what is sinful. The latter belong to the family of Satan, the fallen angel who is in eternal rebellion against God, his Creator. In fact, all human beings belong through natural birth and the presence of sin in the human race to the family of the devil and have to be rescued from it in order to be in the family of God. The reason for the incarnation of the Son of God was that he might be the Lamb of God who takes away the sins of the world (John 1:29). The devil's work is destroyed by the sacrificial atonement of the Son and through the new birth wrought by the Spirit.

A sinner becomes a child of God through the power of the Word of God, which is the gospel message, and by the agency of the Holy Spirit. The Good News is the divine seed which in the power of the Holy Spirit creates new life; from this new life arise new motives and inclinations towards God and his righteousness. No one who is begotten by God, no one in whom God's Spirit dwells, commits sin habitually. Considered as a child of God with a new nature, the believer does not sin; however, considered as a being in this world and still having the old body, mind, and heart, the believer fails to love and serve God perfectly. Thus those who are born of God but are still in their sinful bodies always need to confess their sins and receive the forgiveness of God (1:9). John is not saying that those born of God possess sinless perfection, but that in principle those who are born of God ought not to commit sin.

A tree is recognized by the kind of fruit which appears on its branches. Those who are begotten by God ought to be recognizable by their doing what is right in God's eyes and by their genuinely loving their fellow Christians. It is this practical detail which distinguishes them from the children of the devil. (Since John was combating heretical teaching about rebirth and its effects, he speaks in absolutes to emphasize the profound change that being begotten by God entails. He is not saying that unregenerate people cannot do real good in terms of improving the day-to-day life in this world.)

Dear friends, let us love one another, for love comes from God. Everyone who loves has been born of God and knows God. Whoever does not love does not know God, because God is love. This is how God showed his love among us: He sent his one and only Son into the world that we might live through him. . . . No one has ever seen God; but if we love one another, God lives in us and his love is made complete in us.

We know that we live in him and he in us, because he has given us of his Spirit.
[*I John 4:7–9, 12–13*]

This time John addresses the church members as "beloved" (*agapētoi*) in order to give a solid foundation to his exhortation that they practice genuine Christian love one for the other. The great manifestation and example of love, real love, is the sacrificial death of Jesus, the incarnate Son of God; and Christians are to love one another as Jesus has loved and continues to love them. But such love is not natural; it is supernatural and can be exercised only by those who are begotten of God and in whom God through his Spirit dwells. Because God lives in them and they are members of his family, being his begotten children, they have in their hearts the love of God ready to be released in caring word and deed. Those who have experienced new birth will personify the love of God for others.

Everyone who believes that Jesus is the Christ is born of God, and everyone who loves the father loves his child as well. This is how we know that we love the children of God: by loving God and carrying out his commands. This is love for God: to obey his commands. And his commands are not burdensome, for everyone born of God overcomes the world. This is the victory that has overcome the world, even our faith. [*I John 5:1–4*]

Here we need to note that "believes" is in the present tense, while the Greek word translated "is born [of God]" is in the perfect tense (literally, "has been born"). This indicates that the continuing exercise of faith is the result of having been begotten by God, who is presented as the heavenly Father. Those who have been born of God and who now believe also love God and therefore ought to love all those who are begotten by God and are his *tekna*, "children." Love for God includes the emotions but is basically moral obedience, being and doing what God commands. And what he commands is not irksome because those in whom the Spirit dwells possess a new heart which delights in the will of God and thereby is prepared to overcome the presence and power of Satan in the world. Further, whoever is begotten of God has the faith to triumph over the trials and troubles which arise when one seeks to do what is right in a sinful world.

We know that anyone born of God does not continue to sin; the one who was born of God keeps him safe, and the evil one cannot harm him. [*I John 5:18*]

The perfect participle "having been begotten" is here rendered "born"; it points to something which has happened and which has abiding results. Anyone who has been begotten of God is a child of God and has the obligation not to continue to commit sin. Being a child of God and habitual sinning do not belong together; new birth brings and requires new behavior, that of doing right. However, Christians do not actually stop sinning; rather, they do not sin continually.

The Christian is begotten of God; but Jesus, the incarnate Son, is eternally begotten of the Father. It is he to whom John refers in the words "the one who was born of God." By the guidance and with the help of Jesus Christ, the believer is kept from being led astray or destroyed by Satan. The Lord Jesus is in heaven, watching over the children of his eternal Father. When they are assaulted and tempted by the devil, the Spirit is sent in Jesus' name to help them.

What is very obvious in 1 John is that being born from above is not merely an inward spiritual experience. There is a divinely ordained relation between God's invisible action in begetting children and his requirement that these children visibly reflect their heavenly parentage in the quality of their lives. While the Gospel of John affirms the necessity of the divine begetting, the First Epistle of John goes on to affirm that there are obvious and necessary implications arising from the new birth. Being begotten by God obliges us, as we have seen, to be righteous and do what is right (2:28–29), to seek to be pure (3:2–3), to avoid committing sin against God and habitually do what is right (3:7–10; 5:18), to love God and all the children of God (4:7–9, 12–13), to believe and trust in Christ (5:1–4), and to overcome the world and the devil (5:1–4). Thus, while we cannot generate our own birth from above, we must, once we have experienced it from God, live in a way which reflects our new life.

4

Individual Internal Renewal

Having looked at the Johannine material, we must now decide how to proceed with our investigation of personal regeneration. If we restrict ourselves to the image of begetting and birth, the texts to examine are few. However, if we include dynamic equivalents or very similar images, the list is much greater and selection is necessary. We have chosen (1) to examine other texts in the New Testament where the image of begetting and birth is used to symbolize individual internal renewal, and (2) to notice some dynamic equivalents within the Pauline letters. First, however, we shall make a brief comment on how the theme of begetting and birth is related to the theme of the kingdom of God in the synoptic Gospels.[1]

The New Birth and the Kingdom of God

Mark tells us that "after John was put in prison, Jesus went into Galilee, proclaiming the good news of God. 'The time has come,' he said. 'The kingdom of God is near. Repent and believe the good news!'" (Mark

---

1. For comments on the Gospel of Mark, I am indebted to C. E. B. Cranfield, *The Gospel According to St. Mark,* and William L. Lane, *The Gospel According to Mark.* Studies on the kingdom of God which have been consulted include Herman Ridderbos, *The Coming of the Kingdom;* John Gray, *The Biblical Doctrine of the Reign of God;* and A. M. Hunter, *Christ and the Kingdom.*

1:14–15). John's role as preparer of the way having come to an abrupt end, Jesus stepped onto the scene to announce the drawing near of the kingdom of God, as if it were a mighty army waiting to enter the gates of a city. His announcement of the divine initiative and action (long predicted by the prophets of Israel), and his call for decisive human response, are the two sides of one coin.

The expression "the kingdom of God is near" is to be understood in terms of both space and time. It is near in terms of space because Jesus, who embodies and communicates the gracious reign of God, is now beginning his ministry of confronting Satan, sin, death, and disease, and bringing them into submission to the power of the sovereign rule of God. This rule in its fullness is yet to arrive, but with and in Jesus it has come near. And with its approach in the person and ministry of Jesus, the Spirit will soon be going forth from him (i.e., once he has ascended) to cause new birth in the souls of those who respond to the Good News of God's gracious coming towards them.

And the kingdom is near in terms of time, for the last unmistakable period of time before the arrival of the age of the fullness of the kingdom has dawned with the ministry of the Messiah. Therefore he calls with a new urgency for people to repent and believe the Good News of God's gracious intervention and action. The nearness in time is depicted in the parable of the fig tree: "Now learn this lesson from the fig tree: As soon as its twigs get tender and its leaves come out, you know that summer is near" (Mark 13:28). In this period of grace it behooves *all* to respond to the preaching of the gospel and be born from above. Did not Jesus say to Nicodemus, "You [plural] must be born from above"?

The relationship between the kingdom of God and new birth is made clear in the episode recorded in Mark 10:13–16:

> People were bringing little children to Jesus to have him touch them, but the disciples rebuked them. When Jesus saw this, he was indignant. He said to them, "Let the little children come to me, and do not hinder them, for the kingdom of God belongs to such as these. I tell you the truth, anyone who will not receive the kingdom of God like a little child will never enter it." And he took the children in his arms, put his hands on them and blessed them.

Here Jesus uses the basic nature and characteristics of little children to illustrate important features of the way that the sovereign and gracious rule of God enters human lives. The kingdom belongs to those who, like little children, are ready to receive the salvation of God as *his* gift, donated wholly by grace. For the kingdom of God alone gives and we humbly and gratefully receive. The pride in one's achievements which arises within the sinful heart is the opposite of the attitude God requires. Thus, as the kingdom draws near in the person and ministry of Jesus the Messiah, and as God is ready to work in human hearts through the Spirit, those who hear the Good News are to become like children, openly and confidently believing it and receiving the gift of eternal life that it brings. The action of Jesus in taking the little children and blessing them is a real-life parable signifying that the blessings of the kingdom are freely given by God to those who place a total childlike trust in his Messiah.

It is not necessary for us to pursue this two-sided emphasis of Jesus (God's gift of the kingdom and the call for childlike response) within the synoptic Gospels. Suffice it to say that the gift of the kingdom to each individual believer is a dynamic equivalent of the Johannine teaching on divine begetting, just as the call to repent and believe the Good News is the Synoptics' equivalent of the call in John's writings to believe in the name of the Lord Jesus.

The Concept of Rebirth in Non-Johannine Epistles

We will now look at one text in the Pauline letters, one in the Epistle of James, and three in the First Letter of Peter which contain images of the new birth which are reminiscent of the Johannine material.[2]

> When the kindness and love of God our Savior appeared, he saved us, not because of righteous things we had done, but because of his mercy. He saved us through the washing of rebirth and renewal by the Holy Spirit, whom he poured out on us generously through Jesus Christ our Savior, so that, having been justified by his grace, we might become heirs having the hope of eternal life. [*Titus 3:4–7*]

Here we have the great Pauline emphasis that salvation is wholly by the mercy and grace of God. There is no earning of salvation by personal achievement—"not because of righteous things we had done." It is God alone who saves his people, and he does so *dia loutrou palingenesias,* "through the washing of rebirth." *Loutron* refers to the act of washing or cleansing. *Palingenesia* is a compound noun from *palin* ("again") and *genesis* ("birth, origin"); it means "rebirth" or "regeneration." The washing of rebirth means the end of the old and the origin of new life.

---

2. Sources here include, for Titus, Donald Guthrie, *The Pastoral Epistles,* and J. N. D. Kelly, *A Commentary on the Pastoral Epistles;* for James, James B. Adamson, *The Epistle of James,* and Peter H. Davids, *The Epistle of James;* and for 1 Peter, J. N. D. Kelly, *A Commentary on the Epistles of Peter and Jude,* and Ernest Best, ed., *I Peter.*

This, of course, is what baptism symbolizes (see Acts 2:38; Eph. 5:26). Rebirth is accompanied by *anakainōsis pneumatos hagiou,* "renewal by the Holy Spirit." *Anakainōsis* is the act or process by which something is made new; in this case it is achieved through the inner presence and work of the Holy Spirit (*pneumatos hagiou*). Renewal by the Holy Spirit means renovation of character and personality in preparation for life in the perfection of the kingdom of God. In fact, in Romans 12:2 Paul speaks of transformation of character through the renewal of the mind. We might say that rebirth points to the act of divine begetting while renewal points to the process of growth which occurs after birth.

It is noteworthy that the salvation described here not only brings internal renovation but also brings a new relationship with God. Justification is that work of God whereby he places sinners in a right relationship with himself so that they may have true communion and fellowship with him. And those who are regenerate and justified are also heirs of eternal life. They live in hope of the fullness of joy to be realized in the age of the perfection of the kingdom of God.

> *Every good and perfect gift is from above, coming down from the Father of the heavenly lights, who does not change like shifting shadows. He chose to give us birth through the word of truth, that we might be a kind of firstfruits of all he created.* [*James 1:17–18*]

The new birth is here presented as a good and perfect gift sent from heaven to the believing community. The verb "to give us birth" is not *gennan,* "to beget," but *apokuein,* which was normally used only of the female's giving birth and not of the male's begetting. The reason *apokuein* is used in verse 18 is probably that it has already been used in verse 15 ("sin . . . gives birth to death"). Further, female imagery is applied to God in the Old Testament (e.g., Isa. 66:13) for God was viewed as sexless. James is teaching what John taught: God takes the initiative and causes new life to begin in the soul.

It is by the sovereign will of the Father of the heavenly lights, the God who created the sun, moon, and stars, that new birth occurs as a result of the preaching of the word of truth, which is the gospel concerning the Lord Jesus. Even as God created the physical world, so also he is now, through the power of the Holy Spirit, bringing into being a new creation centered on Christ. The first disciples and converts are the "firstfruits" of this new creation. Firstfruits in the old covenant pointed to (1) God's promise that there would be a larger harvest to come, and (2) God's right to the first part of the harvest, since he had given the seed and the growth. Thus James is here reminding his readers that, as the earliest converts, they belong uniquely to God and that he will eventually bring many others into his kingdom (Jewish teaching often likened the arrival of the kingdom to a harvest).

> *Praise be to the God and Father of our Lord Jesus Christ! In his great mercy he has given us new birth into a living hope through the resurrection of Jesus Christ from the dead, and into an inheritance that can never perish, spoil or fade—kept in heaven for you, who through faith are shielded by God's power until the coming of the salvation that is ready to be revealed in the last time. [I Peter 1:3–5]*

> *For you have been born again, not of perishable seed, but of imperishable, through the living and enduring word of God. [I Peter 1:23]*

> *Like newborn babies, crave pure spiritual milk, so that by it you may grow up in your salvation, now that you have tasted that the Lord is good. [I Peter 2:2–3]*

Peter celebrates the mercy and grace of God the Father, who has caused the risen life of the exalted Lord Jesus to enter the souls of believers and give them new birth, new hope, and a new inheritance. Through the preaching of the gospel of the resurrection of Jesus and by the power of the Holy Spirit, divine seed has sprouted in their souls and they share in the heavenly life of the Lord Jesus. What life will be like in the age to come they do not yet know; but in this world and age they are to live in hope and faith, trusting in God's gracious power to protect them from all evil.

The verb *anagennan,* "to beget again," occurs in participial form in the Greek of 1:3 ("he has given new birth") and 1:23 ("you have been born again"). Christians have been born into a new life which is characterized by a vigorous hope that cannot fail, for that to which it points is a sure future guaranteed by the promises of the living God himself. That future involves both the completion of salvation and inheritance of heavenly life (i.e., the fellowship and communion of the kingdom of God, and life with Christ).

The reference in 2:2 to "newborn babies" should not be taken as a reference to new converts alone. Rather, as Jesus had commended child-likeness (Mark 10:15) as a permanent characteristic of the true disciple, so Peter here insists that believers like newborns are to grow up in the new life by partaking of what he calls "pure spiritual milk" and a tasting of the Lord. Peter is referring to communion and fellowship with the Lord Jesus and spiritually feeding on him through faith. We are reminded that milk is a food that will be abundant in the time of the kingdom (Isa. 60:16; Joel 3:18). With this image in view Peter sees Christ as the provider of the pure spiritual milk by which alone believers can grow in faith, hope, and love.

To sum up: Peter presents the new birth as the marvelous beginning of a new life which has tremendous prospects, prospects to be totally grasped and appreciated only in the fullness of the life of the age to come.

(For the sake of completeness we must look at three verses which indirectly point to new birth through the Spirit and actually use the verb *gennan*. In 1 Corinthians 4:15 and Philemon 11 Paul speaks of his having begotten converts. There is nothing remarkable about this, for when Paul refers to the origin of new life in the believer through the Spirit, he uses the image of birth rather than begetting [Titus 3:5]. Moreover, the image of begetting was used in ancient times in reference to the role of a rabbi in teaching Judaism—"When a man teaches the son of another man the Torah, the Scriptures treat him as if he had begotten him" (Sanhedrin 19b). Further, in Galatians 4:19 Paul uses the dramatic image of birth pangs to describe his care for his converts, and in other places he calls a convert his son [e.g., 1 Cor. 4:17; 1 Tim. 1:2; 2 Tim. 2:1].

In Galatians 4:29, which occurs in an allegory concerning Hagar, Sarah, and their sons, Isaac is called "the son born by the power of the Spirit." He is said to have been born of the Spirit in that he was conceived after Sarah had passed the age of childbearing. Accordingly, his physical conception and birth are often regarded as a type or figure of the spiritual second birth of believers.)

We have seen that the images of new birth which occur in Paul, James, and Peter are in full agreement with what we found in the Johannine writings. There is great emphasis on the divine initiative, mercy, and grace, as well as on the action of the Spirit and Word of God. There is also agreement that rebirth leads to a new life which is characterized by faith, hope, love, and spiritual growth towards full salvation and membership in the future kingdom of God.

Pauline Equivalents of the Concept of Rebirth

It is now our task to see how Paul uses a variety of complementary images to highlight the divine initiative in human salvation. The selection here is not meant to be exhaustive, but rather a basic list of the more obvious parallels to the image of new birth.[3]

God's Call Through the Gospel and the Spirit

Paul makes many references to the divine call to sinners. He is thinking of a call that is effective. That is to say, he does not have in mind a call

3. Herman Ridderbos, *Paul: An Outline of His Theology,* has been most helpful.

that some will hear and others will not, but rather a call that is heard by all those to whom God directs it. He then takes decisive action in them. Thus Paul's conception of God's call is more restricted than the conception in the Matthean text, "Many are called, but few are chosen" (Matt. 22:14, KJV).

Those whom God has elected to salvation in Christ he calls (*kalein*) so that he may justify and sanctify them (Rom. 8:29–30). This call (Eph. 4:1) results in new life and new existence (Rom. 4:17), for it is a call into fellowship with Christ (1 Cor. 1:9), into the kingdom of God (1 Thess. 2:12), and into the church of God, which is the unified body of the faithful (Col. 3:15). Baptism is the outward sign of this internal call. Thus those who have been baptized and are now participating in the life and witness of the local church may be designated as the *klētoi*, the "called ones" (Rom. 1:6; 8:28; 1 Cor. 1:24), and even as *klētoi hagioi*, people "called to be saints [holy]" (Rom. 1:7; 1 Cor. 1:2). This call does not change the external social status of the believer (see 1 Cor. 7:17–24), for it is an internal call into the kingdom of God, the church of God, and fellowship with God and the Lord Jesus Christ. Paul's references to the divine call point to the action of God within the hearts of those who hear and receive his Word, the gospel of the resurrection. Through the working of his Word and Spirit, God grants believers new life and existence in his kingdom and church.

Being Made Alive

Paul uses the verb *zōopoiein*, "to make alive," in Romans 4:17; 8:11; 1 Corinthians 15:22, 36, 45; 2 Corinthians 3:6; Galatians 3:21; and 1 Timothy 6:13. He also uses the verb *suzōopoiein*, "to make alive together with," in Ephesians 2:5 and Colossians 2:13. Though *zōopoiein* usually refers to the new life in the resurrection body of the future kingdom, there is an implied reference to the beginning of that new life within the old body in this age (see especially Rom. 4:17 and 2 Cor. 3:6 ["the Spirit gives life"—the life of the kingdom of God]). The compound verb *suzōopoiein* is used to declare that those who are united to Christ share in his resurrection from the dead into newness of life. Thus it refers to the action of God in this age in giving new life and existence to those who believe—they are made alive in and with Christ (Eph. 2:5).

Incorporation into the Death
and Resurrection of Christ

In Romans 6:1–11 Paul portrays the community of believers as having died, been buried, and been raised with Christ into new life. Participating in the resurrection and sharing in the new life are the same thought as being made alive together with Christ. The picture of death and

burial reinforces the idea that the old life has gone and a new beginning
has been made. Baptism in water is the outward, visible sign of incorporation into Christ and membership in his body. There can be no new
birth from above without union with the Christ who died and has risen,
for the Spirit who regenerates comes from the resurrected and exalted
Lord Christ.

New Creation

In 2 Corinthians 5:17 Paul makes the amazing statement, "Therefore, if anyone is in Christ, he is a new creation; the old has gone, the new
has come!" Paul is teaching that when one becomes a Christian and is
united to the Lord Jesus Christ, an act of creation by God has occurred.
Ktisis, "creation," refers not to the believer as such, but to the making of
a new creation which centers on Christ and of which the believer becomes a part. In Galatians 6:14–15 Paul speaks of "a new creation"
through the cross of Christ.

As God created light before he formed the universe and made man-
kind (Gen. 1:3–5), so "the light of the knowledge of the glory of God in the
face of Christ" (2 Cor. 4:6) is given in the gospel and by the Holy Spirit
before and as the act of new creation occurs in the souls of believers
(2 Cor. 5:17). Thus "new creation" points to the regenerating work of
God within the believer and also (like the word *regeneration* itself) to the
whole work of God in bringing into being a totally new cosmos centered
upon Christ—the future kingdom of God.

Alongside the teaching on new creation, Paul also writes of Christ as
the true image of God (2 Cor. 4:4; Col. 1:15). Since the first man was
made in the image and likeness of God (Gen. 1:26–27) and since Christ
is the second Adam, the head of a new humanity, it is not surprising that
Paul also speaks of believers as being changed to bear the image and
likeness of God that Christ himself perfectly bears and reflects (1 Cor.
15:49; 2 Cor. 3:18; Phil. 3:21; Col. 3:10). Then, in writing to the Ephesian
church, the apostle speaks of God's creating a new kind of man and
nature (2:15; 4:17–32). The change or renewal which is essential if we
are to bear the true image of God and to be a part of humanity as God
intended it to be is the same divine act we refer to as regeneration.

Washing with Water Through the Word

Paul told the church in Ephesus that Christ loved the universal
church and gave himself for her in order to make her holy, "cleansing her
by the washing with water through the word" (5:26). "The word" is the
message of the gospel preached in the power of the Holy Spirit, who
prepares the heart to receive that message and thus brings new life. This
divine activity and the human response are portrayed in the rite of

baptism—"the washing with water." This text recalls both John 3:5 ("born of water and the Spirit") and Ezekiel 36:25–26 ("I will sprinkle clean water on you . . . and put a new spirit in you").

Baptism in the Spirit

Reference to baptism in the Holy Spirit occurs seven times in the New Testament. Six of these occurrences draw a comparison between John the Baptist's baptism with water and the baptism he promised the Messiah would bring (Matt. 3:11; Mark 1:8; Luke 3:16; John 1:33; Acts 1:5; 11:16). Paul used the expression once: "we were all baptized by one Spirit into one body—whether Jews or Greeks, slave or free—and we were all given the one Spirit to drink" (1 Cor. 12:13). Here the Spirit's action of placing believing sinners within the body of Christ, the community of the new covenant, is in view. This action necessarily includes regeneration, the Spirit's coming to indwell the heart.

Paul assumes that the internal work of the Spirit accompanies the external act of baptism. In referring to this internal work the Greek uses the preposition *en* (*en heni pneumati*) rather than *hupo* (i.e., "in" rather than "by one Spirit") because baptism as such is not performed by the Holy Spirit; rather, as believers are washed by water, they receive the gift of the indwelling Spirit. Further, Paul declares that all the members of the body of Christ were given the one Spirit to drink. The verb is in the aorist tense, pointing to a decisive moment of drinking the Spirit, that is, the moment of water baptism. The image of drinking suggests the establishment of a close and intimate communion.

The Pouring of the Love of God into the Heart

"God has poured out his love into our hearts by the Holy Spirit, whom he has given us" (Rom. 5:5). This statement powerfully suggests both the divine act of begetting and the result of that begetting: internal renovation wrought by the presence of the love of God (not our love for God, but God's love for us).

Reception of the Spirit of Adoption

"For you did not receive a spirit that makes you a slave again to fear, but you received the Spirit of sonship. And by him we cry, 'Abba, Father'" (Rom. 8:15). The gift of the Holy Spirit dwelling in the soul constitutes believers adopted children of God. As a result, they are able to have an intimate communion with their heavenly Father, just as a child might address his or her earthly father by a familiar term like the Aramaic *Abba* or the English *Daddy*.

Being Sealed by the Holy Spirit

The verb *sphragizein,* "to seal," is used of the special endowment with the Spirit enjoyed by Jesus (John 6:27; cf. Acts 10:38—"God anointed Jesus of Nazareth with the Holy Spirit"). It is used also by Paul to describe the unction of the Spirit bestowed upon those who receive the gospel (2 Cor. 1:22; Eph. 1:13; 4:30). In the earliest period of patristic literature the image of sealing was applied to the Spirit's coming during baptism to dwell in the believer's heart (see 2 Clement 7:6; 8:6).

The Pauline View of the Relationship Between the Spirit and Baptism

Now that we have examined some of the equivalents of the concept of rebirth which appear in the writings of Paul, it will be useful to comment briefly on his view of the connection between the gift of the Holy Spirit and baptism. The apostle was wholly convinced that if we are to experience new life in union with the exalted Lord Jesus and to live within his body in faith, hope, and love, the Holy Spirit must work within the human soul. For individuals who do not have the indwelling Spirit do not belong to Christ (Rom. 8:9) and cannot receive and appropriate all those truths, gifts, and graces which the Spirit brings from the exalted Lord Jesus (1 Cor. 2:10b–16).

For Paul there was an intimate relation between the gift of the indwelling Spirit and the act of baptism. Paul lived at the beginning of the period of evangelization when the Holy Spirit confirmed the preached word with visible signs and wonders. Baptism was the public rite by which God (acting through the minister who performed the washing) brought believers into his kingdom, his church, and the local congregation (itself a microcosm of the whole church). The act of baptism did not have some special power to bring down the Spirit at that time; rather, it was the divinely appointed sign and symbol of incorporation into Jesus Christ and thus into his body, the church of God. It was performed once and only once and was modeled upon the baptism of Jesus himself in the river Jordan (see pp. 22–23).

Paul's view of the significance of baptism has been elegantly summarized by G. W. H. Lampe:

> The Pauline doctrine treated Baptism as the efficacious sign of a dying with Christ and a rising and ascending with him to a new quality of life, an earnest of the eschatological hope of the total redemption which is to be expected at the Parousia. Of this hope the guarantee is the inward seal set upon the believer's soul by that possession of the Holy Spirit which is the necessary concomitant of the union with Christ which has been brought

about through the response of faith to grace. Baptism is a sacramental rite which looks back to the Messiah-Servant Baptism of Jesus and to the saving and atoning death and resurrection of which His Baptism was a foreshadowing and prefiguring. It represented that Baptism and it was the external symbol through which the atoning work of Christ was applied to the believer and made available for him to share; the convert was figuratively buried and raised with Christ in the baptismal water; and in the union with Christ effected by faith in response to the diving act (whose visible expression was the sacrament itself) he found the realisation of the promise of the remission of sins. At the same time it was a rite which looked forward to the future hope and guaranteed its fulfilment. It pointed not only to the victory of Christ incarnate but to the culmination of that victory at the Parousia. Through being made a partaker of Christ and sharing in his Messianic-Servant character, entering with Him into newness of life, the believer received the assurance of the Holy Spirit, the seal of the covenant of promise, the stamp which marked him as God's own possession awaiting the day of redemption.[4]

It is important for us to be aware of how the intimate connection between baptism and the gift of the indwelling Spirit was understood in the apostolic age. Much was to be made of this understanding in the theology of baptism throughout the following centuries.

(It is possible—and those who are involved in the Pentecostal or charismatic movements would say it is preferable—to interpret the New Testament material on new birth and baptism with the Holy Spirit in a different manner. The essence of this different interpretation is the making of a clear and rigid distinction between birth from above, in which the Holy Spirit comes to indwell the human heart, and a subsequent baptism in the Spirit by the exalted Lord Jesus Christ. The first is a secret act of the Spirit himself; the second is an act of the exalted Christ and is accompanied by some external phenomenon. This interpretation usually includes the following ideas:

1. In the Old Testament there are two distinct promises concerning the Holy Spirit and the people of the new covenant. The first is that they will be indwelt by the Spirit [Ezek. 36:27]; the second is that they will be baptized with the Spirit [Ezek. 39:29; Joel 2:28–29].
2. The prophecy of John the Baptist that the Messiah would baptize with the Holy Spirit relates to the second of the Old Testament promises; it is not concerned with regeneration.

---

4. G. W. H. Lampe, *The Seal of the Spirit,* p. 149.

3. Jesus was already filled with the Spirit and sanctified when he presented himself for baptism, which issued in his being baptized with the Spirit. Thus the life of the Master himself illustrates both experiences.

4. Jesus' promise concerning the gift of the Spirit [Luke 11:13] relates to baptism with the Spirit, not regeneration.

5. When the resurrected Jesus breathed on the disciples (John 20:22), he gave them the indwelling Spirit and constituted them the body of Christ, people of the new covenant.

6. The outpouring of or baptism with the Spirit which is described in Acts 2 was only the first such act of the exalted Christ. The experience is open to all regenerate Christians.

7. The promise in Acts 2:38b–39 ["you will receive the gift of the Holy Spirit"] refers to baptism with the Spirit, not regeneration. So also the special outpourings of the Spirit on the Samaritans [Acts 8:15–17], Saul [Acts 9:17], those assembled in Cornelius's house [Acts 10:44; 11:15–16], and the disciples at Ephesus [Acts 19:6] were baptisms with the Spirit.

8. Paul's teaching on the seal of the Spirit [2 Cor. 1:22; Eph. 1:13] and on the witness of the Spirit [Rom. 8:16] points to the experience of baptism with the Spirit, as does John's teaching on anointing [1 John 2:20, 27].

From these various considerations it is generally argued that the New Testament [especially the Book of Acts] represents the norm to be a secret act of regeneration and then at least one subsequent identifiable experience of baptism with [or outpouring of] the Spirit from the exalted Lord Jesus in heaven.)

5

Cosmic Regeneration

What happens to the individual in terms of new birth and eventually an immortal resurrection body is one important aspect of what God will bring into being when this age and world cease and the new age and world begin. In fact the individual can receive the full inheritance promised in Christ only when there exist a new age and world in which that inheritance can be given to all the saints. The hope of the individual believer is not merely for personal immortality, but it is for a new cosmos, a new human race, and a new fellowship with God; the individual believer longs for the time when heaven will be an integral part of human existence.

While Paul, as we have seen (p. 39), used the noun *palingenesia* of personal, individual regeneration (Titus 3:5), Jesus used it of cosmic regeneration. We shall examine Jesus' teaching on cosmic renewal; then we shall look at what Peter says in the Acts and his Epistles, at what Paul writes in Romans 8, and finally at the visionary insights of John in the Revelation. Examination of these texts will make it very clear that personal regeneration is part of a cosmic activity by God which involves the whole created order and provides the Christian community with wonderful promises in which to rest—especially in these days of talk of nuclear holocaust.

The Teaching of Jesus

At the end of the conversation between the rich young man and Jesus (Matt. 19:16–30) the disciples became involved because they were hor-

49

rified at what Jesus had to say about the difficulty faced by rich people who attempt to enter the kingdom of God. Wondering about the apostolic band of disciples and their prospects, Peter reminded Jesus that they had left everything in order to follow him. "What," Peter asked, "will there be for us?" Jesus replied:

> I tell you the truth, at the renewal of all things, when the Son of Man sits on his glorious throne, you who have followed me will also sit on twelve thrones, judging the twelve tribes of Israel. And everyone who has left houses or brothers or sisters or father or mother or children or fields for my sake will receive a hundred times as much and will inherit eternal life. [Matt. 19:28–29; cf. Luke 22:28–30]

Here the Greek phrase *en tēi palingenesiai,* which literally means "in the regeneration," is translated "at the renewal of all things." *Palingenesia* was used by the Stoics to refer to a future universal restoration after the destruction of the world by fire; thus the idea of universal renewal, restoration, regeneration, or renovation is rightly seen here.[1] Moreover, the way in which Jesus speaks is at least in part conditioned by the apocalypticism which was common in Judaism in the time of our Lord. Jewish apocalyptic literature made a great distinction between this age and the coming age and expected the judgment of the nations and resurrection of all the dead at the end of the present age. Setting these ideas within his own understanding of God's future plans as presented in the Old Testament, Jesus calls himself the "Son of Man" (see Dan. 7:13) and declares himself to be the One who will both judge and rule. Thus he interprets Old Testament prophecy and Jewish expectations as references to himself, presenting himself as determinative, acting in the place of and on behalf of God.

By the phrase *en tēi palingenesiai,* recorded by Matthew alone, Jesus is probably referring to what will happen immediately after the judgment of the nations has concluded (see Matt. 25:31–46). The picture is of the vindicated Messiah, assisted by his apostles, governing the new people of God (described as the twelve tribes) in the new order of the kingdom of God. In this order there is a full inheritance for all those who have been his faithful followers in the old order; they will receive the reward of eternal life and all the blessings of the new relationship with God, with the saints, and with the new order of reality.

Although Matthew 19:28 is the only place where *palingenesia* is used of the new order, the expectation of such an order was conveyed by Jesus in

---

1. Sources utilized in this section include David Hill, ed., *The Gospel of Matthew;* J. C. Fenton, *The Gospel of St. Matthew;* Eduard Schweizer, *The Good News According to Matthew;* and, for New Testament theology, the volumes of that name by Donald Guthrie, Leonhard Goppelt, and Joachim Jeremias.

a variety of other ways. For example, he borrowed the Old Testament and apocalyptic metaphor of the new age as a great feast at which the guests enjoy the food, drink, and fellowship, and are wholly pleased with the host (see, e.g., Matt. 8:11; 22:1–14; Luke 13:29; cf. 14:16–24). Then, also, he made use of the later prophetic and apocalyptic concept that salvation will conclude with the arrival of a new age and new order of creation.

There are three strands to the prophetic expectation that salvation will issue in a new creation. The oldest is the renewal of the natural order, a restoration of the original paradisal state (Isa. 9:2–7; 11:1–9). Secondly, there is the idea of the provision of a new political order wherein all nations bring their gifts to Jerusalem and Israel functions as their light (Isa. 49:5–13). Finally, there is the vision of the new cosmic order of new heavens and new earth (Isa. 65:17; 66:22). In addition to the theme that redemption leads to new creation, Jesus was well aware of the teaching of the resurrection of the dead. Thus he thought of the new order of creation as populated by believers who had been given new resurrection bodies. In his ministry he made people whole in mind and body; this is to be seen as the beginning of the work of salvation and new creation. Thus it is not surprising that Paul, as we have seen, referred to the renewing work of the Spirit as the "new creation" and that, as we shall see, both Peter and John spoke of the new order of the new heavens and earth which would arrive at the end of this present age.

The Teaching of Peter

For Peter's statements on cosmic regeneration we shall look first at Acts and then at 2 Peter.[2] After the healing of the crippled beggar, an amazed crowd quickly gathered around Peter and John. Peter told them of Jesus Christ, in whose power the healing had been performed. And after declaring the gospel of the resurrection of the Lord Jesus he exhorted:

> Repent, then, and turn to God, so that your sins may be wiped out, that times of refreshing may come from the Lord, and that he may send the Christ, who has been appointed for you—even Jesus. He must remain in heaven until the time comes for God to restore everything, as he promised long ago through his holy prophets. [Acts 3:19–21]

The phrase "times of refreshing" translates *kairoi anapsyxeōs;* it points to the age of salvation which is promised to the people of Israel if

2. For comments on Acts, I am indebted to F. F. Bruce, *Commentary on the Book of Acts;* William Neil, *The Acts of the Apostles;* and I. Howard Marshall, *The Acts of the Apostles.* Sources for 2 Peter include Richard J. Bauckham, *Jude, 2 Peter,* and Michael Green, *The Second Epistle General of Peter and the General Epistle of Jude.*

they repent. This time of salvation, the age of the kingdom of God, is centered upon Jesus as Messiah; and so he must be received as Messiah in order for the people to participate in the kingdom he will inaugurate. He is the exalted Messiah in heaven, seated at the right hand of the Father, and there he will remain until the time for his parousia, his arrival on earth as Judge to close the old age and bring in the new one.

"The time . . . to restore everything" translates *chronōn apokatastaseōs pantōn* (literally, "the times of restitution of all things"); it points to the fulfilment of all that God had promised through his prophets concerning the future age of peace and righteousness and the new created order. The word *apokatastasis* seems to have a meaning virtually identical to that of *palingenesia* in Matthew 19:28.[3] Further, the verb *apokathistēmi,* meaning "to reestablish or to restore," is used in the Septuagint to express the promise that the land of Israel will be restored to its former glory with the advent of the Messiah at the end of the age.

While Peter refers to the imperishable inheritance of the new community in his First Letter (1:4), he specifically speaks in the Second Letter of the new order and creation which will follow the day of the Lord:

> But the day of the Lord will come like a thief. The heavens will disappear with a roar; the elements will be destroyed by fire, and the earth and everything in it will be laid bare.
>
> Since everything will be destroyed in this way, what kind of people ought you to be? You ought to live holy and godly lives as you look forward to the day of God and speed its coming. That day will bring about the destruction of the heavens by fire, and the elements will melt in the heat. But in keeping with his promise we are looking forward to a new heaven and a new earth, the home of righteousness. [2 Peter 3:10–13]

Jesus had spoken in similar terms of the end of the present age and order (Matt. 24:29, 35; Luke 21:25). Peter is saying that the solar system and the great galaxies will all be destroyed to make way for the new cosmos, which he describes, echoing Isaiah 65:17 and 66:22, in terms of new heavens and new earth. And he qualifies the latter by insisting that this new cosmos and order will be the permanent home of righteousness—right relationships between God and believers and between believers themselves. Here is genuine cosmic regeneration.

The Teaching of Paul

We noted in the last chapter (p. 44) that while "new creation" refers to the work of God within the individual believer, it also points to the fuller

---

3. *Apokatastasis* became a technical term for universalism. See Peter Toon, *Heaven and Hell,* ch. 10.

reality of which the work within the individual is but one small part. The new creation will be a new cosmos with a new humanity. Paul looks forward in hope to the new cosmic order as well as to the resurrection of the bodies of the individual faithful:

> *The creation waits in eager expectation for the sons of God to be revealed. For the creation was subjected to frustration, not by its own choice, but by the will of the one who subjected it, in hope that the creation itself will be liberated from its bondage to decay and brought into the glorious freedom of the children of God.*
>
> *We know that the whole creation has been groaning as in the pains of childbirth right up to the present time. Not only so, but we ourselves, who have the firstfruits of the Spirit, groan inwardly as we wait eagerly for our adoption as sons, the redemption of our bodies. For in this hope we were saved. But hope that is seen is no hope at all.* [*Rom. 8:19–24*]

Paul is looking at the created order in which he lives.[4] As a Christian who has received the gospel, he sees the present order in relation to God's stated purpose of bringing into being a new creation (Isa. 65:17–25). He pictures the created order as a man or animal eagerly straining forward to see something important. This eager expectation reflects creation's recognition that while it has not fulfilled God's original purpose for it, there is a greater purpose yet to be fulfilled—to be the sphere in which God's kingdom exists wholly and perfectly.

In fact, Paul continues, as the created order painfully but eagerly expects the arrival of the new order, it may be likened to a woman who is giving birth. As a part of this created order, believers, possessing the gift of the Holy Spirit and the seed of eternal life, also inwardly groan as they wait for the putting on of their immortal resurrection bodies (2 Cor. 5:4–5 has a similar thought: "while we are in this tent, we groan and are burdened, because we . . . wish . . . to be clothed with our heavenly dwelling"). Believers long and hope to be in name and in reality the children of God, to dwell in new bodies in a new cosmos and in a permanently new relationship with the Father through the Son.

There is a link between Romans 8:19–24 and 5:12–21, where Paul deals with the renewal of humanity. Christ, the Son of man, is the new Adam, the forerunner of a whole new humanity. In his resurrection we are made new. Then, in the light of Romans 9–11, we can also think of Christians as the new Israel. Therefore, the new Israel, the new humanity, and the new creation are closely related concepts. Obviously the individual regeneration leading to full experience of new life in the

---

4. Sources for the comments on Romans 8 include C. K. Barrett, *A Commentary on the Epistle to the Romans;* F. F. Bruce, *The Epistle of Paul to the Romans;* Ernst Käsemann, *Commentary on Romans;* and Matthew Black, *Romans.*

future kingdom cannot be divorced from the universal regeneration by which the new order of the kingdom of God is brought into being. Each is a necessary part of God's total activity.

The Teaching of John from Patmos

We cannot be certain about the identity of the author of the Apocalypse; we do know that his name was John and that he described himself when writing to the seven churches as "your brother and companion in the suffering" (1:9).[5] He was moved by the Holy Spirit and received a message from the risen, exalted Lord Jesus concerning that which would precede the arrival of the new order of the kingdom of God. The climax of the book is reached in the next to the last chapter:

> Then I saw a new heaven and a new earth, for the first heaven and the first earth had passed away, and there was no longer any sea. I saw the Holy City, the new Jerusalem, coming down out of heaven from God, prepared as a bride beautifully dressed for her husband. And I heard a loud voice from the throne saying, "Now the dwelling of God is with men, and he will live with them. They will be his people, and God himself will be with them and be their God. He will wipe every tear from their eyes. There will be no more death or mourning or crying or pain, for the old order of things has passed away." [Rev. 21:1–4]

John's vision is of an entirely new cosmos for, significantly, there is no longer any sea. The most important feature of the new order is the Holy City, which is the only part of the new creation that John is allowed to see. This new and heavenly Jerusalem is not a city rebuilt in the land of Palestine, but a direct creation of God which is designed to fulfil abundantly for the redeemed the role which the prophets saw earthly Jerusalem as fulfilling for Israel and the Gentile nations (Isa. 2:1–5; 49:14–26; ch. 54). There will be such loving fellowship between God and his people that they will actually see him and live!

It is reasonable to assume that Revelation 21:9–22:5 is an extended comment on the basic vision of 21:1–4. Here it is made clear that in the new order the Lamb of God, the Son of God who became incarnate, suffered, died, and was resurrected to heavenly life, will continue to be the Mediator between God and redeemed humanity. This new order will truly be the kingdom of God and the genuine fulfilment of the prophecies and the hope of the pilgrim people of God—the very people who individually have experienced new birth and are described as "a kingdom and priests to serve his [Jesus Christ's] God and Father" (1:6).

---

5. George R. Beasley-Murray, *The Book of Revelation,* has been most helpful.

6

Old Testament Roots

We learn from the first two chapters of Genesis that human beings were created by God to have a special relationship to him and to his creation—"So God created man in his own image, in the image of God he created him; male and female he created them" (1:27); and "The LORD God formed the man from the dust of the ground and breathed into his nostrils the breath of life, and the man became a living being" (2:7).[1] However, we also read in the third chapter that instead of developing in their relationship and communion of love with God and watching over creation for him, human beings chose to defy him and thereby break their unique relationship. Sin entered into the experience of the human race and prevented fellowship with God.

Though there is no specific statement to the effect, it is surely correct to hold that as created by God, Adam and Eve not only had physical perfection, but also were indwelt by the Holy Spirit. If this is so, then it is also the case that when they chose to disobey God (and thereby experienced spiritual death), they lost the presence of the Spirit from their souls. His presence had made possible and guaranteed their loving communion with their Creator; his absence meant that the human race was now in need of redemption and salvation. Henceforth in the history of the human race, fellowship with God was possible only when God took

---

1. See further Hans Walter Wolff, *Anthropology of the Old Testament*, pp. 159–65.

the initiative, through his Word and Spirit, of restoring the possibilities for such communion.

In the New Testament, Jesus the Christ (i.e., the One anointed by and filled with the Spirit) is presented as the One who truly bears and reflects the image of God; and, therefore, those who are united to him in faith for salvation can be said to be in the process of renewal towards bearing the image of God as God originally intended (Col. 1:15; 3:10; see also 2 Cor. 4:1–6). And, of course, those who are united to Christ in faith for salvation are those in whom the Spirit dwells. One purpose of personal inward regeneration by the Spirit is, therefore, to restore the image of God in believing sinners.

Old Testament Intimations of New Birth

We come now to the Old Testament roots of the New Testament teaching on personal inward regeneration by the Holy Spirit. Jesus apparently did not tell his disciples exactly how he came to choose the image of birth for describing the initial saving work of the Holy Spirit in the human soul. Of course, it is a very basic image; indeed, the rabbis used it to describe the conversion of Gentiles to Judaism. Further, as has already been suggested (p. 29), Jesus meditated upon the idea of the begetting of the King-Messiah as it is set forth in Psalm 2:7 and applied it to himself, as its quotation in Acts 13:33 and Hebrews 1:5 strongly intimates. In addition, the image of new birth wrought in the individual by the Spirit has obvious parallels with the effects which the Old Testament prophets promised the new covenant to be inaugurated in the age of the Messiah would have on individuals. The prophets declared that in this new covenant individuals would have an intimate fellowship with God. Certainly the pious members of old Israel longed for such a fellowship, as the words of the psalmist make clear: "Create in me a pure heart, O God, and renew a steadfast spirit within me" (Ps. 51:10). It is now our task to comment on some of the prophetic promises which parallel the New Testament image of new birth.[2]

"The time is coming," declares the LORD,
  "when I will make a new covenant

---

2. Sources for the comments on Jeremiah include John Bright, *Jeremiah,* and J. A. Thompson, *The Book of Jeremiah;* see also Bernhard W. Anderson, "The New Covenant and the Old," in *The Old Testament and Christian Faith,* pp. 225–42. Sources for the comments on Ezekiel include A. B. Davidson, *The Book of the Prophet Ezekiel,* and Walther Zimmerli, *Ezekiel;* Roy A. Harrisville, *The Concept of Newness in the New Testament,* is useful.

with the house of Israel
  and with the house of Judah.
It will not be like the covenant
  I made with their forefathers
when I took them by the hand
  to lead them out of Egypt,
because they broke my covenant,
  though I was a husband to them,"
                                        declares the LORD.
"This is the covenant I will make with the house of Israel
  after that time," declares the LORD.
"I will put my law in their minds
  and write it on their hearts.
I will be their God,
  and they will be my people.
No longer will a man teach his neighbor,
  or a man his brother, saying, 'Know the LORD,'
because they will all know me,
  from the least of them to the greatest,"
                                        declares the LORD.
"For I will forgive their wickedness
  and will remember their sins no more." [Jer. 31:31–34]

Like the old covenant, the new covenant will create a right relationship between God and his people, center around the law (God's will),
and include all the people of God. However, unlike the old covenant, the
new belongs specifically to the last days ("the time is coming"); further,
it involves creating new people through special divine action. God will
directly implant his will in the hearts of his people through the Holy
Spirit's presence there; and thereby they will come to enjoy a full communion with God, know what he requires of them, and experience the
sense of being forgiven their sins.

From the New Testament we know that this prophecy pointed to
Christ's work on the cross, where the new covenant was inaugurated,
and also to the Spirit's work of bringing the effects of Christ's saving
work into human souls. Personal inward regeneration is, then, a part of
the benefits of the new covenant. (See 2 Cor. 3:7–18 for a comparison of
the glories of the old and new covenants.)

*I will surely gather them from all the lands where I banish them in my furious anger and
great wrath; I will bring them back to this place and let them live in safety. They will be
my people, and I will be their God. I will give them singleness of heart and action, so
that they will always fear me for their own good and the good of their children after
them. I will make an everlasting covenant with them: I will never stop doing good to
them, and I will inspire them to fear me, so that they will never turn away from me. I*

*will rejoice in doing them good and will assuredly plant them in this land with all my
heart and soul. [Jer. 32:37–41]*

These verses are not merely a repeat of Jeremiah 31:31–34, for here
God promises to create a singleness of heart and action within his people
of the new covenant. They will be a people of one heart and one way.
Further, the new covenant is described as an everlasting covenant, and it
is set in the context of the restoration of the land. Thus God's promise
here relates to his work in individual hearts (personal regeneration) in a
new community and place (cosmic regeneration).

*I will give them an undivided heart and put a new spirit in them; I will remove from
them their heart of stone and give them a heart of flesh. Then they will follow my
decrees and be careful to keep my laws. They will be my people, and I will be their God.
[Ezek. 11:19–20]*

God makes a promise to the exiles in Babylonia as they look forward
to their restoration to the homeland (Ezek. 11:14–21). He will so work in
their hearts as to make them a people of undivided loyalty who faithfully
worship and serve him. By divine energy their inner lives will be renewed so that they gladly and freely follow God and walk in his ways,
and thereby enjoy full communion and fellowship with him. Here the
action of God on his people is emphasized, but his action in each individual (the dynamic equivalent of regeneration) is necessarily included.

*I will sprinkle clean water on you, and you will be clean; I will cleanse you from all your
impurities and from all your idols. I will give you a new heart and put a new spirit in
you; I will remove from you your heart of stone and give you a heart of flesh. And I will
put my Spirit in you and move you to follow my decrees and be careful to keep my laws.
[Ezek. 36:25–27]*

Once again God promises to renew the people of Israel. This is part of
a larger promise which includes restoration and renewal of the land
itself (Ezek. 36:22–32) and so fits into what we have called cosmic regeneration. In verse 27 the prophet specifically states that God will place
his Spirit within the souls of his people and thereby directly influence
their wills to follow in his ways and obey his will. This points to the new
birth from above.

*The hand of the LORD was upon me, and he brought me out by the Spirit of the LORD
and set me in the middle of a valley; it was full of bones. He led me back and forth
among them, and I saw a great many bones on the floor of the valley, bones that were
very dry. He asked me, "Son of man, can these bones live?"
I said, "O Sovereign LORD, you alone know."*

> Then he said to me, "Prophesy to these bones and say to them, 'Dry bones, hear
> the word of the LORD! This is what the Sovereign LORD says to these bones: I will make
> breath enter you, and you will come to life. I will attach tendons to you and make flesh
> come upon you and cover you with skin; I will put breath in you, and you will come to
> life. Then you will know that I am the LORD.'"
>
> So I prophesied as I was commanded. And as I was prophesying, there was a noise,
> a rattling sound, and the bones came together, bone to bone. I looked, and tendons
> and flesh appeared on them and skin covered them, but there was no breath in them.
>
> Then he said to me, "Prophesy to the breath; prophesy, son of man, and say to it,
> 'This is what the Sovereign LORD says: Come from the four winds, O breath, and
> breathe into these slain, that they may live.'" So I prophesied as he commanded me,
> and breath entered them; they came to life and stood up on their feet—a vast army.
>
> Then he said to me: "Son of man, these bones are the whole house of Israel. They
> say, 'Our bones are dried up and our hope is gone; we are cut off.' Therefore prophesy
> and say to them: 'This is what the Sovereign LORD says: O my people, I am going to
> open your graves and bring you up from them; I will bring you back to the land of Israel.
> Then you, my people, will know that I am the LORD, when I open your graves and bring
> you up from them. I will put my Spirit in you and you will live, and I will settle you in
> your own land. Then you will know that I the LORD have spoken, and I have done it,
> declares the LORD.'" [Ezek. 37:1–14]

We have already referred to the vision of dry bones several times (see, e.g., pp. 15, 16). Suffice it to say here that it was obviously on Jesus' mind when he spoke to Nicodemus (see especially John 3:5–8). And just as Ezekiel had revitalization of the whole house of Israel in view, so was Jesus pointing to the possibility of new birth for all Israel through the work of the Spirit. This in fact is the force of the plural *you* in "You must be born again" (John 3:7) and "You people do not accept our testimony. I have spoken to you of earthly things and you do not believe; how then will you believe if I speak of heavenly things?" (vv. 11–12).

The Question of Regeneration Under the Old Covenant

Before leaving the Old Testament we must face a question which is often asked and on which there has been controversy within the church: Were the faithful believers within old Israel regenerate? Here one might think of Abraham or Moses, David or Hezekiah, Elijah or Elisha, Jeremiah or Ezekiel, and Elizabeth and Zechariah, the parents of John the Baptist. The reason why the question is asked is that the new birth, while presented as a necessity by Jesus, is also seen as the work of the Spirit, who came in fullness only after the exaltation of Jesus into heaven. Perhaps the best way to come up with an answer is to reflect upon the differences between the old and new covenants.

The provisions of the old and new covenants are not identical for they belong to two different periods of history. God chose two different ways to be in partnership and communion with his people. The truly essential point is that God's people must keep their side of the agreement, whatever that might be.

The Mosaic or old covenant was inaugurated by God and came wholly from his initiative at Mount Sinai. He called the descendants of Abraham into this agreement and relationship, and thus each child born within the community of Israel was born into the covenant and could rightly look to God as his or her God. The requirements for continuing in fellowship and communion with God were carefully set out in the law of Moses. The Israelites were to keep the law both in letter and in spirit, with the emphasis upon the latter. They were to trust and obey the Lord and do whatever he commanded them; as they complied, he would pardon their offenses and protect, bless, and guide them. The Spirit's presence with the faithful was more in the nature of always being available rather than permanently living within. The important point is that true communion and fellowship with God were enjoyed by all those who did what God told them to do.

The new covenant was also inaugurated by God. It came wholly from his initiative in offering his Son, Jesus Christ, as a sacrifice for the sins of the world at Calvary, and in raising him, triumphant over Satan, sin, and death, into heaven as the exalted Messiah. The new covenant is therefore made in Christ with all those who positively respond to the proclamation of the gospel. This proclamation is a continuing duty of the church; thus the new covenant is always open for the entry of new members gained through evangelistic effort.

The big difference between the old and new covenants is that God in the new comes much nearer to his people and offers greater possibilities of fellowship and communion with him. The possibilities are greater because he now relates to his people in and through his incarnate Son, Jesus Christ. In Christ he gives the Spirit to be a permanent presence and helper within the souls of the faithful. All that God has to give to his people is there, as it were, in potential.

The requirements of the new covenant, unlike those of the old, center upon Christ; they relate to believing in him, following him, and looking for his second advent. Enjoyment of the privileges of the new covenant is open only to those who fulfil the conditions of faith, hope, and love. Thus we may say that a faithful believer under the old covenant had a better relationship with God than a halfhearted believer under the new covenant experiences.

We now see why Jesus told Nicodemus that he, and all Jews for that matter, had to be born anew (or from above) through the Spirit. The old covenant was becoming obsolete; the new covenant was about to be inaugurated by Christ's being lifted up on the cross. The Jews had to allow God to transfer them from the old into the new covenant; and for him to effect this transfer, they had to receive the Messiah and believe on his name. In doing so, they would receive the permanent gift of the Holy Spirit to enable them truly to know, worship, love, and serve the Lord.

The answer to our question as to whether the faithful believers of old Israel were regenerate is, then, both yes and no. If by "regenerate" is meant that they had a right relationship with God and enjoyed communion with him, then certainly they were regenerate. They were assisted by the Holy Spirit in their relationship with the covenant God. However, if by "regenerate" is meant that the Holy Spirit was permanently present in their souls, then the answer is that they were not regenerate, for they could not have enjoyed the benefits of the new covenant before it had been inaugurated.

At the beginning of this chapter we noted that Jesus Christ alone is truly the image and likeness of God, for he was permanently filled with the Holy Spirit, and all power and authority in heaven and on earth were given to him. Now in addition to creating fellowship between the Creator-Savior and humans, the Holy Spirit in his work of regeneration under the new covenant also begins to renew humans so that they come to reflect the divine image and likeness, which were perfectly reflected in the person of Jesus. So regeneration leads to a new creation, which, because it is rooted in Christ, is permanent. The new covenant produces a dynamic permanence of fellowship, communion, and service.

Finally, we must add that in the old covenant God occasionally did in fact pour out his Spirit upon selected individuals so that they could perform a mighty work in his name (see, e.g., Judg. 3:9–10; 6:34; 11:29; cf. 16:20). According to the prophecy of Joel (2:28–29) and the evidence of Acts, however, it is God's will within the new covenant that Christ as the Lord should pour out the Spirit upon all flesh, that is, upon all believers.

7

Complementary Doctrines

If we are to appreciate the major ways in which the doctrine of individual regeneration has been developed, expressed, confessed, and defended throughout church history, we must attempt to set the teaching on internal revolution, rebirth, and new creation in some kind of biblical context. To do this properly would mean providing a full-scale biblical theology, which is far beyond the scope of this volume. What we can and must do in the brief compass of one chapter is to offer a general overview of the New Testament teaching on salvation. Our method of procedure will take the form of a series of observations on doctrines which complement the doctrine of regeneration. It is freely admitted that these observations are in large measure based on the way in which the doctrine of regeneration has itself been expressed over the centuries of theological exploration!

Repentance and Conversion

New birth leading to a new life is a gift from God; it cannot be earned. Accordingly, God never commands people to be born again through their own efforts. He does require, however, that they repent of their sins, believe the gospel concerning his kingdom and the resurrection of Jesus, and live as faithful and obedient disciples who look for the age to come. This requirement is found in the preaching of Jesus in the Gospels, in the speeches of the apostles and evangelists in the Book of Acts, and in the exhortations in the Epistles.[1]

The question whether new birth or repentance comes first cannot be definitively answered. There is here a paradox of grace that while we are to continue to work out our salvation reverentially and soberly, we are to remember that it is always God who takes the initiative and supplies the grace (Phil. 2:13). And, as Paul told the church in Ephesus, though we are commanded to believe the gospel and have faith in God and his promises, faith itself is impossible without divine assistance (Eph. 2:8–9). Where the Spirit is present, blessings will follow, including the fruit of the Spirit (Gal. 5:22–23) and the various gifts of the Spirit (Rom. 12:6–8).

Conversion, repentance, and faith are closely associated concepts. Repentance (*metanoia*) and faith (*pistis*) go together since repentance is primarily a turning from sin and faith is primarily a turning to God in trust and commitment. Conversion is a wider concept than either repentance or faith, for it assumes a turning from sin in order to emphasize a turning to God in faith and faithfulness. Thus the concept of conversion (*epistrophē*) usually stands alone (Acts 9:35; 15:3), though it occasionally appears in tandem with faith (Acts 11:21).

A person who has been converted is one who has turned from darkness to light, from the power of Satan to God, and who has received forgiveness of sins and been placed within the new people of God, set apart for God's service (Acts 26:18). Conversion is not a synonym for new birth; however, there can be no conversion without God's granting new life to the soul. New birth, then, is a major part of God's personal involvement in the conversion of sinners into saints.

Forgiveness and Justification

Forgiveness (*aphesis*) is the action of God in restoring sinners to a right relationship with himself; it is the pardoning, canceling, and passing over the guilt of sin, which is guilt before God the Judge.[2] Jesus declared the forgiveness of sins (Mark 2:5–12); indeed, one basic purpose of his sacrificial death was to make it possible for repentant sinners to be forgiven (Matt. 26:28; Mark 10:45). Jesus also insisted (in the Lord's Prayer, for example) that those whom God forgives ought in turn to

---

1. On conversion, repentance, and faith see Colin Brown, ed., *The New International Dictionary of New Testament Theology,* vol. 1, pp. 353–62, 587–606.

2. On forgiveness and justification see Colin Brown, ed., *The New International Dictionary of New Testament Theology,* vol. 1, pp. 697–703, and vol. 3, pp. 352–77; see also Peter Toon, *Justification and Sanctification.*

forgive their fellow human beings. From this insistence it is obvious that Jesus believed that the internal power of the Spirit (i.e., new birth) is given to those whom God forgives—how else could they freely forgive others? Thus, while forgiveness, in the strictest sense of the word, has to do with the external relationship between God and the repenting sinner, it never exists in isolation. It always occurs in combination with the other aspects of salvation; it is one of the vital parts of the arrival of the kingdom in word and in power.

Justification (*dikaiōsis*), as it is expounded in the Letters of Paul, is a larger concept than forgiveness. While forgiveness is primarily concerned with cancelation of guilt, justification is primarily concerned with an external change in one's personal standing before God, a right relationship with him under the new covenant of grace. A term from the lawcourt, justification connotes being placed in the right and judged to be in the right by God the Judge. The doctrine of justification by grace and through faith, as Paul expounds it in Galatians and Romans, is about sinners' believing in the Lord Jesus and being clothed in his righteousness (his perfect obedience and his sacrificial offering) so as to be perfectly acceptable to God as Judge. So justification is not really acquittal; it is being judged and found to be in the right because of being in and with Christ, who is the righteous (i.e., the right) One.

The concept of justification, like forgiveness, never stands alone; it is one of the many aspects of salvation. For example, into those who are justified God also pours his Spirit (hence new birth) and the love of Christ (Rom. 5:5; 8:1–17). Further, what God declares believers to be as he views them in Christ is also what he intends they shall truly be; thus justification leads to their actually being made righteous through the inner renewal of the Spirit (Rom. 6).

The Kingdom of God

We noticed in looking at John 3 that to see and to enter the kingdom of God a person must be born again and from above.[3] The kingdom of God is the fatherly, gracious reign of God in human lives, his rule over his redeemed people. The doctrine of the kingdom includes the ideas of a new Israel, a people of the new covenant, citizenship in the age to come. Personal regeneration does not issue into an individualistic relationship with God the Father through the Son and by the Spirit; rather, it issues into membership amongst a new people, each one of whom has a per-

---

3. On the church and the kingdom of God see Colin Brown, ed., *The New International Dictionary of New Testament Theology*, vol. 1, pp. 291–307, and vol. 2, pp. 376–77, 381–89.

sonal relationship with God. The call of God is a call into his kingdom and into the society of his people, the *ekklēsia,* the church, to become a member of his household of faith, a soldier in his army, and a disciple in the school of Christ. Birth from above is birth into a family whose home is in heaven where Christ is exalted at the right hand of the Father. Growth in new life is growth into Christ within his body, the church; to fellowship one with another within this body is an important aspect of personal growth. It is always salutary to remember that the "You must be born again" of John 3:7 is not in the singular but in the plural. Jesus states that all religious people—adherents of the faith of old Israel and of the newly established Christianity—have of necessity to be born again and together in Christ to become the new people of God.

Baptism in Water

When Gentiles converted to Judaism, they were baptized in a bath of water as an external sign that their impurity was being washed away as they entered the community of Israel.[4] Males were also circumcised and an appropriate sacrifice offered. The rabbis referred to baptized converts as newborn children. John the Baptist also called for baptism as a sign of both a break with the past and a new beginning of loyalty to God and his Messiah.

A survey of the New Testament references to baptism in water leaves us with certain general impressions. First, the rite was seen as intimately related to the work of God within the believer in terms of forgiveness and justification. Converts never baptized themselves! Baptism was administered to them, thereby portraying that God alone is the author and giver of salvation. Second, baptism was a once-for-all rite of entry into God's people; it was not to be repeated at a future date. Thereby the once-for-all nature of the work of Christ for sinners was symbolized. Third, baptism signified and symbolized incorporation into Christ and into his body (Rom. 6:1–14; Gal. 3:26–27). To be baptized was therefore a synonym for being a Christian, a justified sinner, a born-again believer, and a child of God.

This general picture leaves open certain issues which have been hotly contended in the history of the church. Regrettably, there is no clear scriptural teaching on whether or not children and infants were baptized. Were there children in the whole households that were baptized when the head of the family accepted the faith? If the procedure used for

---

4. On baptism see Colin Brown, ed., *The New International Dictionary of New Testament Theology,* vol. 1, pp. 143–54, and vol. 3, pp. 1208–10; see also Michael Green, *I Believe in the Holy Spirit,* pp. 123–47.

converts to Judaism was followed by the young churches, the answer is yes, but we cannot be sure that the churches did in fact adopt the Judaic practice. What we are sure about is that from an early date the baptism of infants born into Christian homes was very widely practiced. Then, also, we do not learn from the New Testament the chronological relationship of baptism to new birth, saving faith, and justification by God. We may think that baptism normally occurs soon after the believer has been justified and born anew; but in the case of infants from Christian homes, where the faith is that of the parents and sponsors, the issue becomes complicated.

Sanctification

It is important that we recognize that sanctification is portrayed by the writers of the New Testament as much more than a process of being made or becoming holy.[5] Take Paul's teaching, for example. The concept of sanctification begins with the idea that believers are in Jesus Christ, who is their holiness: "You are in Christ Jesus, who has become for us wisdom from God—that is, our righteousness, holiness and redemption" (1 Cor. 1:30). In Christ they were chosen by God out of all peoples, placed on his side, and thereby dedicated to his service. In Christ believers have both a right relationship with God (justification) and a place on God's side over against the profane world (sanctification). The church is made up of those who are "sanctified in Christ Jesus" (1 Cor. 1:2; cf. 6:11). Already made holy in Christ, they are also called to be holy in daily living, for in them the Holy Spirit dwells (1 Thess. 4:3–5). Holiness or sanctification, the state of belonging to God and being dedicated to him, issues in a life of service through the power of the Spirit.

In the Letter to the Hebrews, Christ is presented as the Sanctifier of his people: "We have been made holy through the sacrifice of the body of Jesus Christ once for all" (10:10). Here the perfect tense of the verb conveys the idea of something done once for all. In 10:14 two tenses are used to convey the two-sided nature of sanctification: "By one sacrifice he has made perfect forever those who are being made holy." Sanctification is completed in Christ, but in daily service the people of God are being made holy so that they become in practice what they already are in Christ (saints).

The image of sanctification is drawn from the cultus of the temple of Jerusalem where the men and utensils that had a part in the worship of God were set aside and specially consecrated to the service of the Deity. Jesus sanctified himself in that he consecrated himself wholly to God's

5. On sanctification see Peter Toon, *Justification and Sanctification*.

service and cause. To be in him is to be placed on God's side forever, and to be in him is to possess his Spirit and to be involved in becoming holy. Personal regeneration is particularly related to that aspect of the concept of sanctification in which the believer becomes holy through the internal dwelling and ministration of the Spirit. Accordingly, the beginning of this process of becoming holy in soul, heart, mind, and will is usually called regeneration. This said, it must also be said that within the New Testament the concept of sanctification is so broad that it encompasses that which is specially highlighted by the image of new birth through the Spirit. It is unfortunate, then, that much Christian theology has rather simplistically taken regeneration as the beginning and sanctification as the continuation of the process of becoming holy.

Fillings with the Spirit

In the Book of Acts there are six occasions when people are said to be filled with the Spirit. The first was on the day of Pentecost (2:4); that filling was followed by speaking in tongues, praising the Lord, and preaching the gospel of the resurrection. The second involves the apostle Peter, who was filled with the Spirit before he addressed the Sanhedrin (4:8), while the third involves a group of disciples who, having engaged in corporate prayer, were then similarly enabled to speak the word of God with boldness (4:31). Paul provides the fourth example: after Christ had encountered him on the road to Damascus and Ananias had laid hands on him, he too was filled with the Spirit (9:17–19). And Paul knew what it was to be filled with the Spirit during his apostolic ministry, as his experience in confronting Elymas the sorcerer reveals (13:9). Finally, there is the description of the disciples of Jesus who "were filled with joy and with the Holy Spirit" (13:52). To these references we must add the exhortation of Paul in Ephesians 5:18: "Do not get drunk on wine, which leads to debauchery. Instead, be filled with the Spirit." The tense of the verb and the context suggest that Paul is telling his readers that they are to "go on being filled with the Spirit" throughout their Christian life and service. Unlike the new birth, then, which is a one-time occurrence when the Holy Spirit begins to indwell the soul, there can be many fillings with the Spirit.

Cosmic Regeneration

Since we have already studied the theme of cosmic regeneration in chapter 5, we need only restate it here in order to complete our picture of doctrines which complement the doctrine of individual regeneration.

God's purpose for believers is not individualistic salvation but personal salvation in a cosmic and societal setting.

The grace of God is rich and varied and is experienced at different times and in diverse ways. Thus it is not surprising that there is a wealth of images within the New Testament by which each aspect of the gracious work of God is described and emphasized. It is impossible to use all of the images at one time; a choice has to be made. At different times in the history of the church, groups of theologians have decided to make one image prominent and to subsume the others under it. Those that are brought under the chosen "umbrella concept" naturally lose some of their own particularized meaning, for they are trimmed to fit the chosen image. This process is perhaps necessary and inevitable, but historians of doctrine must be aware of how a number of biblical images and concepts have undergone a change in their meaning as a result. That is why the study of the development of doctrine is important.[6]

Before looking at the ways in which personal inward regeneration has been described and understood in the life of the church, it is appropriate to summarize the main points of what we have thus far discovered concerning this act of God. First of all, we have noted that personal regeneration is a part of the action of God in bringing into reality the new covenant of grace; in particular, it is the action of the Holy Spirit bringing the benefit of the saving work of Jesus (on the cross and in his exaltation to heaven) to the individual, who thus becomes a member of the new people of God. That there is need for such an inward work of divine grace reflects the sinfulness of the human heart, a truth we have presupposed but not elaborated.

In the second place, we have noted that the Spirit's inward work of grace is presented in images of birth, rebirth, re-creation (or new creation), and resurrection. These images show that it is the beginning of a new life which will reach its fruition in a new body in the new age of the kingdom of God.

Finally, we have seen that inward regeneration is a decisive act of God which he does only once in each individual believer. Its one-time nature is brought out by the use of the aorist tense in John 1:13, and 3:3, 5, 7. Then, also, that this decisive act has important permanent consequences is brought out by the use of the perfect tense in 1 John 2:29; 3:9; 4:7; and 5:1, 4, 18. Inward new birth leads to a new life of faith and faithfulness, righteousness and love, which anticipates the fullness of life in the age to come after the regeneration of the universe.

---

6. See Peter Toon, *The Development of Doctrine in the Church.*

PART TWO

Theological Interpretations

8

Patristic and Medieval Interpretations

By Water and the Spirit

W‎e turn now to examine the major ways in which the church and her theologians have through the centuries interpreted the doctrine of regeneration. In this chapter we shall look first at early patristic understandings. Then we shall turn to the rite of baptism in the Greek East and in the Coptic church of Egypt. We then move to the Latin West. Having described its rite of baptism, we shall summarize the positions of Augustine, the Council of Orange, and Thomas Aquinas. Finally, we shall take note of a baptismal service in use in Germany on the eve of the Reformation. Against this background we shall be better able to judge the teaching of the Protestant churches, as well as of the Church of Rome, from the sixteenth century to the present day.

Early Patristic Interpretations

In examining how the doctrine of inward regeneration was interpreted in the period from the second to the fifteenth centuries, we must be mentally prepared to encounter an approach and context very different from contemporary Western Protestantism. In particular, we have to be prepared for the fact that virtually all discussion of the new birth is in the context of the rite of baptism. It was taken for granted throughout these centuries that being "born of water and the Spirit" refers to the outward act of baptism (whether of adults or infants) and the inward act of regeneration. This intimate connection between water baptism and spiritual birth is clearly seen in Justin Martyr's *First Apology,* written about 155, as he explains baptism to non-Christians:

> As many as are persuaded and believe that the things are true which are taught by us [Christian teachers] . . . are instructed to pray and entreat God with fasting, for the remission of their past sins, and we pray and fast with them. Then they are brought by us to where there is water, and are born again in like manner in which we ourselves were born again. For in the name of God, the Father and Lord of the universe, and of our Saviour Jesus Christ, and of the Holy Spirit, they then receive the washing of water.[1]

Justin then quotes from John 3 and Isaiah 1:16–20, which contains the exhortation, "Wash and make yourselves clean." He further explains that the new birth illumines spiritual truth. After baptism there followed participation in the Eucharist and full membership in the congregation.

From the *Apostolic Tradition* of Hippolytus we learn of the preparation for baptism in Rome around 200. Converts to Christ and Christianity who expressed a desire to enter the church were rigorously tested, instructed in the faith, tested again, and then baptized. The full catechumenate had four stages lasting three years. First the candidates were given private instruction. Second, they became "hearers," that is, they were allowed into part of the Sunday service to hear the ministry of the Word. Third, they became "kneelers," that is, they were allowed to remain for the ministry of the Word and the prayers. The fourth stage involved examination by the bishop and specific preparation for baptism, a ceremony so rich that the candidates were hardly likely to forget it. For it was as if they had been newly conceived in the womb and had been growing in faith, hope, and love, waiting for their birth in the rite of holy baptism.

Before there were specially built churches with baptistries, baptisms took place in the running water of a stream or river. Candidates took off all their clothing before entering the water. Coming up out of the water after baptism in the triune name, they were garbed in a clean white robe, a symbol of purity (cleansing from sin). The bishop laid his hands

---

1. In E. C. Whitaker, ed., *Documents of the Baptismal Liturgy,* p. 2.

upon their heads and anointed them with oil. Then followed participation in the Eucharist, which could include, on this occasion, not only the sacramental bread and wine, but also milk and honey, symbols of entrance into the Promised Land of the new covenant and family of God.

Of course, the church insisted that the grace of God given before, in, and after baptism came to human beings through Jesus Christ by the Holy Spirit. One favorite way of explaining the nature of this grace and its effect was that the Spirit was restoring the divine image within the human soul. This action was necessary since by their sin Adam and Eve had caused a distortion and defilement of this image. Here is how the great Athanasius explained it in his *De incarnatione,* written about 318:

> 13. So the Word of God came in his own person, in order that, as he is the image of the Father, he might be able to restore man who is in the image. . . . So he was justified in taking a mortal body, in order that in it death could be destroyed and men might again be renewed in the image. For this, then, none other than the image of the Father was required.
>
> 14. For as when a figure which has been painted on wood is spoilt by dirt, it is necessary for him whose portrait it is to come again so that the picture can be renewed in the same material—for because of his portrait the material on which it is painted is not thrown away, but the portrait is redone on it—even so the all-holy Son of the Father, who is the image of the Father, came to our realms to renew man who had been made in his likeness, and, as one lost, to find him through the forgiveness of sins; just as he said in the Gospels: "I have come to find and save that which was lost" (Luke 19:10). Therefore he also said to the Jews: *"Unless a man is born again,"* not referring to the birth from women as they supposed, but indicating the soul which is born again and restored in being in the image.

Thus, for Athanasius, the purpose of the incarnation and saving work of the eternal Son was to bring to humankind renewal of the image of God in their souls together with the forgiveness of their sins. Cleansing and renewal are themes often found in patristic divinity.

The Greek East

By the sixth century the Greek Orthodox rite of holy baptism had reached the form it has retained to the present day.[2] Originally designed for adult converts schooled in the catechumenate, it has been used in modern times more for infants than for adults. In the Eastern churches, baptism has remained unified with what has in the West come to be

---

2. Ibid., pp. 60–82.

called confirmation. Thus the Eastern equivalent of confirmation is administered to all who are baptized, adults and infants.

The service falls into two halves—the formal introduction of a catechumen into the church and the order of holy baptism. In the first are a prayer for the admission of the catechumen, the priest's exorcism of the devil and his influence from the candidate, and the candidate's renunciation of the devil and confession of the true God. The second half begins with the consecration of the baptismal water in order that it might be the means of spiritual birth. After breathing upon the water three times and making the sign of the cross over it three times, the priest prays to God:

> O Maker of all things, declare this water to be a water of rest, water of redemption, water of sanctification, a cleansing of the pollution of the body and soul, a loosening of chains, forgiveness of sins, enlightenment of souls, washing of rebirth, grace of adoption, raiment of immortality, renewal of spirit, fount of life. For you, Lord, have said, *Wash you and make you clean* [Isa. 1:16]. Take away the wickedness from our souls. You have given us the new birth from above by water and Spirit. Be present, O Lord, in this water and grant that those who are baptized therein may be refashioned, so that they may *put off the old man, which is corrupt according to the deceitful lusts* [Eph. 4:22], and put on the new man, which is restored after the image of him that created him: that being *planted together in the likeness of the death* [Rom. 6:5] of your Only-Begotten Son, through baptism, they may share also in his resurrection: and guarding the gift of your Holy Spirit, and increasing the store of grace, they may receive *the prize of the high calling* [Phil. 3:14] and be numbered among *the first-born who are written in heaven* [Heb. 12:23] in Christ Jesus our Lord.

Having prayed for the hallowing of the water of baptism, the priest then prays that the holy oil to be used in the chrism (an anointing with the sign of the cross) will be "a chrism of incorruption, a shield of righteousness, a renewal of soul and body, turning away every work of the devil, unto deliverance from all evil for those that are anointed in faith and partake of it."

Using this holy oil, the priest makes the sign of the cross upon the forehead, breast, and back of the candidate. Following further anointing by the deacon, the priest baptizes the candidate by immersion in the threefold name. After the baptism the singer joyfully sings, "Blessed are they whose iniquities have been forgiven" (Ps. 32:1), as the baptized are robed in white clothing. Then the priest offers another prayer:

> Blessed are you, O Lord God, . . . who even at this moment have been pleased to give new birth to these your servants newly enlightened, by

water and Spirit, and have bestowed upon them forgiveness of their sins, both willingly and unwillingly committed: . . . give to them also the seal of the gift of your holy and all-powerful and worshipful Spirit, and the communion of the holy body and precious blood of your Christ. Guard them in your sanctification: strengthen them in the right faith: deliver them from the evil one and from all his ways, and by your saving fear keep their souls in holiness and righteousness: that being well-pleasing to you in every work and word, they may become sons and inheritors of your heavenly kingdom.

The priest then recites Galatians 3:27, "As many as are baptized in Christ have put on Christ," and proceeds to anoint each newly baptized person. He makes the sign of the cross on the forehead, eyes, nostrils, mouth, and both ears and proclaims it "the seal of the gift of the Holy Spirit." As he retires, he recites Psalm 32:1. Then follows the Eucharist in which the baptized receive the sacramental body and blood of Christ. Thereafter, whether adults or children, they are viewed as members of the body of Christ, children of God, inheritors of the kingdom of Christ.

In this Byzantine rite, the Holy Spirit is seen as being specially present in, through, and with the consecrated water so that, as the candidates are immersed in it, he acts upon and in them to bring them into spiritual union with Christ and into the benefits of his saving death and resurrection. Likewise the Holy Spirit is specially present in, through, and with the oil of chrism so that he begins to indwell the soul when the postbaptismal anointing takes place.

Additional information on how the baptismal liturgy was understood in the early period can be found in the explanations which Cyril of Jerusalem (c. 315–386), John Chrysostom (c. 345–407), and Theodore of Mopsuestia (c. 350–428) offered to catechumens being prepared for baptism at the Easter festival.[3] We learn from Cyril that the sacrament was efficacious only when the candidates were sincere in intention:

If you pretend, men will indeed baptize you, but the Spirit will not baptize you; but if you approach with faith, men will minister to you visibly but the Holy Spirit will bestow upon you what is not visible. . . . It rests with God to bestow grace, but with you to accept and cherish it. Do not despise the grace because it is freely given, but rather cherish it with reverence once you have received it.[4]

---

3. These explanations of baptism are described in Raymond Furnish, *The Meaning of Baptism.*

4. Cyril of Jerusalem, in *The Works of Saint Cyril of Jerusalem*, trans. Anthony A. Stephenson and Leo P. McCauley, vol. 1, p. 93.

He proceeds to explain how each and every part of the rite exhibits at least one of the aspects of the manifold grace of God.

Chrysostom tells of the spiritual effects of baptism in the consecrated water:

> The cleansing is called the bath of regeneration. [God] saves us, says St Paul, through the bath of regeneration and renewal by the Holy Spirit. It is also called enlightenment, and again it is St Paul who calls it this. . . . It is also called baptism. For all you have been baptized into Christ, have put on Christ. It is called a burial, for you were buried, says St Paul, with him by means of baptism into death. It is called circumcision. In him, too, you have been circumcised with a circumcision not wrought by hand but through putting off the body of flesh. It is called a cross. For our old self has been crucified with him, in order that the old body of sin may be destroyed.

He explains in more detail why baptism was called a bath of *regeneration:*

> And why, someone will say, if the bath takes away all our sins, is it not called the bath of the remission of sins, or the bath of cleansing, rather than the bath of regeneration? The reason is that it does not simply remit our sins, nor does it simply cleanse us of our faults, but it does this just as if we were born anew. For it does create us anew and it fashions us again, not moulding us from earth, but creating us from a different element, the nature of water.[5]

Thus baptism is the bath of cleansing and new life by the power of the Spirit.

With help from the illustration of a smelting furnace, Chrysostom gives us further insight into what he believes that God achieves in and through holy baptism:

> This bath does not merely cleanse the vessel but melts the whole thing down again. Even if a vessel has been wiped off and carefully cleansed, it still has the marks of what it is and still bears the traces of the stain. But when it is thrown into the smelting furnace and is renewed by the flames, it puts aside all dross and, when it comes from the furnace, it gives forth the same sheen as newly-moulded vessels. When a man takes and melts down a gold statue which has become filthy with the filth of years of smoke and dirt and rust, he returns it to us all clean and shining. So, too, God takes this nature of ours when it is rusted with the rust of sin, when our faults have covered it with abundant soot, and when it has destroyed the

---

5. John Chrysostom, *Baptismal Instructions,* ed. and trans. P. W. Harkins, p. 138.

beauty he put on it in the beginning, and he smelts it anew. He plunges it into the waters as into the smelting furnace and lets the grace of the Spirit fall on it instead of the flames. He then brings us forth from the furnace, renewed like newly-moulded vessels, to rival the rays of the sun with our brightness. He has broken the old man to pieces but has produced a new man who shines brighter than the old.[6]

So it is that if any man is in Christ he is a new creation.

Theodore made a special effort to convey the thought that baptism looks forward to the resurrection of the body and the life of the age to come:

The power of holy baptism consists in this: it implants in you the hope of future benefits, enables you to participate in the things which we expect, and, by means of symbols and signs of the future good things, it informs you with the gift of the Holy Spirit, the firstfruits of whom you receive when you are baptized.[7]

He saw the baptistry as a womb preparing the candidates for sacramental birth, and he described the water as "the water of second birth," the fluid surrounding the unborn child in the womb.

It is clear from the teaching of these three Fathers of the early Greek church that they took extremely seriously Jesus' dictum that the new birth is by water and the Spirit. As God made water, so also is he able to use that water as the bath of spiritual regeneration. "Great is the baptism that lies before you: a ransom to captives; a remission of offences; a death to sin; a new birth of the soul; a garment of light; a holy indissoluble seal; a chariot to heaven; the delight of Paradise; a welcome into the kingdom; the gift of adoption."[8]

The Coptic Church of Egypt

Claiming an origin through the missionary labors of Mark, the Coptic church went into near isolation after the late fifth century. It has often suffered persecution, but it still exists today, preserving rites and ceremonies that have remained virtually unchanged for more than a millennium.[9]

---

6. Ibid., p. 139.
7. Theodore of Mopsuestia, *Commentary of Theodore of Mopsuestia on the Lord's Prayer and on the Sacraments of Baptism and the Eucharist,* ed. A. Mingana, pp. 53–54.
8. Cyril of Jerusalem, *Works,* vol. 1, p. 82.
9. Whitaker, ed., *Documents of the Baptismal Liturgy,* pp. 83–98.

The baptismal rite is similar to that of other Eastern churches in that it assumes that the candidates have been catechumens, exorcises the devil's claim and influence upon them, and requires them to make a profession of the Christian faith. Three times oil is used in the service— the oil of exorcism (when the priest drives the devil away), the oil of thanksgiving (when the priest anoints the breast, arms, and hands with the "oil of gladness" and then later pours wine into the baptismal waters to sanctify them), and the oil of chrism (when the priest prays for the descent of the Spirit into the soul of the baptized).

After the candidates (or, in the case of infants, their sponsors) have professed the faith, the priest addresses the Lord Jesus Christ in prayer:

> We pray and beseech you to search the chambers of their souls and en-lighten the eyes of their understanding with the light of knowledge. All magic, all sorcery, all workings of Satan chase from them; all traces of idolatry and unbelief cast out of their heart. Prepare their souls for the reception of your Holy Spirit. And let them be worthy of the new birth of the laver, and of remission of sins. Prepar[e] them to be a temple of your Holy Spirit, according to the will of your good Father and the Holy Spirit.

As the candidates come out of the water of baptism and are anointed with the chrism, the priest prays to God to bestow the Holy Spirit upon them so that his presence may be "a living seal and confirmation" to them. Then after they have been clothed in a white "garment of eternal and immortal life," signed with the cross, and breathed upon by the priest, he prays for them, thanking God for their new birth through baptism and their reception of the remission of their sins, and asking that he send down upon them "the grace of the Holy Spirit, the Para-clete," and make them "partakers of life eternal and immortality." Then, "being born again by water and Spirit, they may be able to enter into the kingdom of heaven." After further ceremonies the baptized receive the consecrated bread and wine of the Eucharist. They are now full members of the church, whether they be infants or adults.

Again, as with the Byzantine rite, there is the conviction that the Holy Spirit is specially present in, through, and with both the water and oil so that those who are washed in water and anointed with oil actually receive within their souls the Holy Spirit and the grace he brings.

The Latin West

In the Western, Latin-speaking part of the Roman Empire, baptism was normally administered at the feast of the resurrection and occasion-ally also at Pentecost (Whitsuntide). Candidates were prepared for their baptism by their period in the catechumenate and by suitable fasting in the week before the day of the baptism. At the service the bishop blessed the font by pouring into it a drop of consecrated oil. Then he prayed for the descent of the Holy Spirit upon the water so that those immersed in it would be washed not only physically but also inwardly and spiritually:

> Almighty God . . . breathe kindly upon these waters mixed with the oil of sanctification, bless them with your power, and from your throne pour upon them the grace of holiness: that whoever shall go down into this tide upon which the most exalted Name of the Trinity is called may be loosed from man's ancient offense and pardoned by your everlasting blessing, that being cleansed from all their sins and strengthened with spiritual gifts they may be written in the pages of heaven.[10]

Having prepared the water of regeneration, the bishop next had to prepare the candidates for new birth. He exorcised them of the devil and his influence, invited them to renounce Satan and all his ways, and asked them to confess their faith in the Triune God.

Baptism was by immersion and in the threefold name. Coming out of the water the baptized were covered with a white garment and anointed on the head with oil to signify their incorporation into the kingly and priestly body of Christ. Then a declaration was made by a presbyter:

> Almighty God, the Father of our Lord Jesus Christ, who has regenerated you by water and the Holy Spirit, and who has given you remission of all your sins, himself anoints you with the chrism of salvation, in Christ Jesus our Lord unto eternal life.

Next the bishop laid his hands upon the candidates' heads and prayed:

> Almighty God . . . who have made your servants to be regenerated of water and the Holy Spirit . . . pour upon them your Holy Spirit, the Paraclete, and give them the spirit of wisdom and understanding, the spirit of counsel and might, the spirit of knowledge and godliness, and fill them with the fear of the Lord in the name of our Lord Jesus Christ.[11]

Then the bishop made the sign of the cross on the candidates' foreheads with the oil of chrism. Their initiation into Christ and his church was now complete, except for their first holy communion (and in some cases the symbolic milk and honey).

---

10. Ibid., p. 120. The prayer is from the *Liber ordinum* of Spain.
11. Ibid., p. 178. The prayer is from the Gelasian Sacramentary.

For many who were baptized the experience was the center or the climax of a remarkable conversion from sinful living to loving service of God in Christ. Here is the testimony of Cyprian of Carthage, an important bishop and theologian in the Latin church of the third century:

> I was myself so entangled and constrained by the very many errors of my former life that I could not believe it possible for me to escape from them, so much was I subservient to the faults which clung to me; and in despair of improvement I cherished these evils of mine as if they had been my dearest possessions. But when the stain of my earlier life had been washed away by the help of the water of birth, and light from above had poured down upon my heart, now cleansed and purified; when I had drunk the Spirit from heaven, and the second birth had restored me so as to make me a new man; then straightway in a marvelous manner doubts began to be resolved, closed doors to open, dark places to grow light; what before had seemed difficult was now easy, what I had thought impossible was now capable of accomplishment; so that I could now see that what had been born after the flesh and lived at the mercy of sin belonged to the earth, while that which the Holy Spirit was enlivening had begun to belong to God.[12]

In this piece of personal testimony, which comes from *Ad Donatum,* the spiritual certainty attained in baptism after a long search is given powerful expression.

From the time of Cyprian, and especially after the reign of Constantine the Great, there was an increasing number of infants being baptized. So the custom arose in the Western church—but it was by no means universal at first—of delaying the last part of the rite of baptism. Thus what came to be called the rite of confirmation and in the medieval period was taken to be a separate sacrament began to evolve. And as it did, from the fifth century on there also began to develop a theology to justify and undergird it.

One explanation distinguished between the grace given at baptism (which is sufficient to ensure that an infant who dies goes to heaven) and the grace given at confirmation (which is sufficient to enable the growing child to fight on the Christian side in the battle of life):

> Because those who are to live in this world all their days have to walk among invisible foes and perils, in baptism we are reborn to life, after baptism we are strengthened, and, if the benefits of regeneration suffice for those who immediately after birth pass from this life, nevertheless for

---

12. I have used the translation given in Thomas Weinandy, ed., *Receiving the Promise,* pp. 94–95. There is a translation of all the epistles of Cyprian in *Ante-Nicene Fathers,* ed. Alexander Roberts and James Donaldson, vol. 5.

those who are to live on in this world the graces of confirmation are necessary. Regeneration by itself saves those who are to be received into the peace of the age of bliss, whereas confirmation arms and equips those who are to be kept for the struggles and battles of this world.[13]

This general approach was developed by some of the great theologians of the medieval church. Alexander of Hales argued that "there is the fullness of sufficiency and the fullness of abundance: the first is given in baptism, the second in confirmation. Or there is the fullness in essence and fullness in strength."[14] Thomas Aquinas stated that "man receives spiritual life through baptism, which is spiritual regeneration; but in confirmation man receives a kind of perfect age of the spiritual life."[15]

Augustine

The most influential theologian of Western Christianity was Augustine, who was bishop of the north African town of Hippo from 395 until his death in 430.[16] At the center of all his concerns was the grace of God, whose original manifestation he saw in divine predestination, and whose greatest manifestation he found in the incarnation of the eternal Son, his sacrificial, atoning death, and his glorious resurrection and exaltation. This grace is brought by the Holy Spirit into the church of God, which is the body of Christ. It is the work of the Holy Spirit to bring the elect of God to the forgiveness of sins and internal regeneration via the dominical sacrament of baptism and then to lead them in the life of sanctification within the body of Christ until, having persevered to the end, they enter their inheritance in the kingdom of heaven. As much as Augustine emphasized sovereign grace, he also emphasized that this divine grace is operative only within the catholic church and her ministries and sacraments. Thus baptism is necessary for salvation, and regeneration occurs in connection with the baptism of both infants and adults.

The association of baptism and regeneration is found throughout the writings of Augustine. For example, in a sermon he preached to cate-

---

13. The writer was probably Bishop Faustus of Riez at the end of the fifth century. However, for a long time it was thought that the material came from Pope Melchiades of the fourth century. Thus it was given a greater prominence than its origins warranted. See further J. D. C. Fisher, *Christian Initiation: Baptism in the Medieval West,* pp. 125–26.

14. Cited by Fisher, *Medieval West,* p. 129, from *Glossa in quattuor libros sententiarum.*

15. Cited by Fisher, *Medieval West,* p. 129, from *Summa theologiae,* part 3, question 72, article 1.

16. The best study of Augustine's life is Peter Brown, *Augustine of Hippo.*

chumens who were waiting for their baptism on Easter morning he
asked, "Would you know the Holy Spirit that he is God? Be baptized and
you will be his temple." And he proceeded to tell them that "for the sake
of all sins was Baptism provided," and thus "once for all we have washing
in Baptism" since "God does not remit sins but to the baptized."[17] Further, in his "Enchiridion" Augustine explained that in baptism we die to
sin and rise to new life. But what is the sin to which infants die? Here
Augustine gave an answer which became a common doctrine in the
West: infants are forgiven the sin of Adam, otherwise known as original
sin. Adults at baptism are forgiven two forms of sin by "the grace of
regeneration," since "all their past sins are there and then pardoned,
and the guilt which they contracted in their (physical) birth is removed
in their new birth" (sections 43, 52, 119).[18] However, since not everyone
who is baptized is included in the divine decree of election unto salvation, the grace of regeneration is given only to the elect, whose identity
is known only unto God (sections 98–104).

Though Augustine insisted that the gift of the Holy Spirit with the
forgiveness of sins actually occurs in connection with the act of baptism,
he also was much aware of the prevenient grace of God operative in his
chosen people before their baptism. This is clear in the *Confessions,*
where Augustine reflects upon the way in which God brought him to
new life in Christ.[19] God has a way, and it is different in each particular
case, of bringing his elect to conversion and regeneration. By his sovereign gracious power God turns his people toward him.

Augustine insisted on this point often in his controversy with Pe-
lagius and his supporters.[20] Not only did they deny the doctrine of original sin (i.e., that all human beings were in Adam when he sinned and
therefore are guilty of that sin), but they also denied predestination and
reduced grace to the general help God offers to make it possible to do
what he commands. They viewed the baptism of infants as the means
whereby children enter the kingdom of heaven and are set apart for the
service of the Lord Jesus; in their case no forgiveness of sin occurs. In the
baptism of adults there is forgiveness of the sins for which they alone are
personally responsible. In addition, the Pelagians understood regenera-

---

17. Augustine, "St. Augustine on the Creed: A Sermon to the Catechumens," in *A
Select Library of the Nicene and Post-Nicene Fathers of the Christian Church,* ed. Philip
Schaff, vol. 3, pp. 370–71.

18. Augustine, "Enchiridion," in *Nicene and Post-Nicene Fathers,* ed. Philip Schaff,
vol. 3, pp. 237–76.

19. There are various translations of the *Confessions,* including one by E. M.
Blaiklock.

20. For this controversy see J. N. D. Kelly, *Early Christian Doctrine,* 4th ed., ch. 13.

tion to be nothing more than physical entry into the visible church and into discipleship of Jesus; there is no supernatural work upon the soul.

Augustine insisted, to the contrary, that in baptism God bestows the gift of the indwelling Spirit and cancels the debt of sin—all sin. Augustine himself was what we would call "converted" before he came to baptism. However, as he makes clear in book 9 of his *Confessions,* he believed that it was in his baptism that he received assurance of forgiveness of all his past sins along with the gift of the indwelling Spirit. Further, he recognized the need of infants to be converted at a later age even if they have been baptized: "In baptized infants the sacrament of regeneration comes first; and if they hold fast to Christian piety, conversion in the heart will follow, following as the sacramental sign of it in the body. This all shows that the sacrament of baptism is one thing, the conversion of the heart is another; but the salvation of man is effected by these two."[21] And in another treatise he wrote, "We all know that if one baptized in infancy does not believe when he comes to years of discretion, and does not keep from himself lawless desires, then he will have no profit from the gift he received as a baby."[22] Thus Augustine held that there is no salvation without both baptism (regeneration) and conversion.

The Council of Orange

The position taken by Augustine in the controversy with the Pelagians was not in its totality adopted by the Western church. However, Augustine's doctrine of the grace of God in baptism, regeneration, and conversion was accepted and promulgated by the Council of Orange in 529. This doctrine was set forth in twenty-five canons.

The canons adopted by the Council of Orange insist that Adam's sin affected the whole human race, bringing not only the death of every human being, but also the death of each soul (i.e., deprivation of spiritual communion with God and of ability to do his will). Only by the internal working of the Holy Spirit and his implanting and infusing grace within the soul can there be a genuine desire for salvation and holy baptism, a true and lively faith, and a ready will to do what the Lord requires of his people. In fact, as canon 13 asserts, "the freedom of the will that was destroyed in the first man can be restored only by the grace of baptism, for what is lost can be returned only by the one who was

---

21. Augustine, "On Baptism, Against the Donatists," in *Nicene and Post-Nicene Fathers,* ed. Philip Schaff, vol. 4, p. 462.

22. Augustine, "A Treatise on the Merits and Forgiveness of Sins, and on the Baptism of Infants," in *Nicene and Post-Nicene Fathers,* ed. Philip Schaff, vol. 5, p. 43.

able to give it." Thus salvation is from beginning to end the work of God: we are called to salvation by divine grace and installed in it by holy baptism.

The conclusion to the canons is especially noteworthy:

> According to the catholic faith we also believe that after grace has been received through baptism, all baptized persons have the ability and responsibility, if they desire to labor faithfully, to perform with the aid and cooperation of Christ what is of essential importance in regard to the salvation of their soul. . . . We also believe and confess to our benefit that in every good work it is not we who take the initiative and are then assisted through the mercy of God, but God himself first inspires in us both faith in him and love for him without any previous good works of our own that deserve reward, so that we may faithfully seek the sacrament of baptism and after baptism be able by his help to do what is pleasing to him.[23]

What is interesting from our twentieth-century viewpoint is that, in the case of adults (of which these canons primarily speak), the grace of regeneration is unhesitatingly and without embarrassment tied to the sacrament of baptism. There is recognition that the Holy Spirit works in the soul before and after baptism, but it is in baptism that the high point (as it were) of his saving activity occurs.

Thomas Aquinas

In the Middle Ages, including the century in which Thomas Aquinas (1225–1274) wrote his great works of philosophy and theology, the activity of the God of all grace in the salvation of sinners was very carefully analyzed.[24] The scholastic approach described the presence and work of the Holy Spirit in such categories as actual grace (illumination of the mind and strengthening of the will), efficacious grace (grace which achieves its divinely intended effect), gratuitous grace (a power given so that one may benefit others; e.g., the power given to a priest in ordination), habitual grace (a supernatural gift which works sanctification in the soul), justifying grace (the bringing of a sinner into a right relationship with God through Christ), "sanating" grace (a healing of the ravages of sin in the soul), sanctifying grace (grace infused into the soul to make it holy), and sufficient grace (an adequate amount of help for a particular task or act). Several of these categories could be and were used to explain the biblical idea of regeneration.

---

23. I have used the translation in John H. Leith, ed., *Creeds of the Churches*, rev. ed., pp. 37–45.

24. A helpful introduction to Thomas is F. C. Copleston, *Aquinas*.

Aquinas understood sacraments as symbolic actions given to the church by its head, Jesus Christ. Through them God communicated to his people all that they could possibly need to attain salvation in the world to come. The sacraments were instrumental causes of grace, for through them God acted directly. Baptism, confirmation, holy communion, penance, and extreme unction were the means by which a sinner entered the church, received salvation, and prepared to meet God. The other two sacraments, holy orders and matrimony, ensured that there would be both people to receive and priests to administer the other five sacraments.

With a rare exception here and there, baptisms in thirteenth-century Europe were of newborn infants. Our summation of the theology of Aquinas is offered against this background. Baptism is the first sacrament: it unites a person to Christ and his church. It is the divine instrument (an efficient cause whose action produces a real change) bringing (1) forgiveness, (2) regeneration, and (3) justification to the soul. Where the rite is correctly administered, the grace of the sacrament is effectually imparted to the recipient.[25]

(1) Forgiveness is cancelation of the guilt of the sin of Adam. (2) Regeneration is the Holy Spirit's imprinting on the human soul the image of God in Christ; through baptismal regeneration a supernatural character is stamped on infants, giving them the potentiality in later life to think, will, and feel in the pattern of Christ himself. In other words, there is the potentiality for true faith, hope, and love. Though the initial infusion of grace occurs without the cooperation of the recipient, the development of the potentiality of that grace requires definite cooperation on the part of the baptized individual. The initial character imprinted in baptism becomes Christian virtues only through the active commitment of the recipient. (3) Justification is the process of being made righteous so that at the final judgment God will be able to pronounce one righteous. It begins at baptism when grace is infused into the soul (regeneration) and the sinner is placed in the right with God through forgiveness. It proceeds through the cooperation of the human will with the divine will; and as the two cooperate, grace upon grace is freely given.

Against the background of Aristotelian metaphysics, Aquinas's doctrine of baptismal regeneration, which is a sophisticated way of explaining the operation of God's grace through the Holy Spirit, is perfectly intelligible. However, when popularized at the parish level, it seemed like magic—if the rite is done properly, the grace is given.

---

25. For his teaching see *Summa theologiae* in the Blackfriars edition, vol. 30, 1a2ae. 106–14; and vol. 57, 3a. 66–72.

At the Council of Florence (1438–1445) a clear summary of the teaching of Aquinas concerning the seven sacraments was accepted and promulgated as the teaching of the Western church: "Through baptism we are spiritually reborn; through confirmation we grow in grace and are strengthened in faith. Having been regenerated and strengthened, we are sustained by the divine food of the Eucharist. But if we become sick in soul through sin, we are healed spiritually through penance, and healed spiritually as well as physically, in proportion as it benefits the soul, through extreme unction." Further, the church is governed and grows spiritually through the sacrament of ordination, while it grows physically through the sacrament of marriage.[26]

This is the teaching against which the Reformers were to react in the sixteenth century. It is also the teaching that was to be reaffirmed by the Roman Catholic Church after the division of Western Christendom into Catholicism and Protestantism.

The Magdeburg Rite of 1497

It will be helpful to note the liturgy of a baptismal service used in Germany on the eve of the Protestant Reformation. We have chosen the Magdeburg rite of 1497, for this was the service that Luther was to reform and simplify between 1523 and 1526.[27]

With the male infants on the right and the females on the left at the front of the church, the priest breathed upon each one and called on the unclean spirit to depart. Making the sign of the cross on the forehead, the priest addressed each child concerning the Christian life and then prayed for "this your servant . . . who, seeking the gift of your baptism, desires to obtain eternal grace by spiritual regeneration." He asked that each one, "having obtained the eternal blessing of the heavenly washing, may receive the promised kingdom of your bounty."

Then, after placing salt in the mouth of each child (an action recalling Matt. 5:13 and Col. 4:6), the priest again prayed for the "washing of new regeneration." Offering further prayers, he made the sign of the cross on each child's forehead and in the name of the Lord Jesus drove away all evil powers. Finally, the priest addressed Satan himself:

Be not deceived, Satan, punishment threatens you: torments await you. . . . Come out and depart from this servant of God [here the name of the child was said] . . . so that he may become his temple through the water of regeneration unto the remission of all his sins.

---

26. In Leith, ed., *Creeds*, pp. 60–61.
27. J. D. C. Fisher, *Christian Initiation: The Reformation Period*, pp. 9–16.

Following the renunciation of Satan and the recital of the creed, each infant was anointed on the breast with oil before baptism by immersion. As the godparents held the infant by the feet as he or she stood in the water, the priest declaimed:

> Almighty God, the Father of our Lord Jesus Christ, who has regenerated you by water and the Holy Spirit, and who has given you the remission of all your sins [here the priest anointed the head of each infant with chrism], himself anoints you with the chrism of salvation in Christ Jesus our Lord unto eternal life. Amen.

Uttering appropriate words, the priest then placed a clean white band over the forehead of each child and also gave each one a candle.

The rubrics for this service indicate that it could occur at any time of the year, that it was not followed by the Eucharist, and that at some later date the children would be confirmed by the bishop. There was no blessing of the font because that particular ceremony was specially performed twice a year—at Easter and Whitsuntide.

The Enchiridion of Cologne

For some additional information on what the medieval rite of baptism meant to traditional Catholics and, in particular, on what the devout and serious among them understood the work of the Spirit in baptism and confirmation to be, we turn to a document produced in Cologne in 1538 by the opponents of the reforming movement associated with the name of Martin Luther. The *Enchiridion Christianae Institutionis,* which was produced by John Gropper (1503–1559), shows how traditional Catholics viewed the grace of God operative in the two sacraments.[28] In baptism there is the gift of the remission of all sin, original and actual, the making of a new creature in Christ Jesus, and the weakening of the old nature so that it cannot in the future cause any harm unless its "owner" actually assents to commit sin. Baptism brings innocence and the seed of new life; thus anyone who dies immediately afterwards has a title to heaven. However, those who continue to live in the world after being baptized find that they are involved in a struggle; they have crossed the Red Sea to enter the vast desert of this world, and before they come to the land of promise they have to contend with the world, the flesh, and the devil. They need, therefore, the help of the guarding and protecting Spirit.

---

28. Ibid., pp. 45–53, 187–93.

In baptism we are reborn as sons of God, and we receive the promise of the heavenly inheritance, but in order that we may keep it, the pupils need a tutor. Hence Christ did not think it sufficient that in baptism should be imparted to us the renewing Spirit without also there being conferred upon us through the sacrament of confirmation the protecting and defending Spirit, who, however, is not another Spirit, but is the same Spirit as was given in baptism, each according to the various bestowals of graces and spiritual gifts. For in that he is given in confirmation, he is the Comforter, who to the regenerate in Christ is guardian and consoler and tutor. Therefore the Holy Spirit who comes upon the waters of baptism in a saving descent in the font gives beauty to innocence. In confirmation he provides an increase to grace, because those who are to live to a full age in this world have to walk among invisible foes and perils, wherefore the Spirit has appeared in more than one form. . . .

So in baptism we are regenerated to life; after baptism we are confirmed for battle. In baptism we are washed; after baptism we are strengthened. In baptism we are received as soldiers of Christ and signed. In confirmation we who are to be kept for the struggles and battles of this world are equipped with suitable weapons in order to fight.

Here we encounter belief that the Holy Spirit is given in baptism and again in confirmation. But his arrival on each occasion is for a different purpose—to renew and then to strengthen. We also meet in the *Enchiridion of Cologne* the important late medieval Catholic belief in the objectivity of the sacraments; that is, the view that they are God's appointed means of conveying his grace and that they will always do so when rightly administered. This view, that the sacraments confer grace *ex opere operato,* Luther and the other Reformers rejected.

9

The Reformation
By Word, Spirit, and Water

At the beginning of the sixteenth century, the Latin church of the West, looking to the one vicar of Christ in Rome, was still undivided, even if it had its share of problems and tensions. Christendom was a unity because of its common loyalty to the pope. At the end of the same century, however, Christendom was divided; certain parts of the church in the West no longer looked to the vicar of Christ in Rome. A complex series of events which we call the Protestant Reformation had led to the formation of a number of national or territorial churches (in Scandinavia, Britain, Germany, and Switzerland).[1] There were also small groups of people who wanted radical and far-reaching reformation; they are often referred to as the Radical Reformers, Anabaptists, sectarians, or separatists.[2]

The Protestant national churches claimed to have been reformed by principles which they found in the sacred Scriptures, the written Word of God, and interpreted in the light of the teaching and practice of the church of the early centuries (the patristic period). Adopting such an

---

1. There are many books on the Reformation of the sixteenth century. See, for example, Owen Chadwick, *The Reformation,* and Emile G. Leonard, *A History of Protestantism.*

2. See George Huntston Williams, *The Radical Reformation.*

approach meant that the Protestant churches did not agree amongst themselves on all matters, especially on how much of the received tradition, liturgy, and practice to retain and how much to set aside. Thus while there is a great deal of common ground between Lutheran (Evangelical) and Calvinist (Reformed) teaching and practice, there are also differences. However, in comparison with the Radicals, what the Lutherans, Calvinists, and Anglicans (Church of England) taught and practiced was very conservative. This is especially so with regard to the baptism of infants and the view of the relation of regeneration to baptism.

In this chapter we shall examine the Protestant mind concerning baptism and regeneration by noting (1) the Protestant criticisms of the medieval rites of baptism and confirmation, (2) the liturgy of the new Protestant rites of baptism, (3) the teaching of the Protestant confessions of faith on baptism and regeneration, (4) the specific teaching of Luther and Calvin, and finally (5) the position of the Anabaptists. As we look at these areas, we must always bear in mind that the religious situation then was far different from what it is now both in America and in Europe. All the population was nominally Christian, and it was expected that every baby would be baptized as soon as possible after birth. Another difference is that there could be no reform in the church without the consent of the civil authorities. Further, any renewal of the church was not through evangelization but rather through persuading as many people as possible to take seriously the implications of their baptismal commitment to live as servants and soldiers of Christ. The great watchword of this approach to renewal was "faith"—accepting, laying hold of, and acting on the promises of God made in the sacred Scriptures. All the leading Reformers had a personal experience of discovering the power of this kind of faith—a faith which they saw as the gift of God and a corollary of the fact that in baptism they had already been made children of God the Father and disciples of Jesus the Lord. They had a vision of the whole church reformed and renewed by this faith, the Holy Spirit, and the Word of God.

Protestant Criticism of the Medieval Rites

Martin Luther (1483–1546), the passionate German Reformer and exponent of the doctrine of justification by faith alone, published in 1523 a baptismal service in German (*Taufbüchlein*).[3] It was a very conservative revision of the Magdeburg rite which was described in the last

---

3. Luther's two baptismal services are printed in J. D. C. Fisher, *Christian Initiation: The Reformation Period,* pp. 6–16, 23–25, and in *Luther's Works,* vol. 53, pp. 96–109.

chapter (pp. 86–87). In the epilogue Luther allowed himself the privilege of making a few comments on the service. First, he expressed his hope that by hearing the service in German instead of Latin, the sponsors and bystanders would now understand what was happening and would be moved to faith and reverence. Second, he insisted that the least importance attaches to the external ceremonies. In particular he mentioned breathing under the eyes of the candidates, signing with the cross, placing salt in the mouth, putting spittle and clay on the ears and nose, anointing the breast and shoulders with oil, signing the forehead with chrism, vesting the candidates in the christening robe, and giving them a lighted candle. So as not to disturb people, however, he retained these externals in his service of 1523. Third, he insisted that the service should be conducted by sober and godly ministers and that the sponsors should be people of genuine faith.

In the epilogue to the order of baptism published in 1523 Luther also offered a definition of the "holy sacrament" of baptism: "God himself calls it a new birth, whereby we are freed from all the tyranny of the devil, delivered from sin, death and hell, and become children of life and heirs of all God's good things and his own children and brothers of Christ." Thus it is not surprising that in his radically revised baptismal liturgy of 1526, which has few ceremonies, Luther retains the clear teaching that baptism is the sacrament of regeneration. While the godparents hold the child in a standing position in the font after the baptism, the minister puts a robe on the child and says, "The almighty God and Father of our Lord Jesus Christ, who has regenerated you by water and the Holy Spirit, and has forgiven you all your sins, strengthen you with his grace to eternal life. Amen."

We turn now to Martin Bucer (1491–1551), who after important reforming work in south Germany and Switzerland went to England at the invitation of Archbishop Thomas Cranmer. Here Bucer was asked to critique the new Protestant liturgy being developed for the Church of England. His evaluation of the English Prayer Book of 1549 is known as the *Censura*.[4] Here we are interested only in his comments on the services of holy baptism and confirmation—liturgy which represented a conservative reform of the inherited medieval services. From these comments we can gather his attitude toward the traditional rite of baptism with its many ceremonies. He wanted to retain only a few of the latter, including the sign of the cross, and to hold to the principle that "the utmost simplicity and truth are appropriate in these mysteries." Such things as blessing of the water, exorcism, exsufflation, chrism, and vesting the candidate in a white robe were no longer beneficial:

---

4. Part of the *Censura* is printed in Fisher, *Reformation Period,* pp. 96–105.

The old saints were ablaze with the utmost reverence for God and gratitude for his benefits: the people used to be present at baptism with great devotion: so for them these signs were able to promote reverence towards God and to arouse and sustain more devotion towards so great a mystery.

But for some time we have seen the effect produced by the Romish Antichrists and by the impiety innate in all men, by which they continually turn sacred ceremonies for the worship of God into various wicked shows, so that today those signs among the great majority of people serve more for the maintenance and increase of superstition and show than of piety and religion. Now the occasions for these abuses are to be cut out, not retained.

Bucer did not believe that an attempt to teach the symbolic meaning of the varied ceremonial elements would really help. The mystery of baptism is best kept in a simple and dignified rite so that it is truly the sacrament of regeneration. Like Luther he was quite clear that God gives and works regeneration in the sacrament of baptism. This new birth in a child will eventually be revealed in faith, good works, and a hearty confession of faith. Accordingly, Bucer did not want to see children confirmed by the bishop until they showed these signs of new life.

John Calvin (1509–1564), the French Reformer of Geneva and great biblical exegete, was much in sympathy with Luther and Bucer concerning their criticisms of the Latin rite and likewise felt the need to simplify the baptismal service in order the better to exhibit the nature of the sacrament as a symbol and seal of God's grace through Jesus Christ by the Holy Spirit. Calvin also had some biting criticisms to offer concerning the medieval rite of confirmation. It detracted from the gospel sacrament of baptism and had become a deadly wile of Satan:

> I hasten to declare that I am certainly not of the number of those who think that confirmation, as observed under the Roman papacy, is an idle ceremony, inasmuch as I regard it as one of the deadly wiles of Satan. Let us remember that this pretended sacrament is nowhere recommended in Scripture, either under this name or with this ritual, or this signification.[5]

He was not, however, against the reformed rites of confirmation which came to be written for the Church of England and the Lutheran churches, for they did not claim to be sacramental rites. Rather they were opportunities for a public confession of faith by those baptized in infancy as well as for a prayer, with the laying on of hands, that they might continue in the Christian life through the strength of the Holy Spirit.

---

5. John Calvin, *Acts of the Council of Trent with the Antidote,* p. 183; see also Fisher, *Reformation Period,* pp. 254–60.

What the Reformers were trying to do was to peel away from the received medieval rites all unnecessary ceremonies in order to make the encounter with the living Christ in the sacrament more direct and powerful.

The New Protestant Rites

Luther's second baptismal liturgy, which as we have noted was much simpler than his first, came to be widely used in Germany. It began with a brief command to the unclean spirit to come out of the infant and the making of the sign of the cross on the forehead and breast. There followed a prayer of petition that God grant the gift of his eternal grace and spiritual regeneration. Then the minister offered a second prayer, often called the "flood prayer" because it recalled both the flood that destroyed the world in Noah's day and the flood (of the Red Sea) that destroyed the Egyptians. In this prayer was the request:

> We pray that through your infinite mercy you will graciously look upon this child and bless him with a right faith in the spirit, so that through this saving flood all that was born in him from Adam and all which he himself has added thereto may be drowned and submerged: and that he may be separated from the unfaithful, and preserved in the holy ark of Christendom dry and safe, and ever fervent in spirit and joyful in hope serve your name, so that he with all the faithful may be worthy to inherit your promise of eternal life, through Christ our Lord.[6]

Next there is the exorcism, by the power of the name of the Triune God, of the unclean spirit. This is followed by a reading from Mark 10:13–16, which tells how Jesus received little children. Then come a recital of the Lord's Prayer, a renunciation of the devil, and a confession of the faith by the godparents before the actual immersion in the threefold name. Finally, as the godparents hold the child up in the font, the minister puts a white robe on the child and says, "The almighty God and Father of our Lord Jesus Christ, who has regenerated you by water and the Holy Spirit, and has forgiven you all your sins, strengthen you with his grace to eternal life. Amen."

Luther composed no order of confirmation in German (the Lutheran rites of confirmation do not derive from Luther but came later). His view was that children ought to be baptized in infancy, brought up in a Christian home, taught the faith, and admitted to holy communion as soon as

---

6. Fisher, *Reformation Period,* p. 11. For references to the flood and the Red Sea in baptismal liturgy see Jean Daniélou, *Bible et liturgie,* pp. 104–44.

they know the essentials of their faith and consciously adopt the life of virtue to which they have been committed by their baptism.

Like Luther, Calvin prepared a simplified service for the public baptism of children.[7] This rite is introduced by a lengthy explanation of why baptism is needed and what by the grace of God it achieves. Calvin explains that since we are born with a corrupt nature, we need to be born again. God promises

> to regenerate us by his Holy Spirit into a new life. . . . This regeneration consists in two parts: namely, that we renounce ourselves not following our own reason, our pleasure and own will, but, subjugating and enslaving our desire and our heart to the wisdom and righteousness of God, we mortify all that is of us and of our flesh: and secondly that we follow the light of God to comply with and obey his good pleasure, as he shows it to us by his word, and leads us and directs us to it by his Spirit.

Regeneration has these two parts because in Christ we have both died to sin and been made to share in new life. We die to sin and are forgiven, and we rise to newness of life through the power of the Spirit.

But where does baptism come in? Calvin replies:

> All these graces are conferred on us, when it pleases [God] to incorporate us in his church by baptism. . . . He has appointed the sign of water, to signify to us that, as by this element the bodily defilements are cleansed, so he wishes to wash and purify our souls, so that no more may there appear any stain in them. Again, he there represents to us our renewal, which consists, as has already been said, in the mortification of our flesh and the spiritual life which it engenders and excites in us.

And how does the baptismal representation of regeneration apply to infants? Here Calvin appeals to his covenant theology: the children of Christian believers are heirs to the life which God has promised to his people. As boys in Israel were circumcised on the eighth day, so the infants, male and female, born into the new covenant are to be given the covenant sign, seal, and symbol of baptism in water. The prayer composed by Calvin to be offered shortly before the baptism of an infant reflects this covenant theology:

> Lord God, Father eternal and almighty, since it has pleased you by your infinite mercy to promise us that you will be our God and the God of our children, we pray that it may please you to confirm this grace in this

---

7. Fisher, *Reformation Period*, pp. 112–17, has Calvin's service in English.

present infant, born of a father and mother whom you have called into your church, and, as he is offered and consecrated to you by us, that you would receive him into your holy protection, declaring yourself to be his God and Saviour, remitting to him the original sin of which the whole lineage of Adam is guilty, and then afterwards sanctifying him by your Spirit, so that when he comes to the age of understanding, he may know and adore you as his only God, glorifying you through his life, so as to obtain evermore from you remission of his sins. And so that he can obtain such graces, may it please you to incorporate him in the fellowship of our Lord Jesus to be a partaker of all his benefits, as one of the members of his body. Grant us, Father of mercy, that the baptism which we minister to him according to your ordinance may bring forth its fruit and virtue, such as has been declared to us by your gospel.

The people then say the Lord's Prayer, the parents promise to bring the child up in the Christian faith, and the baptism takes place in the threefold name.

The Book of Common Prayer which appeared in 1552 was basically the work of Thomas Cranmer, archbishop of Canterbury. It was a revision of the earlier book of 1549; the new forms owed something to the critique of Martin Bucer, to which reference has been made. The 1552 edition contains an order for public baptism administered by a priest and an order for confirmation administered by a bishop.[8]

The baptismal rite was to take place within either the morning or evening service on a Sunday. It began with a short explanatory introduction stating the need of everyone to be born of water and of the Spirit, and continued with a prayer by the priest asking that "these infants . . . may receive remission of sins by spiritual regeneration" at their baptism. Following the reading of Mark 10:13–16 and an explanation of its relation to infant baptism, the priest asked the heavenly Father "to give the Holy Spirit to these infants that they may be born again, and be made heirs of everlasting salvation." After the parents and godparents had renounced the devil and his ways and confessed the true faith, the priest again prayed, asking that the children to be baptized would truly die to sin and live unto righteousness, receive the fullness of heavenly grace, and so ever remain in the number of God's faithful and elect children.

Baptism by immersion and signing of the forehead with the cross then followed, the priest observing that since "these children be regenerate and grafted into the body of Christ's congregation," the witnesses ought to give thanks and pray for them "that they may lead the rest of their life according to this beginning." After the Lord's Prayer, the priest thanked God for having been pleased "to regenerate this infant with

---

8. Both the 1549 and 1552 books are printed in the Everyman edition.

your Holy Spirit, to receive him for your own child by adoption, and to incorporate him into your holy congregation." Thanksgiving led to petition that the children might truly live in the strength and light of their baptism.

The children who had been baptized were to be confirmed by the bishop as soon as they were able to recite the Apostles' Creed, the Lord's Prayer, and the Ten Commandments. This rite was seen as affording an opportunity both for the children to commit themselves personally to the promises which had already been made for them by their godparents, and for the bishop to lay hands upon them and pray that the Holy Spirit might strengthen them for service of the Lord in the world. The Church of England made no claim that confirmation was a sacrament; although it may traditionally have been called a sacrament, it was not considered an independent sacrament but the completion of infant baptism.

What is impressive in the Lutheran, Calvinist, and Anglican services of baptism is that the Reformers have not removed the concept that baptism and regeneration are closely related. Their own study of the New Testament led them to believe that the two, by the command and grace of Christ, are intimately related, and so they would not prize them apart. This is not to say, however, that they understood the intimate relation in the same way as did Thomas Aquinas or later Roman Catholic theologians, whose views we shall examine in the following chapter.

The Teaching of the Protestant Confessions of Faith

Our study of what the Protestant confessions have to say on the subject of baptism and regeneration begins with the Augsburg Confession of 1530, written by Philipp Melanchthon (1497–1560) and approved by Luther.[9] Article 2, "Original Sin," reveals how indebted the Protestants were to the theology of Augustine of Hippo:

It is also taught among us that since the fall of Adam all men who are born according to the course of nature are conceived and born in sin. That is, all men are full of evil lust and inclination from their mothers' wombs and are unable by nature to have true fear of God and true faith in God. Moreover, this inborn sickness and hereditary sin is truly sin and condemns to the eternal wrath of God all those who are not born again through Baptism and the Holy Spirit. Rejected in this connection are the Pelagians and

9. Theodore G. Tappert, ed., *The Book of Concord: The Confessions of the Evangelical Lutheran Church,* includes translations of both the German and Latin editions of the Augsburg Confession since the two are not strictly identical.

others who deny that original sin is sin, for they hold that natural man is made righteous by his own powers, thus disparaging the sufferings and merit of Christ.

Here we find the concept of an intimate relation between baptism and one of the effects of regeneration—cancelation of the guilt of original sin. Article 9, "Baptism," declares:

It is taught among us that Baptism is necessary and that grace is offered through it. Children, too, should be baptized, for in Baptism they are committed to God and become acceptable to him. On this account the Anabaptists who teach that infant Baptism is not right are rejected.

This translation is from the German text; the Latin text of the confession is more explicit in regard to the effects of baptism on children: "Our churches condemn the Anabaptists who reject the Baptism of children and declare that children are saved without Baptism." The Protestant leaders in Germany insisted that every infant be presented for baptism, for the Word of God declares that "whoever believes and is baptized will be saved" (Mark 16:15).

Article 13, "The Use of the Sacraments," states:

It is taught among us that the sacraments were instituted not only to be signs by which people might be identified outwardly as Christians, but that they are signs and testimonies of God's will towards us for the purpose of awakening and strengthening our faith. For this reason they require faith, and they are rightly used when they are received in faith and for the purpose of strengthening faith.

In the Latin text there is an addition which reads, "Our churches therefore condemn those who teach that the sacraments justify by the outward act [ex opere operato], and who do not teach that faith which believes that sins are forgiven is required in the use of the sacraments." (We shall note on p. 102 Luther's explanation of how it is that infants can actually exercise faith when they are baptized.)

In the Consensus Tigurinus (the Zurich Agreement) written by John Calvin to unite French- and German-speaking Swiss Protestants on the doctrine of the sacraments, there is clear teaching on the relation of baptism and regeneration.[10] This document, which was published in

---

10. The Latin text of the Consensus Tigurinus is found in Collectio Confessionum in Ecclesiis Reformatis Publicatarum, ed. H. A. Niemeyer, pp. 191–217. There is a translation in the appendix of A. A. Hodge, Outlines of Theology.

1551, is brief, having only twenty-six articles. In article 3 we are told that adoption as God's children

> takes place when we, ingrafted through faith into the body of Christ, and this by the power of the Spirit, are first justified by the gratuitous imputation of righteousness, and then regenerated into a new life, that, new-created in the image of the heavenly Father, we may put off the old man.

Here "regeneration" seems to be used of the process that later divines called sanctification—the re-creation of a person through putting off the old life and putting on the new. Calvin in fact used "regeneration" both of the Spirit's total work in re-creating the image of God within us (as here) and of his initial entry into the soul.

The sacraments fit into the Spirit's work of regeneration (understood as sanctification) for they are the means by which "God attests, presents anew, and seals to us his grace" (article 7). The grace received in the sacraments is from God alone, working in and by the Spirit. "In using the instrumentality of the sacraments, God thereby neither infuses into them his own power, nor abates in the least the efficiency of his Spirit; but in accordance with the capacity of our ignorance [*ruditas*] he uses them as instruments in such a way that the whole efficiency [*facultas agendi*] remains solely with himself." This statement effectively denies the Roman Catholic doctrine of *ex opere operato*.

Though grace is offered to all in the sacraments, it is only elect believers who receive it. In article 20 we learn that this grace may not be received immediately:

> The benefit which we derive from the sacraments should by no means be restricted to the time in which they are administered to us; just as if the visible sign, when brought forward into view, did at the same moment with itself bring God's grace. For those who are baptized in early infancy, God regenerates in boyhood, in budding youth and sometimes even in old age. So the benefit of baptism lies open to the whole course of life; for the promise which it contains is perpetually valid.

Here "regeneration" appears to point to the beginning of "the process of mortifying sin and living unto God in Christ."

The Scots Confession of 1560 owes much to the teaching of Calvin and presents a vibrant summation of the Reformed faith.[11] After stating its doctrine of God the Creator, who made humankind in his own image, it explains original sin (article 3):

---

11. The Scots Confession is printed in Arthur C. Cochrane, ed., *Reformed Confessions of the Sixteenth Century*, pp. 159–62.

By this transgression [of Adam], generally known as original sin, the image of God was utterly defaced in man, and he and his children became by nature hostile to God, slaves to Satan, and servants to sin. And thus everlasting death has had, and shall have, dominion over all who have not been, are not, or shall not be reborn from above. This rebirth is wrought by the power of the Holy Spirit creating in the hearts of God's chosen ones an assured faith in the promise of God revealed to us in his word; by this faith we grasp Christ Jesus with the graces and blessings promised in him.

In article 12 it is again confessed that the Holy Spirit quickens that which is dead, removes the darkness from our minds, and makes our stubborn hearts obedient to God's will. In short, the Holy Spirit regenerates and sanctifies the elect.

In article 21 the view that sacraments are merely "naked and bare signs" is condemned. "We assuredly believe that by Baptism we are engrafted into Christ Jesus, to be made partakers of his righteousness, by which our sins are covered and remitted." And this is as true of the children of believers as it is of adult believers who are being baptized.

In the Scots Confession, then, rebirth is connected with both the cancelation of original sin and spiritual union with Jesus Christ through justifying faith and a life of holiness. The sacrament of baptism is the sign, seal, and symbol that these promises of the gospel have begun to take effect in the heart.

We turn next to the Heidelberg Catechism of 1563 and particularly to questions 69 through 74, which concern baptism.[12]

Q. 69. *How does holy Baptism remind and assure you that the one sacrifice of Christ on the cross avails for you?*

A. In this way: Christ has instituted this external washing with water and by it has promised that I am as certainly washed with his blood and Spirit from the uncleanness of my soul and from all my sins, as I am washed externally with water which is used to remove the dirt from my body.

Q. 70. *What does it mean to be washed with the blood and Spirit of Christ?*

A. It means to have the forgiveness of sins from God, through grace, for the sake of Christ's blood which he shed for us in his sacrifice on the cross, and also to be renewed by the Holy Spirit and sanctified as members of Christ, so that we may more and more die unto sin and live in a consecrated and blameless way.

In the answer to question 71, Mark 16:16 ("He who believes and is baptized shall be saved") and Titus 3:5 ("the washing of regeneration

---

12. In Cochrane, ed., *Reformed Confessions*, pp. 305–31.

and renewal") are cited as evidence that we are as certainly washed with the blood of Christ and the Holy Spirit as with water in the sacrament of baptism. The answer to question 72 insists that the washing with water does not wash away sins.

Q. 73. *Then why does the Holy Spirit call Baptism the water of rebirth and the washing away of sins?*

A. God does not speak in this way except for a strong reason. Not only does he teach us by Baptism that just as the dirt of the body is taken away by water, so our sins are removed by the blood and Spirit of Christ; but more important still, by the divine pledge and sign he wishes to assure us that we are just as truly washed from our sins spiritually as our bodies are washed with water.

Question 74 concerns the right of infants within the covenant to receive holy baptism.

According to the Heidelberg Catechism, then, baptism is to be seen as the divine pledge and sign of (1) the washing away of sin (forgiveness, remission) because of the saving death of Jesus, and (2) new life (renewal, rebirth) because of the presence of the Spirit who raised Jesus from the dead.

Finally, we turn to the Thirty-nine Articles of the Church of England (1563).[13] Regeneration is first mentioned in article 9, which deals with original sin. It is claimed that the infection and corruption of human nature remain even in the regenerate and will do so as long as they have mortal bodies. This is in agreement with Luther and Calvin, who both held that, while the guilt of original sin is forgiven, the actual corruption of human nature is not removed; rather, in regeneration a new nature is created.

Article 27 speaks of baptism and regeneration:

Baptism is not only a sign of profession, and mark of difference, whereby Christian men are discerned from others that be not christened, but it is also a sign of Regeneration or New Birth, whereby, as by an instrument, they that receive Baptism rightly are grafted into the Church; the promises of the forgiveness of sins, and of our adoption to be the sons of God by the Holy Spirit, are visibly signed and sealed; faith is confirmed, and grace increased by virtue of prayer unto God.

The Baptism of young children is in any wise to be retained in the Church as most agreeable with the institution of Christ.

---

13. The Articles are printed in most copies of the Book of Common Prayer (1662); see also John H. Leith, ed., *Creeds of the Churches*, pp. 266–81.

Here a qualification is placed on the relation of baptism and regeneration. Baptism has to be rightly received in order for the sacrament to be effectual.

The Teaching of Luther and Calvin

As we return to Luther's teaching, we must remind ourselves once more that he lived in an age when virtually everyone had been baptized as an infant. Luther carefully examined the practice of infant baptism and, despite the vigorous criticisms of the Anabaptists, affirmed that it is scriptural. Further, he wrote a baptismal liturgy which clearly teaches that in normal circumstances regeneration occurs at the time of baptism.

Now Luther is famous for his eloquent and powerful exposition of the doctrine of justification by faith alone; that is, the teaching that we are justified not by works but solely by a faith that arises in us through the power of the gospel. Since our primary concern is inward regeneration, we must ask, What is the relation of justification and regeneration in Luther's teaching? And when this is answered, we must also ask, What is the relation between the regeneration of infants in baptism and justification by faith alone?[14]

For Luther, justifying faith and being born from above are inseparable, for where there is justifying faith, there are also the beginnings of a new creation in the heart. On account of Christ a believing sinner is forgiven, accepted, and declared to be righteous by the Father; at the same time the Holy Spirit enters the soul to bring Christ and to create new life. Thus Christ, whom faith brings into the heart, is not only our righteousness in heaven—an "alien righteousness"—acceptable to the Father, he is also, and at the same time, an effective living power within our hearts, drawing us into communion with and love of God. The very faith that looks only and solely to Christ and his righteousness, which is outside ourselves, becomes also the presence and the power of Christ within us. In Luther's thinking, justification consists of both the declaration of acceptance in heaven and the inner transformation leading to new obedience. Righteousness is therefore first imputed and then imparted; the two belong together for they come from one and the same Christ, who is present in heaven by virtue of his deity and present in our hearts by virtue of the faith we exercise through the Holy Spirit. For-

---

14. I have relied to a great extent upon Paul Althaus, *The Theology of Martin Luther,* especially pp. 234–42 and 353–74.

giveness and regeneration are inseparable within the one reality of justification.

The fact that Christ is in us and we are regenerate and a part of God's new creation does not mean that we are free from our fallen human nature. Our flesh remains with us until our physical death. Justification by faith means that the Christian is simultaneously just and sinful (*simul iustus et peccator*). Believers are totally righteous through faith, yet in themselves they always remain sinners. With reference to Christ they are righteous; in terms of their fallen nature they are sinful. This means that there is a constant struggle as faith draws Christ into the heart to wage war against the old nature (graphically described, Luther believed, in Rom. 7). The new nature is to grow but the old nature disappears only at death. In this sense, justification is not finished in this life, for though the external aspect (Christ for us) remains constant, the internal aspect (Christ in us) is ever in the process of becoming what God wills it to be.

We turn now to the subject of baptism. Luther held that to be baptized in the name of the Holy Trinity is to be baptized by God himself, even though human hands are used. In connection with baptism God promises salvation (Mark 16:16) and regeneration (Titus 3:5). Thus God's baptism does not give merely this or that particular grace, but rather it gives the whole Christ and the entire Holy Spirit with all his gifts. The Spirit, who is the Spirit of Christ, truly enters the soul at baptism.

But what of infant baptism and the doctrine that justification (and hence regeneration) is by faith alone? Can an infant exercise faith? Luther held that through the intercession of the church, the godparents, and parents the infant receives the gift of faith. This seemed a peculiar claim to many of his contemporaries, but Luther firmly held to it. In his mature thinking on the issue, he suggested that the following statement be made as the infant is presented: "We bring this child to be baptized because we think and hope that it will believe, and we pray God will give it faith; we do not baptize it because of this, however, but only because God has commanded it."

It is the duty of everyone who has been baptized, Luther insisted, daily to die to sin and rise to new life. This was his way of dealing with a society in which almost everyone had been baptized: he did not call upon people to be baptized, but to repeat their baptism each day, as it were, by committing themselves to the overthrow of sin in their lives and to purity and holiness. Luther's use of the image of dying and rising differs from Paul's in Romans 6:1–14 and Colossians 2:12–13. For the apostle the image describes what has already taken place in Christ, while, for the German Reformer, it describes the daily duty and experience of Christians who take their baptism seriously as God's gift and claim upon them. Luther understood regeneration to take place at baptism even though, if the recipient is an infant, the effects and fruit are not immediately visible. Thus he happily baptized infants and insisted that baptism is necessary for salvation. All this is well summarized in his Small Catechism (1529), where he describes the gifts and benefits that baptism bestows: "It effects forgiveness of sins, delivers from death and the devil, and grants eternal salvation to all who believe, as the Word and the promise of God declare."

Though Luther continued to use expressions that could suggest an *ex opere operato* efficacy (as in the baptismal service), he did break decisively with the medieval doctrine that the sacrament when rightly administered has a necessary effect. First of all, he insisted that the work of God in the sacrament is a work of faith and promise, not of sight. The work of the Spirit and its effect are invisible. Second, he claimed that faith is indispensable to the sacrament. Faith in Christ is a prerequisite to effectual baptism. It is also its fulfilment, the response of the soul showing that the sacrament is having its intended effect. Therefore, regeneration and forgiveness are not part of a mechanical or magical process, but occur within a personal relationship with God through Christ by the Holy Spirit. Finally, for Luther the power of baptism is not in the element of water, but in the gracious promise of God's gospel. It is the word of promise which gives to the sign its power and validity.

Thus, while Luther seemed to retain much that belonged to the medieval past, he also gave a dynamic new meaning to the theology of baptism and regeneration. It is to Luther's credit that he restored regeneration to its rightful place of being regarded as the chief grace of baptism. This is not to say that he did not insist that baptism is a sign of forgiveness of sin; rather, it is to say that he taught that God's chief work within his elect is regeneration, re-creating them in his own image by the Holy Spirit through the indwelling of Christ by faith. Late medieval theology had obscured this point by insisting that baptism is primarily the remission of sin and purification of the soul.

Like Luther, Calvin thought of regeneration not only as the result of the saving and redeeming work of Christ for us and in us, but also in the context of original sin and the fall.[15] He was quite clear that a sinner needs a new nature in order to recover the image of God lost in the fall. There must be a work of divine grace within the soul so that we can return to be that which God intends us to be. Regeneration is an instant act of God placing his Spirit within the heart and thereby creating a new

---

15. The following exposition is based chiefly upon the *Institutes of the Christian Religion*, especially 1.15.4; 2.2.7–11, 19–21; 2.3.6–7; and book 3. See further François Wendel, *Calvin*, pp. 234–55.

nature and reestablishing his own image in the human soul. Regeneration may also be viewed as a process whereby sin is mortified and new
life permeates the whole of the heart, will, mind, personality, and
character. The initial act of the entry of the Spirit into the heart cannot
be separated from the continuing work of the Spirit in the soul (which
leads to mortification and vivification). Calvin used the word *repentance*
to refer to putting to death the sinful nature and living according to the
new nature. Thus repentance is the result of initial justification and the
outward accompaniment of the inner formation of the image of God in
the soul, heart, mind, and will.

Before regeneration takes place in the adult, there will have been a
period of preparation in which the Holy Spirit has caused a sense of
conviction of and sorrow for sin and the desire for a right relationship
with God. As a result of this secret work of the Spirit, a person receives
the gift of saving faith and trusts God concerning Christ and salvation.
In being united to Christ by faith through the Holy Spirit, the individual is both justified (forgiven and placed in a right relationship with
God) and regenerated (given the indwelling Spirit and made a new
creation in the image of God after the likeness of Christ).

Like Luther, Calvin had to make sense of the seeming paradox between infant baptism and his claim that this sacrament is a symbol and
sign of internal regeneration. He did not claim that infants are given
faith, but rather put all his emphasis upon the promise of God concerning the place of children within the covenant (Acts 2:39) and upon
the grace of God (salvation, regeneration) given and connected with
baptism. Calvin held that God gives to the elect infant his indwelling
Spirit, and through his presence, as the child is brought up in the nurture and admonition of the Lord, there will in later years be the signs
and fruit of new life. One person may reveal that new life gradually,
while another may have a crisis experience; but as long as the child
baptized is included in the divine decree of election, the life of repentance, mortification, and vivification will begin sooner or later.

Calvin did not claim that baptism is absolutely essential to salvation.
He held, for instance, that a child dying in infancy before a public
baptism can take place will go to be with the Lord in heaven. And
because he was addressing a public who had for the most part been
baptized, Calvin emphasized not that they had to be baptized, but that
they were to live lives of repentance, turning away from sin and turning
towards Christ and holiness. He used the word *conversion* to describe
the turning of the human will by God from selfishness and self-justifica-
tion towards doing the will of the Lord daily and joyfully.[16]

---

16. *Institutes* 2.3.6–7; 3.3.5, 15.

In contrast to medieval theologians, Calvin preferred to speak of the benefits rather than the effects of baptism. Further, he emphasized that baptism is a means of grace, not a gift or work of grace; and because it is a means, it is subordinate to the One who makes use of it to bestow grace. Thus the great need is to concentrate not upon the instrument, which is baptism, but upon the true source of forgiveness and new life—the death and resurrection of Jesus together with the work of the Holy Spirit as Paraclete. That baptism is not an empty sign is precisely because to the elect it is the seal of the promises of God and the gracious work of the Holy Spirit, the Sanctifier.

Perhaps the true root of the differences between Calvin and the medieval schoolmen is their contrasting conceptions of grace. To the latter, grace is a supernatural spiritual substance and energy, while for Calvin it is spiritual union with the living Christ and the fruit of that union.

> For Calvin, baptismal grace was not a spiritual medicine, but the divine favour and promise as we have it in the person and work of Jesus Christ. The office of the sacrament was the same as that of the word: to declare Jesus Christ. In the one no less than the other, Jesus Christ was offered indiscriminately to all. The unbelieving certainly received the sign, and various external benefits. But they missed the true grace of baptism, and the sign itself testified to their unbelief. With the believing the case was different. As they received the sign they perceived Christ himself and therefore they enjoyed the grace. In the normal course, it was the specific function of the sacrament to confirm the faith in Christ already evoked by the word, but in the case of infants baptism could be a powerful adjunct to the word even in the evocation of the faith by which its benefits were subsequently received and enjoyed.[17]

So Calvin was able to hold a definite doctrine of sacramental efficacy without slipping into a static conception of an automatic efficacy with a practical denial of the sovereignty of God the Holy Spirit in his work of grace.

It is important to bear in mind that the sixteenth-century Reformers were not engaged in evangelism to win converts, but in a quest to renew the church by the gospel and the Word of God. They treated the people in much the same way as the prophets of Israel had treated the covenant people of their day. They called upon the people to live in the light of the grace of God promised, offered, and given to them within the covenant. Thus conversion was not to Christianity as such, but to that to which they were already committed by reason of their baptism.

---

17. Geoffrey W. Bromiley, *Baptism and the Anglican Reformers*, p. 189.

The Position of the Anabaptists

It is well known that the Anabaptists rejected infant baptism and thus those who had been baptized as infants were all rebaptized as believers; hence their name (the prefix *ana* means "again"). To illustrate their doctrine of regeneration (which admits of variety) we shall notice the teaching of Obbe Philips, an Anabaptist minister who rejected the revolutionary approach of the Münster episode of 1534–1535. Then we shall look at the Mennonite Confession of 1591.

In his *Confession* (1560) Obbe Philips looks back to the years 1533 to 1536.[18] In a section on "Spiritual Rebirth," he explains what Jesus meant when he told Nicodemus, "You must be born again" (John 3):

> This rebirth does not take place outwardly, but in the understanding, mind, and heart of man. It is in the understanding and the mind that man learns to know the eternal love and gracious God in Christ Jesus who is the eternal image of the Father (2 Cor. 4:4; Col. 1:15) and the brightness of the divine being (Heb. 1:3). It is thus in the heart that man loves this same almighty and living God, fears, honors, and believes in him, trusts in his promise, which cannot take place without the power of the Holy Spirit, who must inflame the heart with divine power which must also give faith, fear with love, hope, and all good virtues of God.

Philips explained regeneration in terms of a re-creation of the image of God in the human soul. Baptism was for "the penitent, believing, reborn children of God." In being baptized they were called by God to live in ways worthy of their new status as the reborn children of God.

In the Mennonite Confession ("A Brief Confession of the Principal Articles of the Christian Faith"), prepared by John de Rys and Lubbert Gerrits in the Dutch language, there is clear teaching on both regeneration and baptism:[19]

> 22. Regeneration is a certain divine quality in the mind of a man truly come to himself, an erection of the image of God in man (Eph. 4:24; Col. 3:9–10), a renovation of the mind or soul (Rom. 12:2; Eph. 4:23), a true illumination of the mind with the knowledge of the truth (John 8:32), bringing with it a change of will and of carnal desires and lusts, a sincere mortification of internal wickedness (Eph. 4:22–24; Col. 3:9–10) and of the

---

18. See George Huntston Williams, ed., *Spiritual and Anabaptist Writers,* pp. 233–37; Dietrich Philip, "Of Regeneration and the New Creature," in his *Enchiridion,* trans. A. B. Kolb, pp. 293–321.

19. This Mennonite Confession is printed in full in William Joseph McGlothlin, ed., *Baptist Confessions of Faith,* pp. 24–48.

old man delighting himself in lust, wickedness and sin. It is, moreover, a
vivification which manifests itself in an honest life according to God, in
true goodness, justice and holiness. It is a removal of the stony heart (Ezek.
36:26), full of vanity, stolidity (Eph. 4:17–18), blindness, ignorance, sin
and perverse pleasures, and, on the contrary, is the gracious gift of the
promised heart of flesh (Ezek. 36:26), replete with the law of God (Jer.
31:33; Heb. 8:10), light, sight, wisdom, understanding, virtue and holy
desires. This regeneration has its rise from God (John 8:47; 1 John 4:1–2,
6–7) through Christ (1 Peter 1:3, 23; James 1:18). The medium or instrument through which it is generated in us is the Holy Spirit (John 3:5–6)
with all his fiery virtues, apart from any co-operation of any creature.
Here concerning the regenerate we affirm that they are born not out of
anything whatsoever which the creature does, but from God (John 1:13;
1 John 3:9); and by it we become children of God (John 1:12), divine, heavenly and spiritually minded, just and holy. We believe and teach that this
regeneration is necessary to salvation according to the words of Christ:
"Verily, verily, I say to you, except a man be born again, he cannot see the
kingdom of God"; and "Except a man be born of water and the Spirit, he
cannot enter the kingdom of God" (John 3:3, 5). . . .

32. The whole action of external, visible baptism places before our eyes,
testifies and signifies that Jesus Christ baptizes internally (Matt. 3:11;
John 1:33), in a laver of regeneration (Eph. 5:26; Titus 3:5) and renewing of
the Holy Spirit, the penitent and believing man: washing away, through
the virtue and merits of his poured-out blood, all the spots and sins of the
soul (1 John 1:7), and through the virtue and operation of the Holy Spirit,
which is a true, heavenly (Isa. 44:3; Ezek. 36:27; Joel 2:28; John 7:38–39),
spiritual and living water, [washing away] the internal wickedness of the
soul (1 Cor. 6:11; Titus 3:5–7), and render[ing] it heavenly (Phil. 3:20),
spiritual (Rom. 8:9) and living (Eph. 2:4–5) in true righteousness and
goodness. Moreover, baptism directs us to Christ and his holy office by
which in glory he performs that which he places before our eyes, and
testifies concerning its consummation in the hearts of believers and ad-
monishes us that we should not cleave to external things, but by holy
prayers ascend into heaven and ask from Christ the good indicated
through it [baptism]: a good which the Lord Jesus graciously concedes and
increases in the hearts of those who by true faith become partakers of the
sacraments.

Here certainly is a high doctrine of regeneration and baptism!

10

Roman Catholic, Lutheran, and Anglican Teaching

Baptismal Regeneration

$\mathbf{W}$e have already noted that for fifteen centuries the church understood baptism as the sacrament of regeneration. It is now our task to ascertain the official doctrine of the Roman Catholic Church since the time that she reacted against the new Protestant teaching, at which we looked in the last chapter. The obvious place to find the official Catholic position is in the doctrine promulgated by the Council of Trent (1545–1563). The decrees and canons concerning original sin, justification, and the sacraments were all set forth in 1547; it is these in which we are primarily interested. Having looked at the sixteenth-century doctrine, we shall then note further matters of interest from the documents produced by the Second Vatican Council (1962–1965). In the second part of this chapter we shall comment on Lutheran and Anglican teaching.

Roman Catholic Teaching

The Council of Trent

The Catholic teaching on original sin was clearly expressed by the Council of Trent.[1] When Adam transgressed God's law, he lost the holi-

---

1. See Philip Schaff, *Creeds of Christendom*, vol. 2, pp. 83–88.

ness and righteousness which he had possessed since his creation by God. Further, through this offense he incurred the wrath of God and became the captive of death and the devil. And because of his position as the first man he injured all his posterity: his original sin has been passed on through human procreation. Thus every newborn infant needs the remission of sin—original sin. It is through the regeneration of baptism that the guilt of original sin is taken away:

> If any one denies, that, by the grace of our Lord Jesus Christ, which is conferred in baptism, the guilt of original sin is remitted; or even asserts that the whole of that which has the true and proper nature of sin is not taken away; but that it is only erased, or not imputed; let him be anathema. For, in those who are born again, there is nothing that God hates; because, There is no condemnation to those who are truly buried together with Christ by baptism into death; who walk not according to the flesh, but, putting off the old man, and putting on the new who is created according to God, are made innocent, immaculate, pure, harmless, and beloved of God, heirs indeed of God, but joint heirs with Christ; so that there is nothing whatever to retard their entrance into heaven.

The reference to those who claim that after baptism the guilt of original sin is merely "not imputed" to the sinner is, of course, a criticism of Luther's doctrine.

There is further criticism of the doctrine of Luther and Calvin as the council's decree concerning original sin continues:

> This holy synod confesses and is sensible, that in the baptized there remains concupiscence, or an incentive (to sin); which, whereas it is left for our exercise, cannot injure those who consent not, but resist manfully by the grace of Jesus Christ. . . . This concupiscence, which the apostle sometimes calls sin [Rom. 6:12; 7:8], the holy Synod declares that the Catholic Church has never understood it to be called sin, as being truly and properly sin in those born again, but because it is of sin, and inclines to sin. And if anyone is of a contrary sentiment, let him be anathema.

The council followed Thomas Aquinas in accepting the idea of a passive bias or tendency to sin residing in the human senses (not in the will), but declared that it is not offensive to God. In contrast, the Reformers insisted (as did the later Jansenists) that it is offensive to God.

The nature of regeneration becomes clearer as we turn to the decree on justification (i.e., the process of making the sinner righteous):[2]

---

2. Ibid., pp. 89–118.

[Justification is] a translation, from that state wherein man is born a child of the first Adam, to the state of grace, and of the adoption of the sons of God, through the second Adam, Jesus Christ, our Saviour. And this translation, since the promulgation of the Gospel, cannot be effected, without the laver of regeneration, or the desire thereof, as it is written: unless a man be born again of water and the Holy Spirit, he cannot enter into the Kingdom of God.

Thus at baptism there is not only the remission of sins, but also the infusion of righteousness into the soul (through the presence and gifts of the Holy Spirit). For this reason baptism is called "the laver of regeneration."

Baptism is the laver of regeneration whether infants or adults are involved. The difference is that in adults there is a preparation for their justification; God helps them to be ready and able to receive the grace of regeneration at their baptism:

In adults, the beginning of the said Justification is to be derived from the prevenient grace of God, through Jesus Christ . . . whereby, without any merits existing on their parts, they are called; that so they, who by sins were alienated from God, may be disposed through his quickening and assisting grace, to convert themselves to their own justification, by freely assenting to and co-operating with that said grace: in such sort that, while God touches the heart of man by the illumination of the Holy Spirit, neither is man himself utterly inactive while he receives that inspiration, forasmuch as he is also able to reject it; yet he is not able, by his own free will, without the grace of God, to move himself unto justice [righteousness] in his sight.

Clearly, the prevenient or anticipatory grace of God must initially move the sinner, but there is no regeneration unless the individual freely consents to this movement of his or her heart and will towards God. Therefore, the individual sinner must accept the teaching of the gospel, turn from sin, look to Christ, and begin to love God as well as be penitent, in order to come to the laver of regeneration for the remission of sins and the gift of the indwelling Spirit, the Spirit of righteousness. As chapter 7 of the decree on justification expresses it:

This disposition, or preparation, is followed by Justification itself, which is not remission of sins merely, but also the sanctification and renewal of the inward man, through the voluntary reception of the grace, and of the gifts, whereby an unjust becomes a just man, and an enemy a friend, so that he may be an heir according to hope of life everlasting.

Regeneration is, therefore, the beginning of sanctification and renewal; and the instrumental cause of this process of being made righteous (i.e., being made holy and totally renewed) is baptism (this is in contrast to the Protestant assertion that the instrumental cause is faith and trust).

It is in canon 8 of the decree on the sacraments that we encounter the highly charged expression *ex opere operato:*[3]

> If anyone says, that by the said sacraments of the New Law [baptism, holy communion] grace is not conferred *through the act performed,* but that faith alone in the divine promise suffices for the obtaining of grace: let him be anathema.

The phrase *ex opere operato* had been used since the thirteenth century to express the conviction that the sacraments operate objectively, that is, independently of the subjective feelings or attitudes of the minister and the recipient. The assertion that a sacrament confers grace *ex opere operato* means that, as an instrument of the Holy Spirit, a sacrament will achieve its intended purpose simply by virtue of being performed. It will be wholly effective regardless of the merits or qualities of the persons in whom it acts or by whom it is performed. Faith on the part of the recipient is not a prerequisite. It is this automatic efficaciousness, so to speak, that distinguishes the sacraments from other ways of receiving God's grace (e.g., hearing a sermon or saying prayers). It should be pointed out, however, that *ex opere operato* was not understood to mean that, in the case of an adult, baptism will achieve regeneration even if the recipient consciously and deliberately resists God's grace.

The Second Vatican Council

Like the Council of Trent, the Second Vatican Council has spoken clearly on the subject of baptism and regeneration. Consider, for example, what it says in "The Dogmatic Constitution on the Church" (*Lumen gentium*):[4]

> 11. Incorporated into the Church by baptism, the faithful are appointed by their baptismal character to Christian religious worship; reborn as sons of God, they must profess before men the faith they have received from God through the Church. By the sacrament of confirmation they are more perfectly bound to the Church and are endowed with the

---

3. Ibid., pp. 118–25.
4. See Austin Flannery, ed., *Vatican Council II: The Conciliar and Post Conciliar Documents,* pp. 350–426.

special strength of the Holy Spirit. Hence they are, as true witnesses of Christ, more strictly obliged to spread the faith by word and deed.

"Baptismal character" is understood as an indelible quality which is imprinted upon the soul and remains forever, even in backsliders.

On the basis of Scripture and tradition the council teaches that baptism is necessary:

> 14. The Church, a pilgrim now on earth, is necessary for salvation. The one Christ is the Mediator and the way of salvation; he is present to us in his Body which is the Church. He himself explicitly asserted the necessity of faith and baptism (cf. Mk. 16:16; Jn. 3:5) and thereby affirmed at the same time the necessity of the Church which men must enter through baptism as through a door.

The council then goes on to acknowledge that in some incomplete yet real way those who are baptized in churches other than the Roman Catholic are thereby "sealed" and united to Christ and to the faithful in the true church, that is, the Roman Catholic.

In "The Decree on the Missionary Activity of the Church" (*Ad gentes*), there is teaching on conversion, rebirth, and baptism.[5] Those who respond seriously to the message of the gospel and wish to enter the catechumenate are called converts:

> 13. Under the movement of divine grace the new convert sets out on a spiritual journey by means of which, while already sharing through faith in the mystery of the death and resurrection, he passes from the old man to the new man who has been made perfect in Christ (cf. Col. 3:5–10; Eph. 4:20–24). This transition, which involves a progressive change of outlook and morals, should be manifested in its social implications and effected gradually during the period of the catechumenate. Since the Lord in whom he believes is a sign of contradiction (cf. Luke 2:34; Matt. 10:34–39), the convert often has to suffer misunderstanding and separation, but he also experiences those joys which are generously granted by God.

During the catechumenate the converts are not only to be taught the faith, but also to be introduced to the liturgy and sacred rites. Then they are to be baptized and confirmed, preferably at Easter (according to ancient practice):

> 14. Having been delivered from the powers of darkness through the sacraments of Christian initiation (cf. Col. 1:13), and having died, been

5. Ibid., pp. 813–56.

buried and risen with Christ (cf. Rom. 6:4–11; Col. 2:12–13; 1 Peter 3:21–22; Mark 16:16), they receive the Spirit of adoption of children (cf. 1 Thess. 3:5–7; Acts 8:14–17) and celebrate with the whole people of God the memorial of the Lord's death and resurrection.

Thus conversion reaches its climax through the sacraments of baptism, confirmation, and holy communion. The grace of regeneration is given only at the end of the catechumenate in the rite of holy baptism. This, it will be recalled, is much the same teaching as we found in the patristic period.

The Roman Catholic Church, like most other churches, has encountered in the Western world both a growing reluctance of parents to bring their children for infant baptism and a demand from some quarters to abandon infant baptism and baptize only adult believers. To face this situation the Vatican Sacred Congregation for the Doctrine of the Faith published in October 1980 a document entitled "Instruction on Infant Baptism" (*Pastoralis actio*).[6] Its purpose was to recall the principal points of doctrine which have justified the church's practice down the centuries and to demonstrate its value in the present climate:

> Baptism is a manifestation of the Father's prevenient love, a sharing in the Son's Paschal Mystery, and a communication of new life in the Spirit; it brings people into the inheritance of God and joins them to the Body of Christ, the Church.
>
> In view of this, Christ's warning—"unless one is born of water and the Spirit, he cannot enter the kingdom of God"—must be taken as an invitation of universal and limitless love, the words of a Father calling all his children and wishing them to have the greatest of blessings. This pressing and irrevocable call cannot leave us indifferent or neutral, since its acceptance is a condition for achieving our destiny.

But how can infants be baptized when they cannot personally exercise faith? To this old question an ancient answer is given. The church baptizes infants in its own faith, as Augustine taught centuries ago and theologians since his day have often repeated. "When children are presented to be given spiritual grace," wrote the bishop of Hippo, "it is not so much those holding them in their arms who present them . . . as it is the whole company of saints and faithful Christians. . . . It is done by the whole of Mother Church . . . it is as a whole that she gives birth to each and every one of them."[7]

---

6. See Austin Flannery, ed., *Vatican Council II: More Postconciliar Documents*, pp. 103–17.

7. Augustine *Epistola* 98.5, in *Patrologiae cursus completus*, ed. J. P. Migne, Series latina, vol. 33, col. 362.

Later on in the "Instruction on Infant Baptism" guidelines are given to govern pastoral practice:

> Concretely, pastoral practice regarding infant baptism must be governed by two great principles, the second of which is subordinate to the first.
> 1. Baptism, which is necessary for salvation, is the sign and the means of God's prevenient love, which frees us from original sin and communicates to us a share in the divine life. Considered in itself, the gift of these blessings to infants must not be delayed.
> 2. Assurances must be given that the gift thus granted can grow by an authentic education in the faith and Christian life, in order to fulfil the true meaning of the sacrament.

Here both the *ex opere operato* aspect of the sacrament and the need to nurture the divine life implanted in the soul are recognized.

Lutheran and Anglican Teaching

We noted earlier that both the Lutheran and Anglican services of baptism included the declaration that in connection with the rite God actually regenerates the infants (pp. 93, 95). This declaration was not based upon an *ex opere operato* view of the sacrament, but upon the sure promise of God concerning the infants born to Christian parents. All infants have inherited the guilt and disease of original sin and need internal regeneration. Because of the promise in the Word of God, they can be brought in confidence to the sacrament of baptism in order to be released from the bondage of their diseased will and enabled then (or later) to exercise true faith.

The question arises as to whether Luther in Germany and Cranmer in England (with their colleagues) actually intended their liturgical prayers of thanksgiving (for regeneration having occurred) to be taken in a simple, literal sense in all cases or whether they were using the language in a hypothetical sense. The answer must be the second alternative. The only possible way to construct a service of holy baptism which seriously reflects the promises of God and the close biblical relationship between faith, baptism, and regeneration is to proceed on the hypothesis that those who are baptized do actually receive the promised blessings from heaven. The assumption must be made that the promised gift is indeed bestowed; at the same time it must be emphasized that the infant is to be brought up in reverence for and in the admonition of the Lord and taught the full meaning of his or her baptism (i.e., death to sin and life in and for Christ). There can be no absolute guarantee that at baptism every infant receives the gift of the indwelling Holy Spirit.

However, there can be a total commitment by the parents and church to treat baptized infants as true Christians and thus to bring them up to be persons of faith, hope, and love.

The resolution to the debates which took place in sixteenth-century Germany amongst the Lutherans concerning the relation of the Holy Spirit to the human will before the moment of regeneration and conversion lent support to the teaching that infants are regenerated at baptism (despite the apparent conversions of adults who had been baptized as infants). This so-called synergist controversy (from 1535 to 1577) concerning in what sense, if at all, the human will cooperates with the Holy Spirit in conversion was settled by the Formula of Concord (1580), a document which in its treatment of original sin, free will, and justification makes use of the words *regeneration* and *conversion* on many occasions.[8] The official Lutheran position presented in the Formula's teaching on free will is that a human being is entirely passive in regeneration and conversion, but is active in the process of sanctification, cooperating with the grace of God. In later Lutheran teaching this position buttressed the doctrine of a hypothetical spiritual regeneration which, ideally, is actuated as the baptized infant matures. We shall see (in chapter 12) that the Pietists, noting that the seed sown was in many cases not producing the fruit that it ought to have produced, rejected the formalized doctrine of infant regeneration which had developed in the German churches.

In seventeenth-century Britain there were many attempts, especially within Puritan teaching, to trace the way in which a person who has been baptized as an infant comes later to conversion and assurance of salvation (see chapter 12). These attempts, as well as the teaching of certain non-Puritan Anglican divines (e.g., Lancelot Andrewes and Richard Hooker), reveal that the one service of baptism which they all used was, in terms of the gift of regeneration, understood in a hypothetical rather than literal sense.

When the regeneration referred to in the Lutheran or Anglican service of infant baptism is understood in this hypothetical sense, there are certain consequences.[9] First, there is a distinction between the re-

---

8. For the controversies leading up to the Formula of Concord see Eric W. Gritsch and Robert W. Jenson, *Lutheranism: The Theological Movement and Its Confessional Writing.* For the Formula itself see Theodore G. Tappert, ed., *The Book of Concord: The Confessions of the Evangelical Lutheran Church.* A very helpful essay is Arthur C. Piepkorn, "The Lutheran Understanding of Baptism," in *Lutherans and Catholics in Dialogue I–III,* ed. Paul C. Empie and T. Austin Murphy, pp. 27–70. For Lutheran teaching on preparation for conversion see Bernhard Citron, *New Birth: A Study of the Evangelical Doctrine of Conversion in the Protestant Fathers,* pp. 115–18.

9. See further the illuminating study by William Goode, *The Doctrine of the Church of England as to the Effects of Baptism in the Case of Infants.*

generation of an infant—or of children who die before they come to use reason—and of those who have reached the years of discretion. In this view the first form may grow into the latter form, or the first may be lost and the latter received later. Second, where there is a strong doctrine of divine election (be it on the basis of sovereign grace or of foreseen faith), baptism is held to be effectual only for the elect; and since we do not know which infants are the elect, we charitably assume that all infants of Christian parents are elect.

Not all Lutherans and Anglicans have accepted that the regeneration in infant baptism is to be understood hypothetically. Accordingly, some have sought for an interpretation of regeneration which is different from that taught by Jesus in John 3. Thus regeneration as received in baptism has been seen as "ecclesiastical regeneration," that is, entry into the visible church with its worship, fellowship, preaching, sacraments, and traditions, and thus into the sphere where true spiritual regeneration and conversion can actually take place.

On the other hand, both High-Church Lutherans and Anglicans have adopted what amounts to an *ex opere operato* view of the sacrament of baptism, even though they have not necessarily used scholastic categories.[10] Where High-Church adherents have been strongly influenced by the charismatic movement, they have tended to speak of the release of the Spirit as the equivalent of what traditional Pentecostalists have called the baptism of the Spirit. The release of the Spirit is, then, a gift beyond that of sacramental regeneration, the baptism with water.

It is perhaps fair to say that, except where there is a clear view of the hypothetical nature of the language, evangelicals in the Lutheran and Anglican churches have been embarrassed by the words of their baptismal services concerning regeneration.[11] Yet they continue to use these services, the modern versions of which still include a "compulsory" prayer giving God thanks for the regeneration of the one baptized. Here, for example, is the final prayer from the American Lutheran service of 1962:

> Almighty and most merciful God and Father: We thank you that you graciously preserve and extend your Church, and that you have granted to this child the new birth in Holy Baptism, and received him as your child and heir to your kingdom; and we humbly beseech you to defend and keep

---

10. See further Peter Toon, *Evangelical Theology 1833–1856: A Response to Tractarianism,* ch. 6.

11. An evidence of this embarrassment is the flood of defensive pamphlets which followed Charles Haddon Spurgeon's sermon on "Baptismal Regeneration" (June 5, 1864), in which he attacked the Anglican Prayer Book for teaching this particular doctrine. See Charles Haddon Spurgeon, *The Full Harvest,* pp. 55–59.

him in this grace, that he may never depart from you, but always live according to your will, and finally receive the fulness of your promise in your eternal kingdom; through Jesus Christ, your Son, our Lord, who lives and reigns with you and the Holy Spirit, one God, world without end. Amen.[12]

And here is the final prayer from the American Episcopal service of 1928:

We yield you hearty thanks, most merciful Father, that it has pleased you to regenerate this child with your Holy Spirit, to receive him for your own child, and to incorporate him into your holy Church. And humbly we beseech you to grant that he, being dead unto sin, may live unto right-eousness, and being buried with Christ in his death, may also be partaker of his resurrection; so that finally, with the residue of your holy Church, he may be an inheritor of your everlasting kingdom, through Christ our Lord. Amen.[13]

Even though both rites do clearly presume that the children are from Christian homes, the depiction of the relationship between baptism and regeneration undoubtedly makes many evangelically oriented Lu-therans and Anglicans quite uncomfortable.

---

12. In *Occasional Service Book*.
13. In *Book of Common Prayer, with the Additions and Deviations Proposed in 1928*.

11

Reformed Theology
Effectual Calling

W herever there are Presbyterian and Reformed churches, the name of John Calvin is honored, for from him came that stream of theology and church polity which characterizes them. No one would seek to prove that Reformed theology of the seventeenth, eighteenth, nineteenth, or twentieth century is identical with that found in Calvin's writings; yet it bears his mark. Here we shall notice the teaching of Arminius, of the Synod of Dort, of the Westminster Assembly and Savoy Declaration, of two types of nineteenth-century divinity, and finally of Emil Brunner.

Arminianism

Reformed theology as it came from Calvin and was expounded by his successors (e.g., Theodore Beza also of Geneva) had to meet the challenge of a renewed Roman Catholicism, of a competitive Lutheranism, of various heretical systems (e.g., Socinianism), and of internal disputes and schisms. One of the most important of these disputes is that associated with the name of Jacobus Arminius (1560–1609), who first questioned, and then rejected, the doctrine of predestination as developed by

Beza and William Perkins.[1] As a professor at Leyden from 1603 Arminius became involved in controversy as he sought to formulate a type of Reformed theology limiting predestination to God's advance knowledge concerning who would actually respond to the call of the gospel. After his death his supporters and friends composed a Remonstrance (1610) of five articles summarizing what they believed, confessed, and taught as the Reformed faith.[2]

The first article describes the divine decree to save those who, for Christ's sake and with the help of the Holy Spirit, believe the Good News concerning Jesus Christ. The second insists that Jesus Christ died for each and every person so that he has obtained for everyone the possibility of redemption; however, to enjoy this salvation the sinner must accept the gospel.

In the third it is emphasized that to believe unto salvation a sinner needs the help of the Holy Spirit:

> 3. That man has not saving grace of himself, nor of the energy of his free will, inasmuch as he, in the state of apostasy and sin, can of and by himself neither think, will nor do anything that is truly good (such as saving faith eminently is); but that it is needful that he be born again of God in Christ, through his Holy Spirit, and renewed in understanding, inclination, or will, and all his powers, in order that he may rightly understand, think, will and effect what is truly good, according to the word of Christ, John 15:5: "Without me you can do nothing."

The fourth article also insists that sinners are dependent upon the direct help of the Holy Spirit if they are to do the will of God:

> 4. That this grace of God is the beginning, continuance, and accomplishment of all good, even to this extent, that the regenerate man himself, without prevenient or assisting, awakening, following and cooperative grace, can neither think, will, nor do good, nor withstand any temptations to evil; so that all good deeds or movements, that can be conceived, must be ascribed to the grace of God in Christ. But as respects the mode of the operation of this grace, it is not irresistible, inasmuch as it is written concerning many, that they have resisted the Holy Spirit. Acts 7, and elsewhere in many places.

The sting here is in the tail, the rejection of the concept of irresistible regenerating grace—a doctrine that had become part of orthodox Reformed theology.

---

1. For Arminius see Carl Bangs, *Arminius: A Study in the Dutch Reformation.*
2. See Philip Schaff, *Creeds of Christendom,* vol. 3, pp. 545–49.

While teaching that Christ wishes to hold on to his regenerate people, the fifth article very cautiously suggests it is possible that they may choose to let go of him:

> 5. That those who are incorporated into Christ by a true faith, and have thereby become partakers of his life-giving Spirit, have thereby full power to strive against Satan, sin, the world, and their own flesh, and to win the victory; it being well understood that it is ever through the assisting grace of the Holy Spirit; and that Jesus Christ assists them through his Spirit in all temptations, extends to them his hand, and if only they are ready for the conflict, and desire his help, and are not inactive, keeps them from falling, so that they, by no craft or power of Satan, can be misled nor plucked out of Christ's hands, according to the word of Christ, John 10:28, "Neither shall any man pluck them out of my hand." But whether they are capable, through negligence, of forsaking again the first beginnings of their life in Christ, of again returning to this present evil world, of turning away from the holy doctrine which was delivered them, of losing a good conscience, of becoming devoid of grace, that must be more particularly determined out of the Holy Scripture, before we ourselves can teach it with the full persuasion of our minds.

This hesitation to affirm that a justified and regenerate sinner bound for heaven might perhaps end up bound for hell was not generally maintained by the Remonstrants in the controversies that followed the publication of the five articles.

Since the year 1610, the term *Arminianism* has been used to describe many types of theology which reject absolute predestination, assert that Christ's atonement was universal, and insist that the human will is free to accept or reject the offer of God in the gospel. In this study we shall primarily use the word to describe the theology of Arminius and his supporters and shall work under the assumption that it is a form— perhaps a deviant form—of Reformed, Calvinistic theology (Arminius believed he was more true to Calvin than were his opponents).

The five Arminian articles had been written as a summary of the position adopted by Arminius and his followers in the controversies within Leyden and the Netherlands. The publication of these articles as the Remonstrance (hence the term *Remonstrants*) in 1610 intensified controversy and led to the calling of the Synod of Dort (Dordrecht) by the States General in 1618. This synod provided a detailed response to the Remonstrance.

The Synod of Dort

The "First Head of Doctrine" in the Canons issued by the Synod of Dort explains in eighteen articles the doctrine of divine predestination, insisting that election unto salvation is of the good pleasure of God and is selective.[3] Thus some people are not included in the decree of election. The "Second Head of Doctrine" is concerned with the death of Christ and the redemption of the elect thereby. Though the atonement of Christ has an infinite value and worth, its efficacy applies only to the elect.

The synod could not find anything wrong with the third article of the Remonstrance taken by itself. Thus the delegates decided to look at the third in the light of the fourth article. Hence the "Third and Fourth Heads of Doctrine" in the Canons of Dort were combined under the title, "Of the Corruption of Man, His Conversion to God, and the Way It Occurs." In this section there are seventeen articles, the first two of which are occupied with the theme of the fall. The third teaches our total inability to do anything to please God: "All men are conceived in sin and born as children of wrath, incapable of any saving good, inclined to evil, dead in sins, and slaves of sin. Apart from the regenerating grace of the Holy Spirit, moreover, they are neither willing nor able to return to God, to reform their depraved nature, or to prepare themselves for its reformation."

Sinners need to hear the gospel in order that they may come to God and receive eternal life. The reason why some do come and others do not come is ultimately to be traced to divine election, for "as God has chosen His own in Christ from eternity, so He calls them effectually in time" (article 10). In article 11 we are told how God brings about conversion, in article 12 we are told of the supernatural character of regeneration, in article 13 of the mystery of regeneration, and in article 14 of the manner in which God gives saving faith:

> 11. When God, moreover, carries out His good pleasure in the elect, or works in them true conversion, He not only sees to it that the gospel is outwardly preached to them, powerfully enlightening their minds by the Holy Spirit so that they may rightly understand and discern the things of the Spirit of God, but by the effectual working of that same regenerating Spirit He also penetrates into the innermost recesses of man, opens the closed and softens the hard heart, circumcises that which was uncircumcised, and pours new qualities into the will. He makes the will which was dead alive, which was bad good, which was unwilling willing, which was stubborn obedient, and moves and strengthens it so that, like a good tree, it may be able to produce the fruits of good works.

> 12. And this is that regeneration, that new creation, that resurrection from the dead, that making alive, so highly spoken of in the Scriptures,

---

3. Ibid., pp. 550–97. I have used a modern translation by Anthony A. Hoekema, which appears in *Calvin Theological Journal* 3 (1968): 133–61.

which God works in us without our help. But this regeneration is by no means brought about only by outward teaching or preaching, by moral persuasion, or by such a method of working that after God has done His work, it remains in the power of man to be regenerated or not regenerated, converted or not converted. It is, however, clearly a supernatural, most powerful and at the same time most delightful, marvelous, secret, and inexpressible work which, according to the Scriptures inspired by the Author of regeneration, is not inferior in power to creation or the resurrection of the dead. Hence all those in whose hearts God works in this amazing way are certainly, unfailingly, and effectually regenerated and do actually believe. Therefore the will so renewed is not only acted upon and moved by God but, acted upon by God, the will itself also acts. Hence also man himself, through the grace he has received, is rightly said to believe and repent.

13. As long as they are in this life believers cannot fully understand the way in which God does this work. Meanwhile, however, they rest content in this, that they know and experience that by this grace of God they believe with the heart and love their Savior.

14. Faith is therefore a gift of God in this way: not that it is merely offered by God to the free will of man, but that it is actually conferred on man, implanted and infused into him. It is not a gift in the sense that God confers only the power to believe, but then awaits from man's free will the consent to believe or the act of believing. It is, however, a gift in the sense that He who works both the willing and the working—in fact, all things in all—brings about in man both the will to believe and believing itself.

Whereas the Arminians had declared that "the mode of the operation of [God's] grace . . . is not irresistible," the Synod of Dort declared that "all those in whose hearts God works in this amazing way are certainly, unfailingly, and effectually regenerated." The decree of election guarantees that the secret and mysterious work of the Spirit is effective and effectual. Both sides believed in the preaching of the gospel to all people; but whereas the Arminians held that, due to human resistance, the Spirit is not always successful in preparing hearts for the climax of regeneration, the synod held that the Spirit's work is irresistible in that he makes a person willing and desirous.

Once the synod had set forth the doctrine of sovereign and irresistible grace in regeneration, it is not surprising that the delegates turned in the "Fifth Head of Doctrine" to "The Perseverance of the Saints," insisting that all those who are regenerated by the Spirit will attain unto final and everlasting salvation: "God is faithful who mercifully confirms them in the grace once conferred upon them, and powerfully keeps them in that grace to the end" (article 3).

The differences between Arminian and Reformed theology are very important, for one's particular stance on the doctrine of predestination has major implications for the other parts of one's system of theology, including the subject of regeneration. Several aspects of the Synod of Dort's view of regeneration will be of interest here. First, the Canons virtually equate regeneration and conversion. We have seen that article 11 in "The Third and Fourth Heads of Doctrine" describes how God works true conversion (Latin *conversio*) in the elect and that article 12 then begins with the words, "And this is that regeneration [*regeneratio*] . . . so highly spoken of in the Scriptures." Calvin had spoken specifically of the conversion of the will;[4] the synod enlarged the concept of conversion to cover both the renewal of the heart and the pouring of new qualities into the will so that it is able to produce decisions and actions pleasing to God.[5]

In the second place, the synod taught that regeneration precedes faith and is the cause of faith (article 14). There can be no saving faith in the Lord Jesus without the infusion and implanting of faith in the heart, which is an action of the regenerating Spirit.

Third, as article 17 makes clear, the Spirit works through and with the Word of God as that Word is made known by the preaching of the gospel, the administration of the sacraments, and the exercise of discipline within the congregation. This insistence upon the Word, and not baptism, as "the seed of regeneration and food of the soul" is fundamental to the whole presentation of conversion. The modern reader of the "Third and Fourth Heads of Doctrine" would hardly guess that the synod spoke for a church which practiced infant baptism and embraced a confession of faith stating "that every man who is earnestly studious of obtaining eternal life ought to be once baptized." Further, this statement immediately follows the affirmation:

> Our Lord gives that which is signified by the sacrament, namely, the gifts and invisible grace; washing, cleansing, and purging our souls of all filth and unrighteousness; renewing our hearts and filling them with all comfort; giving unto us a true assurance of his fatherly goodness; putting on us the new man, and putting off the old man with all his deeds.[6]

---

4. John Calvin, *Institutes of the Christian Religion* 2.3.6–7.

5. In Reformed theology, conversion may be understood as either (1) God's work of turning the individual from sin to righteousness by placing a new principle of life within (in this sense conversion is an equivalent of regeneration), or (2) the renewed, regenerated individual's response (a new faith, genuine repentance, and loving obedience) to this internal action of the Holy Spirit. The passivity of the human subject in (1) is conveyed by the Latin expression *conversio habitualis seu passiva,* and the activity of the subject in (2) by *conversio actualis seu activa.*

6. Belgic Confession 34, in Arthur C. Cochrane, ed., *Reformed Confessions of the Sixteenth Century,* pp. 185–219.

The delegates to the synod described conversion (regeneration) as if they were addressing a missionary situation; they had in view that which occurs when pagans respond to the gospel. This can be explained in part by the fact that the theologians of Dort used the New Testament as their basic source of information, and of course the New Testament was clearly addressed to a missionary situation. It can also be explained in part by the fact that the theologians had not wholly integrated their thinking on the relation of infant baptism to the work of the regenerating, converting Spirit. What was stated at Dort appears to rule out for infant baptism anything other than the minimal beginnings of the operation of the regenerating Spirit. In fact, baptism is not mentioned in the whole discussion—an omission that would have been impossible for Roman Catholic as well as many Anglican and Lutheran theologians at that time.

The Westminster Assembly

The teaching of the Synod of Dort had an important influence on the development of the Reformed tradition and fixed the way in which the doctrine of regeneration would be taught in those churches for the next two or three centuries. Thirty or so years after the Synod of Dort another synod of Reformed theologians met in London. This gathering became known as the Westminster Assembly, and it produced a Confession of Faith, a Larger and Shorter Catechism, and a Directory for the Public Worship of God.[7] The basic theological position in these documents, which have been very influential in Scottish Presbyterianism and those churches derived from Scottish origins, is much the same as that of the document produced by the Synod of Dort. There is the same great emphasis upon divine predestination and election in Christ unto salvation; there is the same doctrine of regeneration and identification of it with conversion; and there is the same stress upon irresistible grace working within the elect to bring them to faith, repentance, and union with Christ.

However, partly because the Westminster documents are longer and more comprehensive than the Canons of Dort, and partly because the issue was explicitly discussed in the assembly, there is specific treatment of the relation of baptism and regeneration. Chapter 28 of the Westminster Confession defines baptism as "a sign and seal of the covenant of grace, of [one's] ingrafting into Christ, of regeneration, of remission of sins, and of [one's] giving up unto God, through Jesus Christ, to

---

7. These documents are all printed in *The Confession of Faith*.

walk in newness of life." It is emphasized that infants of believing parents are to be baptized. Then we read:

> Although it be a great sin to contemn or neglect this ordinance, yet grace and salvation are not so inseparably annexed unto it, as that no person can be regenerated or saved without it, or that all that are baptized are undoubtedly regenerated.
>
> The efficacy of baptism is not tied to the moment of time wherein it is administered; yet, notwithstanding, by the right use of this ordinance, the grace promised is not only offered, but really exhibited, and conferred by the Holy Ghost, to such (whether of age or infants) as that grace belongeth unto, according to the counsel of God's own will, in his appointed time.

Thus it is admitted that it is possible to be regenerate without having been baptized; further, the time of regeneration is not necessarily tied to the time of baptism.

In chapter 10 of the same Confession, the following statement is made: "Elect infants, dying in infancy, are regenerated and saved by Christ through the Spirit, who worketh when, and where, and how he pleaseth. So also are all other elect persons who are incapable of being outwardly called by the ministry of the Word." It is here taught that God can and does achieve regeneration (i.e., inner renewal and renovation of the sinner into the true image of God through the action and presence of the Holy Spirit) without the preliminary work of causing (1) conviction of and sorrow for sin and (2) a searching after the God of grace. An obvious conclusion is that regeneration can take place in the heart of an infant at baptism, and the fruit of that divine work and presence will be seen later in life when he or she turns from sin and unto Christ. (There is very clear teaching on infant baptism and regeneration in the Directory of 1644).

The Westminster Confession presents regeneration under the headings of "Effectual Calling" (ch. 10), "Sanctification" (ch. 13), and "Baptism" (ch. 28). Those whom God truly calls through the ministry of the Word in the power of the Spirit, he regenerates. Such individuals may or may not already have been baptized. Those whom he thus calls and regenerates are afforded the gift of saving faith and belief on the Lord Jesus and are justified; they also begin a life of faith, hope, and love, the starting point of which is their inward regeneration. In a missionary situation baptism takes place when the individual confesses the Lord Jesus Christ (i.e., is regenerated, justified, and adopted into God's family); but in the Britain of the 1640s it had already taken place when the individual was an infant, and so the grace exhibited and sealed by the sacrament actually became effectual later in life. Regeneration may also be called conversion by God in that he turns sinners from being children of the devil to being his own children. Regeneration (or conversion, or renewal) is wholly the act of God and occurs within the elect through irresistible grace.

The Savoy Declaration of 1658

A number of Congregational ministers and theologians, who had been well treated under the Commonwealth and Protectorate in Britain, gathered at the Savoy Palace in London in 1658 to produce a confession of faith and a statement of their church polity. While their Declaration of the Institution of Churches was a new creation, their Declaration of Faith was to a large extent a rewrite of the Westminster Confession of Faith. However, some changes were made, and a new chapter entitled "Of the Gospel, and of the Extent of the Grace Thereof" (ch. 20) was added.[8] After stating that the promise of salvation in Christ is revealed only in the Word of God and that the preaching of the gospel is therefore necessary, this new chapter concludes:

> Although the gospel be the only outward means of revealing Christ and saving grace, and is as such abundantly sufficient thereunto; yet that men who are dead in trespasses may be born again, quickened, or regenerated, there is moreover necessary an effectual, irresistible work of the Holy Ghost upon the whole soul, for the producing in them [of] a new spiritual life, without which no other means are sufficient for their conversion unto God.

Later we shall look at the teaching of one of the major authors of this document, John Owen (pp. 141–43). Here we may note that in line with this emphasis on regeneration and conversion the Declaration of the Institution of Churches specifically teaches that only the regenerate should be admitted into church membership. Such a position was very different from that of the Church of England, as restored in 1662, where all baptized persons were regarded as members. The churches of the Congregational Way looked for a personal testimony to the work of God in the soul.

---

8. For the text see Arnold G. Matthews, *The Savoy Declaration of Faith and Order, 1658.* And for the differences in theology between the Westminster Confession and the Savoy Declaration see Peter Toon, *Puritans and Calvinism,* chs. 4 and 5. It is important to note that the Particular (i.e., Reformed, Calvinistic) Baptists in their Confessions of 1677 and 1689 (England) and 1742 (Philadelphia) expressed the same theology as that of the Westminster Confession and Savoy Declaration. For these Baptist documents see William L. Lumpkin, ed., *Baptist Confessions of Faith.*

Scottish Divinity

Reformed doctrine of the type delineated by the Canons of Dort and the Westminster symbols, especially in its emphasis on sovereign grace, has had able defenders and exponents in the Netherlands, Switzerland, England, Scotland, and America.[9] Classic Puritanism, with its stress on purity of church life and vital religion, is itself, as we shall see in chapter 12, a particular expression of Reformed doctrine. Among the well-known exponents of Reformed theology since the period of Puritanism are such Scottish divines as Thomas Chalmers (1780–1847), William Cunningham (1805–1861), and George Smeaton (1814–1889), a professor of exegetical theology at New College, Edinburgh. To this list may be added such American divines as Charles Hodge (1797–1878) and his son Archibald Alexander Hodge (1823–1886). We shall focus on Smeaton's *Doctrine of the Holy Spirit* in order to discover how a leading nineteenth-century theologian understood regeneration and what he saw as the major threats to purity of this doctrine in both Europe and America.[10]

Smeaton's exposition of regeneration follows his study of the personality and procession of the Spirit, the work of the Spirit in the anointing of Christ, and in connection with divine revelation and the inspiration of the Bible. In approaching the topic of new birth he insists that human beings need regeneration because their souls are deprived of the Holy Spirit. On the stately ruins of the soul is the doleful inscription, "Here God once dwelt." By his apostasy Adam drove the Holy Spirit from his soul and from the souls of his descendants. "Thus detached from his primeval ties by the forfeiture of the Spirit, man follows the natural rather than the spiritual, the human rather than the divine" (p. 166). Though physically alive, humankind is spiritually dead; this means that all the faculties of the soul—the understanding, affections, and will—are seriously affected. In terms of the will we are free to choose but we uniformly choose that which is not pleasing to God; this is because the will itself is diseased and vitiated.

Having insisted on the fact of human depravity and the need for the return of the Spirit to the house in which he once dwelt, Smeaton examines three scriptural texts—John 3:3–6; 6:63; and 16:8–11. He understands "born of water" (3:5) not as a reference to water baptism, but as "the ceremonial expression for the cleansing of our person by [Christ's] own obedience or atoning sacrifice" (p. 170). In this work of cleansing

---

9. For citations from Reformed divines see Heinrich Heppe, *Reformed Dogmatics Set Out and Illustrated from the Sources*, pp. 510–42.

10. This work was first published in 1882 by T. & T. Clark. I have taken the quotations from the 1958 reprint (Banner of Truth), which has identical pagination.

and regeneration "the Spirit's agency is sovereign . . . the mode of his activity is inscrutable . . . the efficacy is irresistible, and the effects indubitable" (p. 172). Thus in the phrase "born of water and the Spirit" Smeaton takes "water" to point to the *meritorious* cause of salvation and "the Spirit" to point to the *efficient* cause.

John 16:8–11 is for Smeaton "the most conclusive passage on the Spirit's work in connection with conversion in the whole compass of Scripture." After a full discussion of the meaning of our Lord's words in this passage, he concludes that in regeneration the Spirit's operations take effect upon the whole soul and thus influence every faculty directly, and that the inhabitation of the Spirit in the soul means that he becomes the "indefectible source of light and life and fruitfulness, as well as of perseverance and progressive holiness" (p. 187). He becomes the efficient cause of all spiritual activity in the understanding, will, and conscience:

> With regard to the *understanding,* all spiritual light is derived from the Spirit of wisdom and revelation in the knowledge of the Lord Jesus enlightening the eyes of the understanding (Eph. 1:17). . . . In the first act of illumination, the Spirit acts much in the same way as when he commanded light to shine out of darkness (2 Cor. 4:6). But when the man has received the power of vision, he uses it for the further increase of his knowledge in the way of co-operating grace. The truths which he believed to the saving of the soul had reference to God, to himself, and to the adaptation of the atonement. By the illumination of the Spirit, he acquires wholly different views of all these points and of God, who is no longer regarded as an indulgent being, nor as a tyrant, but as a gracious Father, all whose perfections are glorified by the atonement. As to ourselves, the Spirit shows us the ruin and the remedy.
>
> The Spirit's operation is not less conspicuous on the *will.* The principal effect of the Spirit's activity is seen in a new principle of spiritual life diffused through all the mental powers, and inclining the soul to yield itself to Christ in the exercise of faith and subjection, as now enabled or made fit both to will and to do.
>
> And as to the *conscience,* the sanctification of the Spirit contributes to a good conscience. In other words, the conscience purged with the sprinkling of the blood of Christ by the effectual application of the Spirit, is then committed to the Spirit, who corrects and teaches it, who purifies and comforts it, from day to day. [pp. 188–89]

Those in whom the Spirit works in this manner become the adopted children of God, for they have been effectually called by the gospel and the Spirit into the kingdom and family of God.

Well aware of the various questions that had been raised over the centuries concerning the relationship between the human will and the work of the Spirit in regeneration (conversion), Smeaton made his own position very clear:

> The leading principle which helps us to find our way through all the difficulties of these questions is, that *the Spirit* in returning to the human heart, *anticipates the will*—that is, *works in us to will,* at the first moment of conversion and at every subsequent step. The first desire, wish, or resolution to return to God, as well as the first prayer offered with this end in view, is from the Holy Spirit. That all spiritual good emanates from the Spirit of God is a simple formula which keeps every inquirer in this department right. That the Spirit's power and grace precede the will is a maxim to be carried with us, unless we are prepared to ascribe a merit to the first step, or to view the first step as originated on the man's own side.
>
> And from the moment that the soul begins to act in spiritual things, it acts with its *newly acquired spiritual powers,* imparted by the Spirit of God. . . . The expression *spiritual powers* does not imply a change in man's essential nature, or the donation of faculties which were never found in the human mind before, but simply a *new aptitude and power* to comply with what is truly good, as derived from the Holy Spirit. With a new will, that is, a will renovated and endowed with a spiritual capacity, the soul becomes active, and co-operates with God. [p. 198]

Thus regeneration is from first to last the work of the Holy Spirit.

The Holy Spirit is given to each elect believer by the exalted Lord Jesus, for, having fulfilled the Father's will, he has received as a reward an inexhaustible supply of the Spirit to impart to his people. And the Spirit, sent from the Lord Jesus, "will not abandon the souls which he has regenerated, and which he will use effectual means to reclaim when they are prone, from inward feebleness or listless indifference, to vacillate or waver" (p. 201).

As we would expect, Smeaton strongly opposed what he called Pelagianism, Arminianism, Socinianism, and rationalism. He was also opposed to Pajonism (after Claude Pajon [1626–1685], a professor of theology at Saumur who denied any immediate influence of the Holy Spirit in conversion). Nineteenth-century Reformed theologians used the term to denote the view that regeneration is caused by the moral power of the preached word of God alone, without any special direct involvement of the Holy Spirit. They associated Pajonism not only with the University of Saumur, but also with the influential late-eighteenth-century Lutheran theologian J. L. Z. Junckheim, who, following Immanuel Kant, claimed for humans the power of amending their lives by their own will as persuaded and empowered by the preached word of God. According to Smeaton, Junckheim "asserted that the operation of God in men's regeneration and conversion was not to be designated supernatural. . . . The moral power of the word effected all." Smeaton lamented that this approach had infected most German theology up to his own time (the late nineteenth century).

Smeaton also held the teaching from Saumur—in this case from its most famous theologian, Moise Amyraut (Amyraldus [1596–1664])— responsible for another error, which had deeply infected American and British theology after having been reiterated by Jonathan Edwards himself.[11] This was the distinction between natural and moral ability to believe the gospel of Jesus Christ. Amyraut contended that the sinner has the former, but not the latter. Smeaton comments:

> Had Edwards fully known the place which that mischievous theory oc-
> cupied in the Amyraldist system, it would probably never have been pro-
> pounded in the manner in which it is set forth by him in his essay on the
> freedom of the will and elsewhere. For the practical ends for which he
> appeals to it, it is safe enough; when it is used speculatively, it is dan-
> gerous. [p. 342]

Smeaton maintained that the revivalists used the distinction in the wrong way: on the grounds that everyone has at least a natural ability to believe, they claimed that there is no excuse for not receiving the gospel. Responses of unbelief meant simply "that men *would not,* not that they *could not,* repent and believe the gospel. The [revivalists] wished to exhibit that the entire turning-point was with the will, and they threw the responsibility on the man to make him feel that he would not come and be saved."

Thus Smeaton argued against both Pajonism, the view that moral suasion alone is needed in the process of regeneration and conversion, and the Amyraldian distinction between natural and moral ability. While the first denied any direct involvement of the Holy Spirit in the new creation, the second diminished his role by minimizing his work in the process of conversion, emphasizing instead the ability of the human will. For Smeaton, however, the whole of human nature was corrupted by sin and thus in every part—understanding, affections, will, and con-science—needed supernatural grace. And what Smeaton asserted in Scotland the Princeton divines argued in America. Yet they could not hold back the tide of erroneous teaching, as they discerned it, in the revivalism of the so-called New School theology associated with Nathaniel Taylor (1786–1858), Albert Barnes (1798–1870), and Charles G. Finney (1792–1875). Perhaps the most distinguished of the New School theologians of the middle of the nineteenth century was

---

11. See further Brian G. Armstrong, *Calvinism and the Amyraut Heresy.*

Henry Boynton Smith (1815–1877), whose work at Union Theological Seminary helped to give that school its distinguished reputation.

New School Theology

Henry Boynton Smith shared with Calvin an emphasis upon Christ and the union of believers with Christ. And he sought to construct his systematic theology around this central point.[12] We shall use his *System of Christian Theology* as our source for his views on regeneration. But first we need to recall that he differed with the Old School Presbyterians (represented by the Princeton divines) on various points; for example, on the extent of the atonement (they taught limited atonement; he taught universal), on divine election (they taught a double decree of election and damnation; he taught a single decree of election), and on the nature of the will (they did not accept his distinction—taken from Jonathan Edwards—between natural and moral ability).

Smith's discussion of God's call through the gospel to the sinner and of regeneration certainly belongs to Reformed, Calvinist thought rather than to any other theology, but we must also remember that it was written in the mid-nineteenth century. Doctrinal treatises produced at that time were informed not only by theological reflection but also by new trends in philosophy and psychology. For example, Smith notes the various views that the truth of Scripture (as the sword of the Spirit) has in itself the moral power not merely to convince but also to change the heart of the sinner; there is no need for extra help of a *direct* action of the Spirit in and upon the soul. Smith vigorously rejects these views:

> Besides all that can be put under the head of moral suasion and of super-natural influence through the truth, there is in the renewal of the soul, according to Scripture, a divine, secret, and direct influence . . . of the Spirit. . . . In speaking of the truth as a means of regeneration, we should be careful to use it in its specific Scriptural sense. The Scriptures never disjoin it from Christ and God and the Holy Spirit. Christ is the Truth. . . . To talk of man's being renewed by the truth without the Spirit is the same as to talk of a man's being killed by a sword when the sword is in nobody's hands. [pp. 519, 569]

Smith also maintained that regeneration is subjective in nature:

> Regeneration is not a physical change. The term physical, as used in respect to regeneration, is differently defined. It may mean what belongs

---

12. See further George M. Marsden, *The Evangelical Mind and the New School Presbyterian Experience,* ch. 8.

to the external material world, or what belongs to the essence and faculties of man. Regeneration is not physical as implying a change in the essence or faculties of man. . . . Those who hold strictly to the exercise scheme reason thus: There are in man (1) the essence, (2) the faculties, (3) the acts or exercises of the faculties. Regeneration is not in the 1st or 2nd, therefore it must be in the 3d.—A better analysis gives this statement: There are in man, 1st, the essence, 2dly, the faculties, 3dly, the generic tendencies, 4thly, the actions. The regeneration then will take effect in the third and fourth,—not merely in the specific acts, but in the ground or source of those acts. [pp. 560–61]

In sinful humans there is a generic tendency towards sin—a bias towards evil. In the regenerate, through the mighty action of the Spirit, there is a generic tendency towards God, righteousness, and holiness. Thus the state or direction of the faculties has been renewed and redirected. "In short, regeneration in its full measure and extent involves a new direction of all the human powers from the world and towards God—an illumination of the understanding, a current of the affections, and a choice of the will" (p. 562). And this divine work must be instantaneous even though in human conscious experience it may not seem so. There must be some point at which the soul is turned and turns from darkness to light.

Smith taught what he called "the general evangelical doctrine of regeneration":

(a) Regeneration is a supernatural change of which God is the author, which is wrought by the Holy Spirit.

(b) In its idea it is instantaneous, although not always so in conscious experience.

(c) In adults it is wrought most frequently by the word of God as the instrument. Believing that infants may be regenerated, we cannot assert that it is tied to the word of God absolutely.

(d) It involves the renewal of the whole man—not merely of one of his faculties. It gives a new direction to all his faculties.

(e) There is no antecedent co-operation on man's part in the change itself. The efficiency in the change is not human, it is in the Holy Spirit. The act of the will on man's part does not produce, but indicates the change.

(f) Regeneration, in the New Testament sense, is on the basis of Christ's work, and consists essentially in the application of what Christ has done, to the human soul, through the Holy Spirit.

(g) This new state shows itself in faith, repentance, and good works. Negatively—

(h) Regeneration is not a physical change but a change in the moral state. It does not impart new faculties, it gives direction to our faculties.

(i) It does not consist in the executive acts of the will as distinguished from the immanent preference, but it is essentially found in the latter. Nor is it in the conscious, as distinguished from the unconscious, moral states of man. We know it in its results, not in its essence. [pp. 556–57]

This "evangelical" doctrine was shared by many in the Presbyterian, Congregational, Baptist, and Episcopalian denominations who called themselves "evangelical" and in a general sense "Reformed" or "Calvinist." A virtually identical doctrine was taught by the influential Baptist theologian Augustus Hopkins Strong (1836–1921) in part 3 of his *Systematic Theology,* where he treats regeneration in between his discussions of union with Christ and conversion.[13] In fact, this moderate Reformed theology had earlier been expressed in the New Hampshire Confession (1833), a statement of faith widely accepted by Baptists.[14]

Dialectical Theology

As we turn to Heinrich Emil Brunner (1889–1966), professor of theology at the University of Zurich from 1924 until 1955, we encounter a modern form of Reformed theology, a form that many traditionalists refuse to recognize as genuinely Reformed.[15] It has been said of Brunner:

> He stands between the worlds of the waning liberalism and the advancing new liberalism, between the decline of the old orthodoxy and the forward march of neo-orthodoxy. He broke with the traditional theology (liberal and orthodox both) in order to become a dialectical theologian. He took issue with the advocates of impersonal dogmas in order to engage man in the existential encounter of personal truth. He will perhaps be remembered most for the impact he gave to theology by his stress upon dialecticism and personal correspondence.[16]

We shall make use of his *Dogmatics,* in which he assumes that revelation is not doctrine as such, nor is it the disclosure of facts and information.

---

13. See further Grant Wacker, *Augustus H. Strong and the Dilemma of Historical Consciousness.*

14. For the text see Lumpkin, ed., *Baptist Confessions.* Note especially sections 7 ("Of Grace in Regeneration") and 8 ("Of Repentance and Faith").

15. There is a useful introductory article on Brunner by Robert D. Linder in Walter A. Elwell, ed., *Evangelical Dictionary of Theology,* pp. 175–77. See also Paul G. Schrotenboer, "Emil Brunner," in Philip E. Hughes, *Creative Minds in Contemporary Theology,* pp. 99–130.

16. Schrotenboer, "Emil Brunner," pp. 99–100.

Rather, it is God's once-for-all unique disclosure of himself, an encounter with humans which has a dual character of address (*Zuspruch*) and claim (*Anspruch*).

In section 2 of the third volume of the *Dogmatics,* Brunner has chapters on both regeneration and conversion. These occur in between his discussions of justification and sanctification. It is obvious that his main emphasis is upon the God who justifies, but he feels it necessary to look briefly at the concept of regeneration because (1) though a different figure, it is synonymous with justifying faith, and (2) it has been grossly misunderstood and misused in the church over the centuries, being interpreted as if it referred to a natural process. Brunner emphasizes that what the figure of new birth points to "in a specially impressive way is the *totality* of the new creation of the person," since Jesus Christ is not only the Word who justifies, but also the Life who begets and vivifies (p. 269).

Rejecting traditional Roman Catholic and some Lutheran theology which gives the impression that a new substance or being is infused into the soul through holy baptism, Brunner attempts to follow Luther:

> But how is rebirth related to the fact that even the believer, the justified man, is a sinner? Faith is that event through which the sinful man, in spite of his sin, is declared righteous, that event in which he receives the new personal being. Therefore this new being is at first limited to the fact of faith. . . . This new being does not [immediately] come into evidence as such . . . empirically we are still sinners, and . . . it only becomes empirically visible in the strenuous battle for sanctification. . . .
>
> [So regeneration means that in the] invisible core of personality the great, eternally decisive change takes place, that "Christ is formed in us" through the death of the old man and the creation of the new, and that from this origin something new, even if only relatively new, comes into visible existence also. [pp. 272–74]

Thus it is the very faith by which we believe and are justified, and not baptism, that is the sign and the expression of the beginnings of new creation in us.

Brunner is reasonably happy to speak of regeneration as passive and conversion as active as long as we recognize that "we are not dealing with a temporal sequence, an order of salvation (*ordo salutis*) which begins with one thing, let us say regeneration, and continues with another, let us say conversion" (p. 281). By faith in the Word we are justified and created as new persons, children of God. In keeping with his emphasis that we are responsible beings, Brunner does not interpret human passivity in regeneration as the classic Reformed theologians had done; rather, he insists:

The creation of the new man, in faith in the new created Word of God in Christ, does not happen without our presence as responsible persons. . . . It is once again the same paradox as everywhere appears where faith is the theme: the new life is effected on the one hand only through the repen- tance of man, and on the other hand only through the act and speech, or the speech and act, of God. Both are true: we must repent, and it is God alone who creates the new life. [pp. 282–83]

Although he rejects all views of baptismal regeneration, as well as the view that baptism is a sacrament, Brunner does see a place for baptism of believers as well as the children of believers. However, this baptism is not fundamental and therefore not absolutely obligatory.[17] What mat- ters to him is the correlation of Christ's word and act with faith. There must be personal response to the God who discloses himself, addresses sinners, and makes a claim upon them. In that response, as the Spirit of God is present, faith arises and regeneration and conversion occur. And these will lead on to holiness and righteousness.

---

17. See the appendix "On the Doctrine of Baptism," in Brunner, *Dogmatics*, vol. 3, pp. 53–57.

12

Puritans, Pietists, and Evangelists

Puritanism, originating in England in the late sixteenth century, and Pietism, beginning in Germany in the late seventeenth century, are linked by both personalities and concerns. The writings of various English Puritans (e.g., Lewis Bayly, William Ames, and Richard Baxter) helped some Lutherans to see the great need for an emphasis on godliness and practical Christianity. In turn the teaching and examples of several German Pietists (e.g., Philipp Jakob Spener and August Hermann Francke) influenced both the theological and practical concerns not only of such prominent American Puritans as Cotton Mather (1663–1728), but also leaders of the Great Awakening such as Jonathan Edwards and George Whitefield. The influence of Pietism on the Wesley brothers, John and Charles, is well known. Puritanism and Pietism, coming from two different traditions, did nevertheless agree that theology is not only true propositions, but also the art of living unto God, and that this begins with the divine act of regeneration.

Puritanism was first and foremost a movement for the purification of the national Church of England; secondly, it was a movement of practical divinity for the sanctification of congregations, families, and individuals.[1] It flourished from the reign of Queen Elizabeth I to the Protectorate

1. There is a useful article on Puritanism by Mark A. Noll in Walter A. Elwell, ed., *Evangelical Dictionary of Theology*, pp. 897–900. See also Peter Toon, *Puritans and Calvinism*.

of Oliver Cromwell; however, in 1662 it was virtually forced out of the national church and became the basic spirit of Protestant Nonconformity in England and Wales. Earlier it had crossed the Atlantic Ocean to create a new form of church life in New England, where it had a mixed success for over a century. Further, it entered the Scottish church to marry happily with the Reformed theology of the Westminster Confession. We shall look at the teaching on regeneration of three of Puritanism's most able exponents—William Perkins and John Owen of England and Jonathan Edwards of New England.

Pietism was initially a movement within German Lutheranism; it insisted that the reformation of doctrine which had been initiated by Martin Luther be consummated by a reformation of life in individuals, homes, and congregations.[2] Pietism was concerned with the regeneration of individuals, the renewal of parishes, and practical acts of charity. Cotton Mather described it as "the fire of God which flames in the heart of Germany." We shall look at the teaching of Spener and Francke as well as that of Count Zinzendorf and the Moravians.

We will conclude this chapter with the evangelical revival in England and America in the mid-eighteenth century. Itinerant preachers stressed that everyone in their audiences, including those who had been baptized as infants, stood in need of the new birth and conversion. We shall look particularly at the teaching of George Whitefield and John Wesley.

Puritanism

William Perkins

William Perkins (1558–1602) was the most widely known theologian of the Elizabethan Church of England.[3] As lecturer at Great St. Andrews, Cambridge, he gave much time to writing, and his works were published not only in Britain but in several other European countries as well. His theology was in the tradition which flowed from John Calvin and Theodore Beza in Geneva, and he made a specialty of practical divinity (preaching, cases of conscience, writings on the nature of conversion and the Christian life). He would have been able to subscribe to those chapters of the Westminster Confession (1647) which set forth the sovereign grace of God in election, effectual calling, and the Christian life of mortification and vivification.

---

2. There is a useful article on Pietism by Mark A. Noll in Elwell, ed., *Evangelical Dictionary*, pp. 855–58. This may be supplemented by a steady stream of articles printed in the *Covenant Quarterly*.

3. For the life and writings of Perkins see *The Work of William Perkins,* ed. Ian Breward.

We are particularly interested in what Perkins has to say about regeneration and conversion. His use of these terms is similar to Calvin's
and thus less precise than that of later Reformed theologians. Happily
he set out his views in a short piece entitled "A Grain of Mustard Seed."[4]
Against the background of both the work of Christ and the depravity of
humankind, he explains that "the conversion of a sinner . . . is not the
change of the substance of man or of the faculties [the understanding,
will, and affections] of the soul, but a renewing and restoring of that
purity and holiness which was lost by man's fall, with the abolishment of
that corruption that is in all the powers of the soul." And he insists that
"this is the work of God, and of God alone." It is a work which has a
definite beginning but which also must continue; in this sense conversion and regeneration are a process of making new:

> The conversion of a sinner is not wrought all at one instant, but in con-
> tinuance of time and that by certain measures and degrees. And a man is
> in the first degree of his conversion when the Holy Ghost, by the means of
> the word, inspires him with some spiritual motions and begins to regener-
> ate and renew the inward powers of his soul.

This is like the first dawning of morning light when the darkness is still
dominant.

As a practical theologian, Perkins distinguished between preparation
for and the actual beginnings of regeneration by God, and also between
restraining grace and renewing grace. Preparation for regeneration and
conversion consists of the ministry of the law of God acting upon the
conscience and causing us to know not only our guilt before God, but also
the wrath of God directed against our sin. In contrast the beginnings of
true conversion and regeneration are those Spirit-caused motions and
inclinations by which we see in the gospel our life and hope.

By restraining grace Perkins meant much the same as what later
theologians have called common grace—the help given by God to all
people so that they can act in a sober, just, and merciful way ensuring a
peaceful society. Renewing grace, however, is not for all: it is "not common to all men, but proper to the elect and is a gift of God's Spirit
whereby the corruption of sin is not only restrained, but also mortified,
and the decayed image of God restored in righteousness and true holiness." This definition includes what later theologians (and what Perkins
himself elsewhere) called regeneration, mortification of sin and vivification, or regeneration with sanctification. The point to observe is that he
saw the entry of the Spirit into the soul to quicken the understanding,

---

4. Ibid., pp. 387ff.

will, and affections as the beginnings of a process whose originator is God himself. The end of the process is conformity to the image of God as that is revealed in Christ Jesus.

Perkins connected inner regeneration and conversion with union with Christ, adoption into the family of God, and justification by God. "These four are wrought all at one instant, so as for order of time neither goes before or after the other; and yet in regard of order of nature, union with Christ, justification and adoption go before the inward conversion of a sinner, it being the fruit and effect of them all."

We must now look at what Perkins had to say about baptism and regeneration in the case of infants. He deals with this subject in *A Golden Chain, or the Description of Theology*.[5] First, we note his definition of baptism:

> 33. Baptism is a sacrament by which such as are within the covenant are washed with water in the name of the Father, the Son and the Holy Ghost, that being thus engrafted into Christ they may have perpetual fellowship with him. Within the covenant are all the seed of Abraham, or the seed of the faithful. These are either of riper years or infants. Those of riper years are all such as adjoining themselves to the visible church do both testify their repentance of their sins and hold the foundations of religion taught in the same church. Infants within the covenant are such as have one at the least of their parents faithful.

Baptism therefore is effectual only for those who are the elect of God. Though Perkins did not deny the possibility of the regeneration of an infant at baptism, he did expect that normally those baptized in infancy would in riper years come to a deep conviction of guilt of sin and then actually experience inner regeneration. Like Luther, he held that all those who are converted ought to look back to their baptism as a seal of their incorporation into Christ.

As to the spiritual state of babies who die at birth or soon after birth Perkins wrote:

> 35. The declaration of God's love towards infants is on this manner. Infants being elected, albeit they in the womb of their mother before they were born, or presently after (birth) depart this life, they, I say, being after a secret and unspeakable manner by God's Spirit engrafted into Christ, obtain eternal salvation. I call the manner of infants' salvation secret and unspeakable, because they want actual faith to receive Christ: for actual faith necessarily presupposeth a knowledge of God's free promise, the

5. Ibid., pp. 169ff.

which he that believeth doth apply to himself: but this infants cannot
anyways possibly perform.

So, unlike Luther, he did not believe that infants can actually have
saving faith. He elaborated further on this point: "Infants are said to be
regenerated only in regard of their internal qualities and inclinations,
not in regard of any motions or actions of the mind, will or affections.
And therefore they want those terrors of conscience which come before
repentance, as occasions thereof, in such as are of riper years."

Before leaving Perkins we should observe his description of the normal route from being a child of darkness to being a child of the light,
from nominal Christianity to vital Christianity. In chapter 36 of the
Golden Chain he sets out a broad outline of this route, the route of God's
effectual calling:

1. The hearing of the word of God: first, the law to reveal sin and its
   punishment, and second, the gospel to offer salvation in Christ
   Jesus.
2. The mollifying of the heart, which must be bruised that it may be
   fit to receive God's saving grace. This breaking of the stony heart is
   achieved by four hammers—knowledge of the law of God, knowledge of sin, the pricking of conscience, and a deep recognition that
   salvation cannot be gained by man's powers or ingenuity.
3. Apprehension and incorporation of the living Christ through
   faith, a supernatural faculty of the heart. This is brought about
   through the special operation of the Holy Spirit. Faith of this kind,
   saving faith, has five degrees: (a) spiritual knowledge of the gospel
   (serious meditation on, full understanding of, and belief in the
   promises within the gospel); (b) hope of pardon; (c) hunger and
   thirst after the grace of God; (d) an approach to the throne of grace
   to lay hold of Christ and find favor with God; and (e) a persuasion
   imprinted in the heart by the Holy Spirit that the promises of God
   actually apply to oneself.

Inner conversion or regeneration occurs within the last of these
stages: the origin and exercise of faith. It is not surprising that in a
period when the doctrine of divine election was seriously taught, believed, and confessed, there was great interest not only in the actual
process of conversion, but also in evidence of genuine regeneration. Nor
is it surprising that many believed that there could be no genuine internal regeneration without lengthy spiritual preparation.[6] This widely

---

6. See further Norman Pettit, *The Heart Prepared: Grace and Conversion in Puritan
Spiritual Life.*

held view (preparationism) within English and American Puritanism was to be severely challenged by the preaching ministry of George Whitefield and others in the eighteenth century.

John Owen

After a period as vice-chancellor of Oxford University during the Protectorate of Oliver Cromwell, John Owen (1616–1683) became the theological leader of the Puritans who adopted the Congregational Way; he also continued his career as a major exponent and defender of both Reformed theology and Puritan practical divinity.[7] In his *Pneumatologia: A Discourse Concerning the Holy Spirit* (1674) he addressed himself to the topic of the regeneration and conversion of the elect.[8] He begins this treatise by looking at the nature and personality of the Spirit and his work in the old creation; then he looks at the work of the Holy Spirit in the new creation, especially in and upon the human nature of Jesus Christ, and in the preparation of a mystical body for him. The latter work involves the calling, regenerating, sanctifying, and glorifying of all the elect, who have been given to the Son by the Father. And this, says Owen, is to be brought about together with the creation of a new universe: "The Holy Spirit undertaketh to create a new world, new heavens and a new earth, wherein righteousness shall dwell" (p. 207). Thus his doctrine of regeneration is set in a cosmic and eschatological framework centered upon union with Christ and membership in his spiritual, mystical body.

In terms of the human race, Owen's doctrine of regeneration, which he expounds in the third part of his treatise, is set in the context of the Augustinian doctrine of original sin and depravity. In the seventeenth century a growing number of churchmen in Europe were rejecting this view and insisting that we are not guilty of Adam's sin and we are not wholly infected by evil. To Owen such views were Socinian, Pelagian, or Arminian (depending upon their context) and were to be strenuously opposed. "The reason why some despise, some oppose, some deride the work of the Spirit of God in our regeneration or conversion," he wrote, "or fancy it to be only an outward ceremony, or a moral change of life and conversation, is their ignorance of the corrupted and depraved estate of the souls of men, in their minds, wills and affections, by nature" (p. 328).

Owen defines regeneration as "the infusion of a new, real, spiritual principle into the soul and its faculties, of spiritual life, light, holiness and righteousness, disposed unto and suited for the destruction or ex-

---

7. For Owen see Peter Toon, *God's Statesman: The Life and Work of Dr. John Owen.*

8. John Owen, *Pneumatologia: A Discourse Concerning the Holy Spirit,* in *The Works of John Owen,* ed. William H. Goold, vol. 3.

pulsion of a contrary, inbred, habitual principle of sin and enmity against God, enabling unto all acts of holy obedience, and so in the order of nature antecedent to them" (pp. 219, 329). The Holy Spirit himself enters the soul, bringing the power, holiness, righteousness, and love of God to renew and redirect the mind, heart, and will. Citing many biblical texts, Owen shows how the faculties of the soul—mind, heart, and will—are given new knowledge, love, and power by the presence of the Holy Spirit. Thus a process of sanctification necessarily flows from one's initial regeneration.

Owen further insists that what he is teaching is the historic, received doctrine of the church and not the result of Puritan "enthusiasm":

> The ancient writers of the Church, who looked into these things with most diligence, and laboured in them with most success—as Augustine, Hilary, Prosper, and Fulgentius—do represent the whole work of the Spirit of God towards the souls of men under certain heads or distinctions of grace; and herein were they followed by many of the more sober schoolmen, and others of late without number. Frequent mention we find in them of grace as "preparing, preventing, working, co-working and confirming." Under these heads do they handle the whole work of our regeneration or conversion unto God. [pp. 300–01]

Noting that in Augustine's *Confessions* the divine act of regeneration and conversion is "nobly and elegantly exemplified," Owen devotes a whole chapter to Augustine's depiction of the nature of conversion. Owen was right to insist that the Fathers and Schoolmen had a high doctrine of regeneration; however, as he explained in other places, they did also tend to conflate regeneration with justification. Further, they posited a much closer tie between regeneration and baptism than did Owen. While Owen accepted that some infants are born from above at their baptism, he believed with Perkins and most Puritans that it is as young adults that the majority are regenerated and come to the faith of their baptism.

As an exponent of practical divinity, Owen paid particular attention to the normal preparation in adults for regeneration and conversion, the difference between genuine regeneration and false conversion, and the internal and external changes caused by God's irresistible grace in this saving event. While he insisted that "God in our conversion, by the exceeding greatness of his power (as he wrought in Christ when he raised him from the dead), actually works faith and repentance in us, gives them to us, bestows them on us—so that they are mere effects of his grace in us" (p. 323), he also insisted that we have duties in relation to God and his gospel. For example, we are to pray that God will do what he has promised—to regenerate and convert; we are to attend the ministry of the word and the means of grace; and we are to pay heed to the commands of God within the gospel to repent and to believe. Further, we are to examine ourselves to see whether or not we are of the faith.

Owen also offered advice to pastors and preachers of the gospel. They ought to master the whole doctrine of regeneration and its practical implications so that they know how to preach to and deal with those who, moved by the Spirit, are desirous of being born of God and converted to him. We should observe that the kind of practical divinity taught by Owen might easily lead people to despair of ever being true Christians unless they have a wise pastor to help them discern the true motions of the Spirit within them.

Together with this teaching concerning regeneration went a view which insisted that the church is an assembly and fellowship of the regenerate. In 1658 Owen, with other Congregational pastors, had written, as a part of the Savoy Declaration, a Declaration of the Institution of Churches.[9] Article 8 reads:

> The members of these churches are saints by calling, visibly manifesting and evidencing (in and by their profession and walking) their obedience unto that call of Christ, who being further known to each other by their confession of the faith wrought in them by the power of God, declared by themselves or otherwise manifested, do willingly consent to walk together according to the appointment of Christ, giving up themselves to the Lord and to one another by the will of God, in professed subjection to the ordinances of the gospel.

This makes clear that evidence of regeneration was required before admittance to church membership. In New England the Congregationalist authors of the Cambridge Platform (1648) insisted, "The doors of the churches of Christ upon earth do not by God's appointment stand so wide open, that all sorts of people, good or bad, may freely enter therein at their pleasure; but such as are admitted thereto as members, ought to be examined and tried first."[10] Such a requirement naturally led to the need for a practical divinity concerning conversion, a practical divinity of the kind that Owen (with others before and after him in Old and New England) provided.

Jonathan Edwards

Recognized as the greatest philosopher-theologian to be born in the American colonies, Jonathan Edwards (1703–1758) spent most of his

---

9. In Williston Walker, ed., *The Creeds and Platforms of Congregationalism*, pp. 403ff.
10. In Walker, ed., *Creeds*, pp. 194ff., ch. 12.

working life as a Congregational pastor.[11] When the Puritans of the Congregational Way had left England for America in the seventeenth century, they had intended to transplant the national Church of England in a transformed state, reformed and renewed by the Word of God. Thus the "state church" in New England was congregational in polity. While everyone was expected to attend worship, only those who could testify to the saving work of God in their souls were admitted into the church covenant and to the Lord's Supper. Edwards became a pastor at a time when the churches faced the problem of what they should do with regard to the infant children of baptized members who themselves had not been admitted to the church covenant and full membership. Were the children of parents who had not given evidence of regeneration and conversion entitled (within the doctrine of the covenant of grace) to baptism? Most churches believed that they were, and thus arose the theology of the Halfway Covenant. Edwards's predecessor at Northampton, Massachusetts, his grandfather Solomon Stoddard, also advocated that the Lord's Supper should be open to all baptized members who lived decently, even if they did not profess to have gone through an experience of conversion.[12]

For the first part of his ministry in Northampton, Edwards followed the practice of Stoddard, but revivals within the congregation and town caused him to change his mind and argue against his grandfather's teaching as well as against the Halfway Covenant. Church membership and admittance to the Lord's Table were for those who could testify to regeneration. After the First Great Awakening (or Revival) Edwards wrote *A Faithful Narrative of the Surprising Work of God in the Conversion of Many Hundred Souls in Northampton.*[13] In contrast to the belief that there is often a long period of preparation before regeneration and conversion Edwards recorded what he had witnessed:

God has seemed to have gone out of his usual way in the *quickness* of his work, and the swift progress his Spirit has made in his operations in the hearts of many. It is wonderful that persons should be so *suddenly* and yet

---

11. There is a good introductory article on Edwards's life and thought by Mark A. Noll in Elwell, ed., *Evangelical Dictionary,* pp. 343–46. For his theology see Conrad Cherry, *The Theology of Jonathan Edwards: A Reappraisal,* particularly ch. 4 ("Conversion"). Also useful is John H. Gerstner, *Steps to Salvation: The Evangelistic Message of Jonathan Edwards.*

12. For the Halfway Covenant see Walker, ed., *Creeds,* pp. 238ff. See further the illuminating article by David Laurence, "Jonathan Edwards, Solomon Stoddard, and the Preparationist Model of Conversion," *Harvard Theological Review* 72 (1979): 267–83; and Richard Lovelace's excellent chapter "The Experience of Rebirth" in *The American Pietism of Cotton Mather,* pp. 73–109.

13. In *Works of Jonathan Edwards,* ed. Edward Hickman, vol. 1, pp. 344ff.

so *greatly changed.* Many have been taken from a loose and careless way of living, and seized with strong convictions of their guilt and misery, and in a very little time old things have passed away and all things have become new with them. [*Works,* vol. 1, p. 350]

Edwards proceeds to describe the two initial effects of the work of the Spirit of the Lord in human hearts. First, people immediately give up their sinful practices; second, they apply themselves to Scripture reading, prayer, meditation, attendance at ordinances of worship, and seeking counsel. Their cry is, "What shall we do to be saved?" Then, in the manner of Puritan practical divinity, Edwards provides a description of the way in which people come to true faith and repentance:

Conversion is a great and glorious work of God's power, at once changing the heart and infusing life into the dead soul; though the grace then implanted more gradually displays itself in some than in others. But as to fixing the precise time when they put forth the very first act of grace, there is a great deal of difference in different persons: in some it seems to be very discernible when the very time was; but others are more at a loss. . . .

In some, converting light is like a glorious brightness suddenly shining upon a person, and all around him: they are in a remarkable manner brought out of darkness into marvellous light. In many others it has been like the dawning of the day, when at first but a little light appears, and it may be is presently hid with a cloud; and then it appears again, and shines a little brighter, and gradually increases, with intervening darkness, till at length it breaks forth more clearly from behind the clouds. And many are, doubtless, ready to date their conversion wrong, setting aside those lesser degrees of light that appeared at first dawning, and calling some more remarkable experience, that they had afterwards, their conversion. This often, in a great measure, arises from a wrong understanding of what they have always been taught, that conversion is a great change, wherein old things are done away and all things become new, or at least from a false inference from that doctrine. [p. 355]

What really matters, he holds, is the life that flows from regeneration.

One of Edwards's greatest books is his *Treatise Concerning Religious Affections,* in which he reflects upon true and false conversion.[14] However, his clearest and most delightful presentation of the nature of regeneration is found in his *Treatise on Grace,*[15] which he left amongst his unpublished papers at his sudden death soon after he had become president of the College of New Jersey (now Princeton University). Edwards

---

14. Ibid., pp. 234ff.
15. Jonathan Edwards, *Treatise on Grace,* ed. Paul Helm.

begins the study by distinguishing clearly between common and saving grace:

> *Common grace* is used to signify that kind of action or influence of the Spirit of God, to which are owing those religious or moral attainments that are common to both saints and sinners, and so signifies as much as common assistance; and sometimes these moral or religious attainments themselves that are the fruits of this assistance, are intended.

In contrast to this basic help offered by God to all persons there is special or saving grace:

> *Special* or *saving grace* is used to signify that peculiar kind or degree of operation or influence of God's Spirit, whence saving actions and attainments do arise in the godly, or which is the same thing, special and saving assistance; or else to signify that distinguishing saving virtue itself, which is the fruit of this assistance. [p. 25]

As a theologian in the Reformed tradition, Edwards held that only in the elect does God act with saving grace to produce saving virtue.

Having made this distinction, Edwards proceeds to provide eight arguments to show that saving grace and virtue are not a part of the basic human nature we all possess. God must act decisively in us in order for there to be saving grace and virtue within us. The last of the eight points is that conversion is presented in the Scriptures as a work of creation. And, he explains, "when God creates he does not merely establish and perfect the things which were made before, but makes wholly and immediately something entirely new, either out of nothing, or out of that which was perfectly void of any such nature, as when he made man of the dust of the earth" (p. 33). Further, conversion is often compared to resurrection, to new birth, and to an opening of the eyes of the blind as well as to a replacing of a heart of stone with a heart of flesh.

On the basis of his eight arguments Edwards insists that "conversion is wrought at once":

> That knowledge, that reformation and conviction that is preparatory to conversion may be gradual, and the work of grace after conversion may be gradually carried on, yet that work of grace upon the soul whereby a person is brought out of a state of total corruption and depravity into a state of grace, to an interest in Christ, and to be actually a child of God, is in a moment. [p. 34]

It will have become obvious that Edwards uses "conversion" as a synonym for "regeneration," thinking of it as an internal change leading to external change in attitude, behavior, and speech.

In the second part of the treatise Edwards seeks to answer the question, What is the nature of the divine principle in the regenerate soul? His answer is that it is the principle of divine love, which is the summary of all grace, holiness, and virtue, and a complete change from everything that is inherent in the soul. This divine love, as it has God for its object, may be described as "the soul's relish of the supreme excellency of the divine nature, inclining the heart to God as the chief good." Edwards explains that

> the first effect of the power of God in the heart in REGENERATION is to give the heart a divine taste or sense; to cause it to have a relish of the loveliness and sweetness of the supreme excellency of the divine nature; and indeed this is all the immediate effect of the divine power that there is, this is all the Spirit of God needs to do, in order to a production of all good effects in the soul. [p. 49]

In the third and final part Edwards seeks to show that the divine principle in the soul, which consists in divine love, is the actual presence of the Spirit of God himself—nothing less, nothing more. At this point Edwards calls into active use his profound understanding of the theology of the Holy Trinity in order to show that what enters the soul in regeneration is the Holy Spirit himself, the very essence of divine love:

> Though we often read in Scripture of the Father loving the Son, and the Son loving the Father, yet we never once read either of the Father or the Son loving the Holy Spirit, and the Holy Spirit loving either of them. It is because the Holy Spirit is the Divine love itself, the love of the Father and the Son. Hence also it is to be accounted for, that we very often read of the love both of the Father and the Son to men, and particularly their love to the saints; but we never read of the Holy Ghost loving them, for the Holy Ghost is that love of God and of Christ that is breathed forth primarily towards each other, and flows out secondarily towards the creature. This also will well account for it, that the apostle Paul so often wishes grace, mercy and peace from God the Father, and from the Lord Jesus Christ, in the beginning of his epistles, without even mentioning the Holy Ghost, because the Holy Ghost is Himself the love and grace of God the Father and the Lord Jesus Christ. He is the deity wholly breathed forth in infinite, substantial, intelligent love; from the Father and Son first towards each other, and secondarily freely flowing out to the creature, and so standing forth a distinct personal subsistence. [p. 63]

Thus the Spirit who enters the soul in regeneration is the eternal divine love; and from him, and the love that he is, all grace, virtue, holiness, and power proceed to change the understanding, the will, and the affections. It will be observed that such a doctrine of regeneration of necessity includes a change in life, for "the love of God is shed abroad in our hearts by the Holy Spirit who is given unto us."

The Spirit of God, who is also called the Spirit of Christ, is given to the elect because of the saving work of Christ himself, who is their Head and Redeemer. The Spirit, who fills Christ's human nature as well as unites Christ's divine nature with that of the Father, is the inheritance and possession of those who belong to Christ. Thus, to conclude, "saving grace is no other than the very love of God—that is, God, in one of the persons of the Trinity, uniting himself to the soul of a creature, as a vital principle, dwelling there and exerting himself by the faculties of the soul of man, in his own proper nature, after the manner of a principle of nature" (p. 72). Is it possible to have a higher doctrine of regeneration than this?

Before we leave Jonathan Edwards, we need to note his teaching concerning the human will. This he explained in his justly famous *Careful and Strict Inquiry into the Modern Prevailing Notions of That Freedom of Will, Which Is Supposed to Be Essential to Moral Agency, Virtue and Vice, Reward and Punishment, Praise and Blame* (1754).[16] His aim was to defend and illustrate the Augustinian and Reformed doctrine of the bondage of the will to sin. In the process he made the distinction, which had previously been made by theologians of the Academy of Saumur in the seventeenth century (see p. 130), between natural ability to will and moral ability to will. Unlike Amyraldus and his colleagues, however, Edwards's commitment to the teaching of the Synod of Dort could not be doubted. Edwards found the distinction very useful in dealing with Arminian objections (as they were called) to the doctrine of the bondage of the will. This distinction between natural and moral ability was then taken up by many in both Britain and America, and it proved of especial importance to those whose preaching aimed at instantaneous conversions. On the grounds that, though lacking moral ability to repent and believe, humans do nonetheless possess a natural ability to do so, it was concluded that they can and should be called upon to repent and believe immediately. The Holy Spirit will then give them power to overcome their moral inability.

Pietism

Philipp Jakob Spener

Philipp Jakob Spener (1635–1705) is often called the father of Lutheran Pietism.[17] Serving as a pastor in Strasbourg, Frankfurt am

---

16. In *Works of Jonathan Edwards,* ed. Edward Hickman, vol. 1, pp. 1ff.

17. There is a brief life of Spener by Theodore G. Tappert in his translation of the *Pia desideria.*

Main, Dresden, and Berlin, he was very familiar with the cold and rigid orthodoxy that characterized Lutheranism in both university and parish.[18] He spoke from both heart and mind in his *Pia desideria (Pious Desires)*, written originally as a long preface to the sermons of Johann Arndt (1555–1621) but published in its own right in 1675.[19] In the first part of this book Spener discusses the failings of the civil authorities, the clergy, and the ordinary people in matters of religion. In the second he offers proposals to set right the defects and weaknesses of the churches. In the last part the themes of Pietism are clearly set forth:

> Our whole Christian religion consists in the inner man or the new man, whose soul is faith and whose expressions are the fruits of life, and all sermons should be aimed at this. On the one hand, the precious benefactions of God, which are directed towards this inner man, should be presented in such a way that faith, and hence the inner man, may be strengthened more and more. On the other hand, works should be set in motion that we may by no means be content merely to have the people refrain from outward vices and practice outward virtues and thus be concerned only with the outward man, which the ethics of the heathen can also accomplish; but that we lay the right foundation in the heart, show that what does not proceed from this foundation is mere hypocrisy, and hence accustom the people first to work on what is inward (awaken love of God and neighbor through suitable means) and only then to act accordingly. [p. 116]

Here is emphasis on the new person, the new birth, the new faith, and its fruit. True good works are to proceed from the faith of a born-again Christian. Pietism assumes a congruity between the inner and outer person:

> One should, therefore, emphasize that the divine means of Word and sacrament are concerned with the inner man. Hence it is not enough that we hear the Word with our outward ear, but we must let it penetrate to our heart, so that we may hear the Holy Spirit speak there, that is, with vibrant emotion and comfort feel the sealing of the Spirit and the power of the Word. Nor is it enough to be baptized, but the inner man, where we have put on Christ in Baptism, must also keep Christ on and bear witness to him in our outward life. Nor is it enough to have received the Lord's Supper externally, but the inner man must truly be fed with that blessed

---

18. See Heinrich Schmid, *The Doctrinal Theology of the Evangelical Lutheran Church,* 3d ed. rev., pp. 407ff.

19. For further detail see Allan C. Deeter, "An Historical and Theological Introduction to P. J. Spener's *Pia Desideria:* A Study in German Pietism." Our quotations are from the Tappert translation.

food. Nor is it enough to pray outwardly with our mouth, but true prayer, and the best prayer, occurs in the inner man, and it either breaks forth in words or remains in the soul, yet God will find and hit upon it. Nor, again, is it enough to worship God in an external temple, but the inner man worships God best in his own temple, whether or not he is in an external temple at the time. So one could go on. [p. 117]

The key concept is *Wiedergeburt,* "new birth." And on this topic Spener preached many sermons, publishing a collection of sixty-six of them as *Der höchwichtige Articul von der Wiedergeburt.* In the first of these he insists that new birth is an act of God in which man is passive. The Holy Spirit enters the human soul and kindles faith leading to justification and adoption. But from this new birth there also begins a new life of growth in holiness, a topic expounded in other sermons:

> Although Spener knows of repentance and temptations as the birth pangs of *Wiedergeburt,* he insists that *Wiedergeburt* is the beginning of faith. Faith does not bring forth *Wiedergeburt;* rather, *Wiedergeburt* brings forth faith. *Wiedergeburt* is the beginning of a process of growth, a growth from within man's restored soul. Out of God's initial act, the creation of a new inner man, comes a continuing process in which man himself now begins, through the Holy Spirit, to direct the growth of the new man within him until his entire existence reflects that of Jesus Christ.[20]

Spener did not deny the doctrine of regeneration at baptism but held that the grace given at infant baptism was more often than not actually lost by its recipients because they failed to keep their side of the baptismal covenant (*Pia desideria,* p. 66). Thus most church members stood in need of *Bekehrung,* "conversion," and *Wiedergeburt,* "inward regeneration." This meant that they needed to be justified by living faith in the Lord Jesus Christ. The concept of justification by faith, however, had been reduced in much popular teaching to mere assent to the doctrines of the Lutheran (Evangelical) church and to a nominal Christianity. Consequently, Spener and his fellow Pietists decided to emphasize instead the making of true believers by the divine act of regeneration. As is clear from the *Pia desideria,* Spener certainly shared Luther's view of justification:

> We gladly acknowledge that we must be saved only and alone through faith and that our works or godly life contribute neither much nor little to our salvation, for as a fruit of our faith our works are connected with the

---

20. M. W. Kohl, "*Wiedergeburt* as the Central Theme in Pietism," *Covenant Quarterly* 32 (Nov. 1974): 16.

gratitude which we owe to God, who has already given us who believe the
gift of righteousness and salvation. Far be it from us to depart even a
finger's breadth from this teaching, for we would rather give up our life and
the whole world than yield the smallest part of it. [p. 63]

Spener chose, however, to focus more particularly on the intimate connection between true saving faith and regeneration.

August Hermann Francke

What Philipp Melanchthon was to Luther, so was August Hermann
Francke (1663–1727) to Spener.[21] Francke was appointed professor at
the newly established university at Halle in 1692 through Spener's
influence, and he also became a pastor at nearby Glaucha. In 1696 he
founded his *Paedagogium* and orphanage; each one grew rapidly, bringing to him both fame and opposition. The opposition subsided after the
visit in 1713 of the Prussian king, Frederick William I, who was much
impressed by Francke's educational and charitable institutions.

Francke's theology was deeply affected by his own experience of conversion, which he described in some detail. When twenty-four years of
age he had been studying the Bible and theology at the university level
for six years. Desperately wanting to be a true believer and to seek after
holiness of life, he had begun to make very serious use of the means of
grace in the churches. Yet all he experienced was anguish:

> In this state of anguish I kneeled down again and again, and prayed ear-
> nestly to that God and Saviour in whom I had, as yet, no faith, that if
> indeed he existed he would deliver me from my misery. At last he heard
> me! He was pleased, in his wondrous love, to manifest himself, and that,
> not in taking away by degrees my doubts and fears, but at once, and as if to
> overpower all my objections to his power and faithfulness. All my doubts
> disappeared at once and I was assured of his favor. I could not only call him
> God, but my Father.[22]

So deeply did he feel the need for conversion that he geared the instruction and discipline at Halle in such a way as to prepare young people for
conversion and then to assist them in going on with the Lord in dedica-
tion and sanctification. He never taught that his system itself could
convert and bring the new birth, but he did fervently believe that the

---

21. The best introduction in English to Francke's life and theology is Gary R. Sattler,
*God's Glory, Neighbor's Good: A Brief Introduction to the Life and Writings of August
Hermann Francke.*
22. The description of the conversion is in Sattler, *God's Glory*, pp. 29–33.

right context and preparation made new birth and conversion more likely.[23]

Among Francke's published sermons is "The Doctrine of Our Lord Jesus Christ Concerning Rebirth," preached on Trinity Sunday, 1697.[24] It is a full statement of his understanding of inward regeneration. In the introduction he insists that "no doctrine of Christianity is more necessary than the doctrine of rebirth," for "this is the very ground upon which Christianity stands," and "a person without this is not to be called a Christian." And though this teaching is truly understood only by those whose minds have been enlightened by the Holy Spirit, it must still be preached from the pulpits.

In the body of the sermon Francke sets himself five tasks. His first task is to answer the question, "From whom does rebirth come?" Since it is a birth from *above,* "the whole Holy Trinity is the One to whom we must ascribe the new birth and the One from whom we receive a new character and nature." When this spiritual renewal takes place, we will know in our heart that we are children of God, having Christ as Brother, God as Father, and the Holy Spirit as Comforter. We will experience glory in our heart and soul, and will know that we have received a greater gift than the world can ever offer.

The second task is to consider the means by which the Lord gives or causes rebirth. The first is the Word of God, which has power to strike us down and then make us alive again. The law kills and the gospel makes alive. Second, there is holy baptism: one has to be born of water and the Spirit to enter the kingdom of God. However, Francke explains, water baptism is not absolutely necessary since God can baptize a person in the Spirit without baptizing also in water. Further, baptism in water is ineffectual unless it is accompanied by living faith on the part of the person who is baptized. Thus, unless one who is baptized as an infant actually comes to exercise living, saving faith, one loses the grace of baptism and needs to be born anew by the Holy Spirit. Put another way, unless the individual who is baptized and has entered into the baptismal covenant with God actually keeps his or her side of the covenant in faith and love, God removes his grace from the soul. Those people who, though baptized as infants, do not grow, through nurture and admonition, into living, saving faith, but rather turn to sinful ways, must be slain by the law and resurrected by the gospel if they are to be brought to regeneration, true faith, and conversion, and thus to a restoration of their baptismal covenant.

---

23. See further Kohl, *"Wiedergeburt,"* pp. 22–23.
24. In Sattler, *God's Glory,* pp. 133–53.

The third task is to examine "the manner and way of rebirth," which is "a true birth and not an empty word." Francke agrees with Luther that the creation of true, living faith in the heart is regeneration:

> When a person recognizes his sinful nature, not only outwardly and according to appearance . . . but also inwardly, feeling the bite of the snake in the heart and the wrath of God in conscience, becoming aware of what an abomination sin is, there the person truly sees according to the grace and mercy of God. . . .
>
> If it is shown to this person from the Word of God that Jesus Christ is the Mediator who has reconciled us to God with his blood and then this individual seeks refuge in the wounds of the Lord Jesus and the grace of God the Lord that he may have mercy upon him, in such a crushed heart made ill with remorse and sorrow will be awakened a childlike trust in the overwhelming mercy of God in Christ Jesus. And through that trust God is known and honored in the heart as the true Father—a bottomless fountain of mercy and love; and with sincere humiliation of self, the believer will feel great unworthiness of all such grace and mercy. This believing trust is, then, no idle thought, but rather something true and living that formerly we had not experienced in our hearts. We may well have prayed an "Our Father" and thus called God our Father, but that only went without power over the tongue and not "from the heart." But once faith is truly worked in the heart, the person can truly say through the Holy Spirit, "Abba, dear Father."

This living faith created in regeneration grasps God in Christ for forgiveness and justification. The regenerate person seeks God and "has completely different thoughts, hopes and aspirations," but can never satisfactorily explain the nature of rebirth, which is a secret activity of God and is known in its fruit of holiness.

The fourth task is to establish who needs to be told that they must be born from above by the Holy Spirit. Here Francke mentions Nicodemus, a faithful Jew who taught his religion to others. If such a person had to be told of the necessity of inward regeneration, so also must they who trust in their baptism, their church attendance, their knowledge of the Bible and theology, and their morality.

The fifth task is to set forth the goal of rebirth, which is eternal life. "Rebirth would not be necessary for us," Francke explains, "had we remained in innocence, but after man fell in sin and thus lost the image of God, it is now necessary that we be born again and become true children of God renewed in the image of Jesus Christ and sharing in his glory." Rebirth is the narrow gate, spoken of by Jesus in the Sermon on the Mount, which leads to life—eternal life.

The sermon closes with a call to the hearers to go home and there in private plead with God in earnest prayer to lead them through the narrow gate, for God who sees in secret will reward openly. Finally, in the prayer after the sermon, Francke entreats God to work rebirth in the hearts of the unregenerate: "May you, O faithful God and Father, spread your grace and mercy over us, that those who until now stand in their old sinful birth, may now be born of you. Let even this word be blessed that it may be even now a means of rebirth to many to become new men in heart, soul, mind and thoughts."

Both Spener and Francke believed that the world would be transformed through the regeneration, conversion, and sanctification of individuals. According to their concept of *Wiedergeburt,* a new form of humanity would emerge through the creation of new life within the sinners of this world and lead to a new church and a period of latter-day glory before the second coming of Christ.

Nicholas Ludwig von Zinzendorf

Count Nicholas Ludwig von Zinzendorf (1700–1760) was a brilliant pupil at the Halle school from 1710 to 1716, but it was judged that he was not truly converted when he left.[25] From 1727 he devoted himself wholeheartedly to the vision of Christian renewal and evangelization through both the religious colony of Herrnhut on his personal estate and the dispatch of Moravian missionaries to various parts of the world. For the count the sovereignty and absolute love of Christ were increasingly important, and he eventually concluded that sinners may come to the Savior, who died for them, without fulfilling any preconditions or prerequisites. They need only come in faith to the loving Savior. To become a Christian, then, is an easy procedure, which results in true joy and happiness. Thus the community at Herrnhut was characterized by celebration, cheerfulness, and variety (in contrast to the strictness and sobriety of the Halle of Francke). The Moravians, as their hymns testify, sought to see and feel their crucified Savior, who by virtue of their faith lived in their regenerate hearts.

Various collections of Zinzendorf's sermons were printed in English. Here is an extract from a volume entitled *Sixteen Discourses on the Redemption of Man,* which was published in 1740:

---

25. There is nothing in English to compare with the three-volume biography of Zinzendorf by Erich Beyreuther. See also A. J. Freeman, "The Hermeneutics of Count Nicholas Ludwig von Zinzendorf," especially part B, ch. 3 ("The New Man"). For Zinzendorf's relationship with Methodism see Howard Snyder, "Pietism, Moravianism and Methodism as Renewal Movements: A Comparative and Thematic Study." Then there is the little book by A. J. Lewis, *Zinzendorf: The Ecumenical Pioneer.*

Our Saviour must begin the work; we must first hear the voice of the Son of God, then we begin to live, and when we live, then we learn to believe.

If we have any of the virtue and energy of Baptism still left within us, and do not live according to the mind of our Redeemer, that will condemn us. He that doth never feel the wrath of God is dead in sin. Has he been baptized then is he twice dead.

The moment a soul begins to live, and the Spirit of God overshadows her, she hears the voice of the Son of God, which speaks of nothing but the Blood of propitiation. Whoever lives and has heard the voice of the Son of God, he soon is sensible of his being lost if he doth not acknowledge Jesus to be his Lord and Master.

But whoever believes, shakes off all, doth not consult with flesh and blood, but immediately follows the conviction of his heart, can in a moment be rescued from his perdition and become a child of God, if he doth cast himself down at the feet of our Saviour as a poor, miserable sinner. Then one can say, "He has loved and washed us from our sins in his own blood."

The divine effort in the heart which drives the sinner to the Cross of Christ doth effect all this. Here one need not go about to ransack one's passions and corruptions, nor anxiously endeavour to mend one's self. For Grace overflows all our sins; they are all covered with the Blood of the Lamb.

He that hath once tasted the saving sweetness of the name of Jesus will give him his whole heart and can be pleased with nothing else but with our Saviour and with following him.

Here, despite the occasionally awkward translation, it is possible to recognize the emphasis on the direct route to the Savior, the feeling of being lost and then being renewed by Christ, and the ever flowing source of grace in the blood of the Lamb.

The doctrine of the new birth as understood by the Moravians was well summarized at their American Synod of 1857:

It has been the earnest desire of our church, from the beginning, that each individual member of it should be led, in the school of the Holy Ghost, to a deep and thorough knowledge, not only of his sinfulness, but of his exposedness to condemnation before God, as the desert of sin; and so be brought to a genuine repentance, and to the conviction of his need of a Saviour; whence will result, through living faith in Jesus, a thorough renewal of the inward man, consisting not in the mere laying aside of some sinful habits, but in an entire change of views and dispositions, and in a full surrender of the heart to the Lord.[26]

---

26. In Edmund A. de Schweinitz, ed., *The Moravian Manual,* pp. 114–16.

The same synod laid heavy emphasis upon the cross: "The word of the cross—that is, the testimony of [Christ's] voluntary offering of himself to suffer and to die, and of the treasures of grace purchased thereby—is the beginning, middle and end of our ministry, and to proclaim the Lord's death we regard as the main calling of the Brethren's Church." Regeneration comes when there is faith in the cross and the blood of Christ.

The Evangelical Revival

Traveling preachers were not unknown in Britain and her American colonies in the early eighteenth century. However, with the itinerant evangelism of George Whitefield and John Wesley (and those associated with them) from around 1740 a new era began.[27] Not only did this produce specifically religious results in terms of revivals, converts, new societies and churches, and the cherishing of vital, experiential Christianity, but it also helped to create general political awareness and interest.[28] Never before had so many people eagerly gathered together to hear sermons concerning salvation.

All new movements begin in a given context and are influenced by other contemporary movements. As members of the "Holy Club," a group of young men at Oxford who took their religion seriously, Whitefield and John and Charles Wesley were heavily influenced by the spiritual discipline associated with the daily offices and services of the Book of Common Prayer (1662) and by books on spirituality by such authors as Thomas à Kempis, William Law, Richard Baxter, and Henry Scougal. The devotional systems of both the High Church and Puritanism molded the piety of the members of the Holy Club. Later, the Calvinism of the Puritans was to influence Whitefield more than the Wesleys, and the Arminianism of the Anglican divines was to influence the Wesleys more than Whitefield.

Though Whitefield learned much from the Wesley brothers, especially from Charles, he was, in fact, the first to experience what he believed to be the new birth. Their experience came several years later, not in Oxford but in London. In the spring of 1735 in the quiet of his own room in Oxford, Whitefield felt the joy of having entered into a new, dynamic relationship with God:

---

27. For Whitefield see Arnold Dallimore, *George Whitefield;* for Wesley see Martin Schmidt, *John Wesley: A Theological Biography,* especially vol. 2, part 2, ch. 7.

28. See further the interesting suggestions of Harry S. Stout, "Religion, Communications and the Ideological Origins of the American Revolution," in Gary B. Nash and Thomas Frazier, eds., *The Private Side of American History: Readings in Everyday Life,* vol. 1, pp. 155ff.

After having undergone innumerable buffetings of Satan, and many months of inexpressible trials by night and day under the spirit of bondage, God was pleased at length to remove the heavy load, to enable me to lay hold on his dear Son by a living faith, and, by giving me the spirit of adoption, to seal me, as I humbly hope, even to the day of everlasting redemption. But oh! with what joy—joy unspeakable—even joy that was full of, and big with glory, was my soul filled, when the weight of sin went off, and an abiding sense of the pardoning love of God, and a full assurance of faith broke in on my disconsolate soul! Surely it was the day of my espousals,—a day to be had in everlasting remembrance. At first my joys were like a spring tide and, as it were, overflowed the banks; afterwards it became more settled—and blessed be God, saving a few casual intervals, has abode and increased in my soul ever since.[29]

Henceforward the very site of this experience was sacred to him: "I know the place; it may perhaps be superstitious, but, whenever I go to Oxford, I cannot help running to the spot where Jesus Christ first revealed himself to me, and gave me new birth."[30]

Soon afterwards Whitefield was ordained and preached his first sermon. He would later recall that first sermon, which, not surprisingly, was on the new birth:

I remember when I first began to speak against baptismal regeneration— in my first sermon, printed when I was about twenty-two years old . . . the first quarrel many had with me was because I did not say that all people who were baptized were born again. I would as soon believe the doctrine of transubstantiation! Can I believe that a person who, from the time of his baptism to the time, perhaps, of his death, never fights against the world, the flesh and the devil, and never minds one word of what his godfathers and godmothers promised for him, is a real Christian? No, I can as soon believe that a little wafer in the hands of a priest is the very blood and bones of Jesus Christ.[31]

As we shall see, Whitefield's criticism of the doctrine of baptismal regeneration led to much opposition from both clergy and laity.

John Wesley's search for peace with God and assurance of personal salvation took him to Georgia and back to London. His fellowship with Moravians both during the Atlantic crossing and back in London gave

29. George Whitefield, *George Whitefield's Journals*, p. 58.
30. From the sermon "All Men's Place," cited by Dallimore, *George Whitefield*, vol. 1, p. 77.
31. From the sermon "The Necessity and Benefit of Religious Society," cited by Arthur Skevington Wood, *The Inextinguishable Blaze: Spiritual Renewal and Advance in the Eighteenth Century*, pp. 88–89.

direction to his search. His brother Charles came to assurance of salvation on Whitsunday, May 21, 1738; then on Wednesday, May 24, it was John's turn to receive a heavenly experience. He has himself described it:

> In the evening I went very unwillingly to a society in Aldersgate Street, where one was reading Luther's preface to the Epistle to the Romans. About a quarter before nine, while he was describing the change which God works in the heart through faith in Christ, I felt my heart strangely warmed. I felt I did trust in Christ, Christ alone, for my salvation; and an assurance was given me that he had taken away my sins, even mine, and saved me from the law of sin and death. . . . I then testified to all there what I now first felt in my heart.[32]

What were the words from Luther? They were probably the following, the reading of which reminds us of the dynamic nature of Luther's teaching on new creation:

> Wherefore let us conclude that faith alone justifies, and that faith alone fulfilleth the Law. For faith through the merit of Christ obtaineth the Holy Spirit, which Spirit doth make us new hearts, doth exhilarate us, doth excite and inflame our hearts, that it may do those things willingly of love, which the Law commandeth; and so, at the last, good works indeed do proceed freely from faith which worketh so mightily, and which is so lively in our hearts.[33]

The fire that had been lit in his heart Wesley took to his compatriots over a period of fifty years. Further, from his experience of the assurance of personal salvation he came to the belief that personal regeneration and justification by faith are the two most important doctrines. "If any doctrines within the whole compass of Christianity may properly be called 'fundamental,'" he once wrote, "they are doubtless those two—the doctrine of justification and that of the new birth: the former relating to the great work which God does for us in forgiving our sins; the latter, to the great work which God does in us, in renewing our fallen nature."[34]

It hardly needs stating that the vivid experience of the grace of God forgiving and renewing, justifying and assuring, was of paramount importance to the careers and message of the Wesleys and Whitefield. Though their own route to assurance of personal salvation had been

---

32. John Wesley, *The Journal of the Rev. John Wesley*, ed. Nehemiah Curnock, vol. 1, pp. 475–76.

33. Luther's preface to Romans appears in a variety of English translations, including *The Reformation Writings of Martin Luther*, ed. Bertram Lee Wolff, vol. 1.

34. John Wesley, *Sermons on Several Occasions*, sermon 39, pp. 514–26.

tortuous, when that assurance came, it was dynamic and unforgettable. They quickly learned that not everyone—perhaps only a few—needs to go through a long period of preparation, and so they confidently preached the possibility of an instant change, immediate new birth and conversion. Further, since there appeared to be little obvious relation between their baptism as infants and their assurance of salvation as adults, they preached that most, if not all, of those baptized as infants need to be born from above, to be converted, and (certainly) to experience the assurance of sins forgiven and peace with heaven. More radically than in Pietism and more definitely than in Puritanism, the need for new birth was emphasized. It was also maintained that by its very nature the new birth can be felt and known—even pinpointed in time. Though Whitefield and the Wesleys retained infant baptism and justified it on traditional grounds, they in effect separated it from God's act of regeneration.

George Whitefield

We will now deal specifically with the ministry of Whitefield (1714–1770). Arnold Dallimore has written that "the one great truth which had been the foundation of Whitefield's ministry from the first was that of the new birth. His most widely circulated sermon, *The Nature and Necessity of Our New Birth in Christ Jesus,* could almost be regarded as the manifesto of the [evangelical] movement."[35] So we are not surprised to read in that sermon Whitefield's contention that "it is plain beyond all contradiction, that comparatively but few of those that are 'born of water' are 'born of the Spirit,'" or, put in another way, "many are baptized with water which were never baptized with the Holy Ghost." For to be in Christ is more than water baptism. It is

> to be in him not only by an outward profession, but by an inward change and purity of heart, and cohabitation of his Holy Spirit. To be in him, so as to be mystically united to him by a true and lively faith, and thereby to receive spiritual virtue from him. . . . [In the new birth] our souls, though still the same as to essence, yet are so purged, purified and cleansed from their natural dross, filth and leprosy, by the blessed influences of the Holy Spirit that they may properly be said to be made anew.[36]

Whitefield's message that those who had been baptized but were not living as new creatures in Christ Jesus needed to be born from above by

---

35. Dallimore, *George Whitefield,* vol. 1, p. 345.
36. In George Whitefield, *Sermons on Important Subjects,* new ed., ed. Joseph Smith, pp. 496–97.

the Spirit of Christ was not popular with his brother clergy. Both in England and the colonies appeared booklets criticizing his views. Alexander Garden of South Carolina published *Six Letters to the Rev. George Whitefield* complaining that "the populace have been strangely amused of late with the doctrine of regeneration as a sudden instantaneous work of the Holy Spirit in which the subjects are entirely passive." Contradicting this Calvinist approach, Garden took the line of many Anglican clergymen of his day: "Regeneration is not a sole, critical or instantaneous, but a gradual, co-operating work of the Holy Spirit; commencing at Baptism and gradually advancing throughout the whole course of the Christian life." To most respectable clergy and laity what Whitefield was preaching was "religious delusion" leading to dangerous "enthusiasm"![37]

Whitefield's preaching of instantaneous conversion occurred in the context of that Reformed theology he had inherited from the English Reformers and Puritans of the sixteenth and seventeenth centuries. It is doubtful, however, whether any of those divines would have pressed for immediate repentance and faith as did Whitefield. That Whitefield was aware of this difference is evident in a sermon on the conversion of Zaccheus:

> It would seem that Zaccheus was under soul distress but a little while; "perhaps," says Guthrie . . . "not above a quarter of an hour." I add, perhaps not so long; for as one observes, sometimes the Lord Jesus delights to deliver speedily. God is a sovereign agent, and works upon his children in their effectual calling, according to the counsel of his eternal will. It is with the spiritual, as the natural birth. All women have not the like pangs; all Christians have not the like degree of conviction. But all agree in this, that all have Jesus Christ formed in their hearts: and those who have not so many trials at first, may be visited with the greater conflicts hereafter; though they never come into bondage again, after they have once received the spirit of adoption.[38]

Practical experience had taught him that new birth and conversion can occur with a minimum of preparation and searching.

In the light of his great desire to see souls converted and of his sure belief that they could be converted instantaneously, if God so please, Whitefield ended his sermons with dramatic appeals to the people to turn from their guilt and sin to the Lord Jesus in repentance and faith. For example:

---

37. See further R. H. Pierce, "George Whitefield and His Critics," ch. 3.

38. In John Gillies, *Memoirs of George Whitefield . . . and an Extensive Collection of His Sermons and Other Writings*, pp. 407–08. "Guthrie" is William Guthrie, the author of *The Christian's Great Interest*, which was originally published in 1658.

O that God would wound you with the sword of his Spirit, and cause his arrows of conviction to stick deep in your hearts! O that he would dart a ray of divine light into your souls. . . . O that we felt the power of Christ's resurrection. . . . The power of his resurrection is as great now as formerly, and the Holy Spirit, which was assured to us by his resurrection, as ready and able to quicken us who are dead in trespasses and sins, as any saint that ever lived. Let us but cry, and that instantly, to him that is mighty and able to save.[39]

And Whitefield expected God to begin the great process of salvation in human souls there and then by regenerating them in order that they could enter the highway of holiness and walk in the Spirit towards the Lord.

If asked why everyone who wishes to see God must be born again and thereby gain a pure soul and heart, Whitefield would answer in terms of original sin and the depravity of the human soul: "If it be true, then, that we are all by nature, since the fall, a mixture of brute and devil, it is evident, that we all must receive the Holy Ghost, ere we can dwell with and enjoy God." The salvation Whitefield preached was that "Jesus Christ came to save us not only from the guilt but also from the power of sin"; thus he emphasized that regeneration leads to sanctification and holiness.

According to Reformed theology, as we noted earlier, regeneration, a work of the Spirit in which the soul is passive, leads to saving faith and repentance. Virtually all the evidence that we used was taken from formal theological documents. By contrast, because Whitefield's published material consists entirely of sermons (apart from small pamphlets, journals, and letters), we find that in line with the apostolic preaching he calls upon people to repent and believe in order to receive the gift of the indwelling Spirit: "Whosoever believeth on Jesus Christ with his whole heart, though his soul be as black as hell itself, shall receive the gift of the Holy Ghost." He had in mind such texts as Acts 2:38; 3:19; 5:32; and 10:43–44, which appear to teach that the gift of the indwelling Spirit follows initial saving belief in Jesus.[40]

However, Whitefield also told his hearers on some occasions that the author of the new birth and conversion is the Holy Spirit. For example, in a sermon on Acts 3:19 he declared that "the author of this conversion is the Holy Ghost; it is not their own free will; it is not moral suasion; nothing short of the influence of the Spirit of the living God can effect this change in their hearts."[41] Certainly there can be no regeneration,

---

39. In Gillies, *Memoirs,* pp. 412–13.
40. Ibid., p. 427.
41. In George Whitefield, *Sermons on Important Subjects* . . . , p. 664.

no conversion, no saving faith, and no genuine repentance unless the Holy Spirit takes the initiative and provides the will and the power. But just how all these fit together in either a logical or chronological order does not seem to have been of too great interest to Whitefield. He was primarily the preacher, not the systematic theologian.

John Wesley

Like Whitefield, John Wesley (1703–1791) preached often on the new birth. In fact one of his published sermons is entitled "The New Birth" and based on John 3:7, "You must be born again."[42] He begins by asking the question, "Why must we be born again?" In answer, in order to show what the fall, the origin of sin, has caused, he provides a careful statement of what it meant for Adam to have been made in the image of God:

> God created man in his own image—not barely his *natural image,* a picture of his own immortality; a spiritual being, endued with understanding, freedom of will, and various affections; nor merely in his *political image,* the governor of this lower world . . . but chiefly in his *moral image,* which, according to the apostle, is "righteousness and true holiness" (Eph. 4:24).

No wonder God pronounced his creation to be "very good"! However, man was not made immutable.

In the day that Adam ate of the forbidden fruit he also died spiritually. The love of God was extinguished in his soul, and he was alienated from the life of God. Under the power of servile fear he, both unholy and unhappy, having sunk into pride and self-will, fled from the presence of God.

> In Adam all died, all human kind, all the children of men who were then in Adam's loins. The natural consequence of this is, that every one descended from him comes into the world spiritually dead, dead to God, wholly dead in sin; entirely void of the life of God; void of the image of God, of all that righteousness and holiness wherein Adam was created. Instead of this, every man born into the world now bears the image of the devil, in pride and self-will; the image of the beast, in sensual appetites and desires. This, then, is the foundation of the new birth—the entire corruption of our nature. Hence it is that, being born in sin, we must be "born again." Hence every one that is born of a woman must be born of the Spirit of God.

So the need for inward regeneration from heaven is based on the fact of the entire corruption of our nature. Here we may add that Wesley did not

---

42. Wesley, *Sermons on Several Occasions,* sermon 39, pp. 514–26.

draw from this doctrine the corollary that the human will is unable, when attracted by the power of the gospel, to choose the gospel. His "bondage of the will" was not as severe a bondage as that which Luther and the Puritans taught.

Wesley now answers a second question, "What is the nature of the new birth?"

> It is that great change which God works in the soul when he brings it into life; when he raises it from the death of sin to the life of righteousness. It is the change wrought in the whole soul by the almighty Spirit of God when it is "created anew in Christ Jesus"; when it is "renewed after the image of God in righteousness and true holiness"; when the love of the world is changed into the love of God; pride into humility; passion into meekness; hatred, envy, malice, into a sincere, tender, disinterested love for all mankind. In a word, it is that change whereby the earthly, sensual, devilish mind is turned into the "mind which was in Christ Jesus." This is the nature of the new birth: "So is every one that is born of the Spirit."

Wesley held the classical Arminian theology that it is possible to lose this new state of the soul through willful sin against God. Further, Wesley held that regeneration and justification are simultaneous acts of God: "In order of *time,* neither of these is before the other; in the moment we are justified by the grace of God, through the redemption that is in Jesus, we are also 'born of the Spirit'; but in order of *thinking,* as it is termed, justification precedes the new birth. We first conceive his wrath to be turned away and then his Spirit to work in our hearts."

Wesley turns his attention to a third question, "To what end is it necessary that we should be born again?" Once more his answer is very clear. First, it is necessary for holiness. "Gospel holiness is no less than the image of God stamped upon the heart; it is no other than the whole mind that was in Christ Jesus; it consists of all heavenly affections and tempers mingled together in one." Second, it is necessary for eternal salvation. Being harmless, virtuous, honest, and moral is not enough; unless we are born again we will go to hell. Finally, it is necessary for true happiness in this world as well as in the world to come. A sinful heart gives more pain than pleasure, but a regenerate heart gives true joy and peace.

To close the sermon, Wesley adds a few inferences. Against much popular theology in the Church of England, he asserts that "baptism is not the new birth: they are not one and the same thing." He also emphasizes that the new birth does not always accompany the baptism of adults; "the tree is known by its fruits." He admits that the service of baptism for infants presupposes that they are regenerated in connection with baptism, but he makes no further comment on whether or not he holds this to be always the case. Finally, he expresses disagreement with William Law, whose writings had been so influential upon the young Wesleys at Oxford, over his definition of regeneration. In *Grounds and Reasons of Christian Regeneration* (1739) Law had defined regeneration as a process of sanctification and renovation of the soul. Wesley insists that the new birth is one thing and the life of holiness another; the latter flows from the former but must not be confused with it.

What Wesley took to be "The Marks of the New Birth" are found in his sermon of that title, which is based on John 3:8.[43] The first mark, which is the foundation of the rest, is faith: "The true living faith, which whosoever hath is born of God, is not only assent, an act of the understanding; but a disposition, which God hath wrought in his heart; 'a sure trust and confidence in God, that, through the merits of Christ, his sins are forgiven, and he reconciled to the favour of God.'" The fruits of such faith include power over sin and peace with God. The second mark is hope. It arises from both the word of Scripture and the internal testimony of the Spirit of God that "we are the children of God . . . heirs of God, and joint heirs with Christ." The indwelling Holy Spirit is the earnest of our inheritance. The third mark of those who are born of God is love, "the love of God shed abroad in their hearts by the Holy Ghost which is given unto them" (Rom. 5:5). Those who love God and have his love in their hearts actually keep God's commandments and do not sin.

Wesley was deeply conscious that "without holiness no man can see the Lord." He saw Christian perfection and full sanctification as "the grand depositum which God has lodged with the people called Methodist; and for the sake of propagating this chiefly he appeared to have raised us up." How he understood scriptural holiness may be gathered from his sermons on the topic and from his *Plain Account of Christian Perfection*. Unlike the Puritans Wesley did not speak of a postregeneration growth *towards* holiness, but of a growth *in* holiness. Holiness is not something for which the regenerated individual must strive; rather, it is given in the act of internal regeneration and renewal of the soul. True believers are to grow in the holiness and righteousness given to them at their new birth. Their goal, which is perfect love, is truly attainable. Indeed without true holiness it is not possible to enter into the presence of the Lord after the death of the body. Thus believers are to aim at purity of motive and a life controlled by the love of God. Of course, they will be fallible in judgment, and they will not be exempt from ignorance, bodily sickness, and temptation. However, the state of perfection in motive and love is possible, though some will attain it only just before their death. Entry into this higher state, which itself is capable of growth into deeper

---

43. Ibid., sermon 14, pp. 162–74.

love of God and humankind, is usually by some definite experience distinct from, but similar to new birth.

It is important to recall that Wesley's doctrine of justification (unlike that of Whitefield) does not include the reckoning of the righteousness of Christ to the believer (i.e., the concept of imputation). Thus the righteousness and holiness which believers need to enter the presence of the Lord cannot be the righteousness of Christ reckoned to them; it has to be that holiness which was implanted in the soul at regeneration and fully permeates the mind, will, and affections. That justification was for Wesley only the forgiveness of sins and acceptance with God also explains why he believed it possible to lose not only the state of Christian perfection but also the enjoyment of initial salvation.

Following Wesley, there have been many denominations, groups, and individuals who have taught the necessity of a second work of grace distinct from, but related to initial inward regeneration. Few of these, however, have presented it in the precise context which informed Wesley's thinking—the necessity of genuine personal holiness to enter God's holy presence. Most of the others who speak of a second work of grace have in view a special strength to witness for the Lord, to enjoy the gifts of the Spirit, or to have a deeper communion with God.

13

Modern Evangelism

A Decision for Christ

In the preceding chapter we referred to the Great Awakening in New England in the eighteenth century and to the teaching of Jonathan Edwards and George Whitefield on regeneration as they were involved in that revival. In this chapter we will be concerned with the phenomenon of revivals, evangelistic campaigns, and crusades from the early nineteenth century to the present day. We will confine ourselves to the teaching of American evangelists and discover that for the majority of them (and probably for their supporters as well) the following observations are accurate: (1) The expressions "to be born again," "to be converted," and "to make a decision for Christ" tend to run into each other and mean much the same. Particularly, to be born again is seen not as a passive but an active experience. (2) It is held that regeneration can occur immediately in the context of the evangelistic service: there are no requisite preparations to delay one's decision for Christ. (3) It is maintained that regeneration has no meaningful connection with infant baptism and little vital relation to adult (believers') baptism. To these three points the only notable exceptions were the founding fathers of the Christian Church (Disciples of Christ).

The Second Awakening

Revival occurred in the period of the rapid western expansion of the new nation.[1] By 1829 more than a third of the population lived west of the Allegheny Mountains. There were revivals in the East and West, from Maine to Tennessee. Naturally, there were less sophistication and more excitement on the frontier, where in the religious exercises known as camp meetings thousands professed to be born again and converted. Peter Cartwright (1785–1872), a Methodist itinerant preacher, published his autobiography in 1856, in which he provides vivid accounts of dynamic preaching, spiritual awakenings, instant conversions, and great emotional excitement with striking physical accompaniments: "I have known these camp-meetings to last three or four weeks, and great good resulted from them. I have seen more than a hundred sinners fall like dead men under one powerful sermon . . . and I will venture to assert that many happy thousands were awakened and converted to God at these camp meetings."[2]

The phenomenon of the camp meeting, which was well suited to the basic conditions of the frontier, was the brainchild of James McGready (1758–1817), a Presbyterian minister in Kentucky. One of McGready's converts, Barton W. Stone (1772–1844), recorded what happened at a typical camp meeting in 1801:

> Many, very many, fell down as men slain in battle, and continued for hours together in an apparently breathless and motionless state, sometimes for a few moments reviving and exhibiting symptoms of life by a deep groan or piercing shriek, or by a prayer for mercy fervently uttered. After lying there for hours they obtained deliverance. The gloomy cloud that had covered their faces seemed gradually and visibly to disappear, and hope, in smiles, brightened into joy. They would rise, shouting deliverances and then would address the surrounding multitude in language truly eloquent and impressive. With astonishment did I hear men, women and children declaring the wonderful works of God and the glorious mysteries of the gospel.[3]

Later, Stone himself preached at such meetings and saw thousands professing new birth.

---

1. For an introduction to the period of the Second Great Awakening see George C. Bedell, Leo Sandon, Jr., and Charles T. Wellborn, *Religion in America*, ch. 3.
2. Peter Cartwright, *The Autobiography of Peter Cartwright*, p. 75. For the phenomenon of the camp meeting see Charles A. Johnson, *The Frontier Camp Meeting*.
3. Cited by Leonard Woolsey Bacon, *A History of American Christianity*, p. 234.

It has been observed that in this period three important characteristics were incorporated into evangelical Christianity and the ethos
of the churches affected by revival: pietism, individualism, and reductionism.[4] The incorporation of pietism does not refer to a transportation
of classical Lutheran Pietism to America. Rather it refers to a personal
appropriation of God's grace in Christ and thus to a subjective experience of religion, beginning with a profession of conversion or a decision
to follow Christ. This immediate and very personal experience of God's
grace tended to become an authority in its own right.

To survive on the frontier, self-reliance was necessary. Frontier life
tended to be individualistic, and so the revivalists' stress on the individual's being personally loved and saved by God fit right in. Having experienced new birth—a very individual matter—the recipient was then
responsible for the cultivation of a personal walk with God. Every convert was deemed to have the right to interpret the Bible for himself or
herself.

By reductionism is meant that creeds, rituals, and ceremonies were
pared down to a minimum set of (apparently) simple, basic convictions,
beliefs, and styles of worship. Thus regeneration was seen as merely
another way of talking about conversion or about making a decision for
Christ; further, "Ye must be born again" (KJV) was taken to be an imperative and thus a virtual equivalent of "Repent and believe" or "Receive
the Lord Jesus into your heart."

The Disciples of Christ

The characteristics of pietism, individualism, and reductionism are,
to a greater or lesser extent (depending on denomination, ethnic background, and political circumstances), still obvious in American evangelical Christianity. This said, it would be wrong to assume that all
those involved in the revivals and evangelistic campaigns of nineteenth-
century America were without any theological sophistication. While the
preaching avoided complicated doctrine and provided practical illustrations and exhortations, some of the preachers gave themselves to serious
biblical study and theological reflection. One such was Alexander
Campbell (1788–1866), who with Barton Stone and others (e.g., Walter
Scott) founded the new denomination called the Disciples of Christ,
which enjoyed phenomenal growth on the frontier in the mid-nineteenth century.[5]

---

4. These points are made concerning Methodism in Edwin S. Gaustad, *A Religious
History of America*, pp. 144–45, and utilized in Bedell, Sandon, and Wellborn, *Religion
in America*, pp. 165–66.

5. See W. E. Garrison and A. T. DeGroot, *The Disciples of Christ*, for a basic account of

The founding fathers of the Disciples of Christ came to see that, if they were truly to restore authentic primitive Christianity, baptism had to be intimately related to faith and repentance, regeneration and conversion. This was obvious to them from their close study of the text of the New Testament. They came up with the schema of faith, repentance, baptism for the remission of sins, the gift of the Holy Spirit, and the promise of eternal life. Faith was understood as trust and confidence in Jesus as the Christ and Lord, repentance was understood as serious and sincere amendment of life on the basis of the gospel, and baptism by immersion was understood as a God-appointed ordinance for salvation ("he that believeth and is baptized shall be saved"—Mark 16:16 [KJV]).

Campbell explained this schema in his *Christian System*. On the subject of baptism he wrote:

> Baptism is designed to introduce the subjects of it into the participation of the blessings of the death and resurrection of Christ. . . . But it has no abstract efficacy. Without previous faith in the blood of Christ, and deep and unfeigned repentance before God, neither immersion in water, nor any other action, can secure to us the blessings of peace and pardon. It can merit nothing. Still to the believing penitent it is *the means* of receiving a formal, distinct and specific absolution, or release from guilt. Therefore, none but those who have first believed the testimony of God and have repented of their sins, and that have been intelligently immersed into his death, have the full and explicit testimony of God, assuring them of pardon. [p. 58]

Such a position had an immediate appeal: had not Peter in his very first sermon called upon his hearers in these terms, "Repent and be baptized, every one of you, in the name of Jesus Christ for the forgiveness of your sins. And you will receive the gift of the Holy Spirit" (Acts 2:38)?

In chapter 18 ("Conversion & Regeneration") Campbell makes clear the different aspects of the change which is consummated by baptismal immersion. He explains that the New Testament refers to this change by a variety of terms—"being quickened," "being made alive," "passing from death to life," "being born again," "having risen with Christ," "turning to the Lord," "being enlightened," "conversion," and "repentance unto life." Then he provides this careful statement:

the movement; and Byrdine Akers Abbott, *The Disciples: An Interpretation,* for its principles and practices. It is important to bear in mind that the early Disciples were influenced by the distinctive teachings (on ecclesiology and conversion) of John Glas, Robert Sandeman, and the Haldane brothers, James Alexander and Robert. For this influence see W. A. Gerrard, "Walter Scott, Frontier Disciples' Evangelist."

> The entire change effected in man by the Christian system consists in four
> things: a change of views; a change of affections; a change of state; and a
> change of life. . . . As a change of *views* it is called "being enlightened" . . .
> as a change of affections it is called "being reconciled" . . . as a change of
> state it is called "being quickened" or "being born again" . . . and as a
> change of life it is called "repentance unto life" or "conversion." [p. 60]

He proceeds to insist that regeneration and conversion must not be
made into synonyms (as they had been, he believed, in both classical
Reformed theology and popular frontier preaching, for different reasons
in each case):

> We ought, then, to use this word [*regeneration*] in its strict and scriptural
> acceptation, if we would escape the great confusion now resting upon this
> subject. The sophistry or delusion of this confusion is that making *re-
> generation* equivalent to the entire change, instead of to the one-fourth
> part of it, the community will be always imposed on and misled by seeking
> to find the attributes of conversion in the new birth, or of the new birth in
> conversion; and so of all the others. Being born again is not conversion, nor
> a change of views, nor a change of affections, but a change of state. [p. 61]

Whether such a precise distinction can be maintained in popular teaching and preaching is another matter!

Campbell insisted that the gift of the Spirit is bestowed on the believer only after baptism by immersion. Certainly the Spirit has been
active in bringing the believer to faith and repentance, but this specific
activity is not his actual indwelling.

> God gives his Holy Spirit to them who ask him according to his revealed
> will; and without this gift no one could be saved or ultimately triumph over
> all opposition. . . . To those, then, who believe, repent, and obey the gospel,
> he actually communicates of his Good Spirit. The fruits of that Spirit in
> them are "love, joy, peace, long-suffering, gentleness, goodness, fidelity,
> meekness and temperance." The attributes of character which distinguish
> the new man are each of them communications of the Holy Spirit, and thus
> are we the sons of God in fact, as well as in title, under the dispensation of
> the Holy Spirit. [p. 66]

Receiving the Holy Spirit the believer also is endowed with the gift of
eternal life and can henceforth live in genuine Christian hope.

Campbell and his associates insisted that the schema of faith, repentance, baptism, the gift of the Spirit, and the promise of eternal life
correctly describes the actual progression of the work of God in saving
the individual. From the perspective of the history of doctrine, it is of

great interest that this restorationist movement tied very closely together, as the patristic and medieval church had done, baptism, regeneration, and the gift of the Spirit. For the Disciples, baptism is the consummation of faith and repentance, leading to forgiveness, regeneration, conversion, and the indwelling of the Spirit.

Charles Grandison Finney

Leaving the frontier where Campbell had his successes, we return to the growing urban centers of the East Coast in order to notice the teaching of Charles Grandison Finney (1792–1875), who may be described as the first great professional evangelist of North America.[6]

Having served a brief apprenticeship as a lawyer, Finney applied both the principles and the techniques of the courts to his calling as a preacher. He adopted methods employed by attorneys in pleading their cases before the bar. These included a powerful appeal to his hearers for *immediate* decision. Further, his principles of theology were arrived at by applying legal reasoning to the text of Scripture. He abandoned the traditional Calvinism of New England and the Presbyterian denomination of which he was initially a member to put forward his own system of theology, based on the idea that conversion is a decision to submit to God's moral government, an act of will of which all are naturally capable. One of his earliest published sermons, "Sinners Bound to Change Their Own Hearts (1834)," conveyed his particular emphasis upon human duty and ability under God. Here as elsewhere he insisted that people are responsible agents whose relationship to God is wholly ordered according to rational principles of divine moral government. Changing one's heart means a radical change in ultimate choice and intention—that is, choosing God, Christ, and heaven.

Finney's most sophisticated theological treatise is his *Lectures on Systematic Theology*. This volume along with his *Lectures on Revival* presents a severely moderated New School Calvinism which is (by no means accurately) often termed "Arminianism."[7] There are four lectures on regeneration (27–30), although the substance of the doctrine is fully explained in the first two.[8] In these he rejects the old-style New England Reformed theology with its teaching that regeneration is wholly a work of God with the subject passive, while conversion is a

---

6. See Charles Grandison Finney, *An Autobiography of Charles G. Finney*, and the recent helpful study by David L. Weddle, *The Law as Gospel: Revival and Reform in the Theology of Charles G. Finney*.

7. See George M. Marsden, *The Evangelical Mind and the New School Presbyterian Experience*, pp. 76–80.

8. Charles Grandison Finney, *Lectures on Systematic Theology*. The Eerdmans reprint of 1964 is the edition used here.

work of God in which the subject is active, exercising faith, repentance, hope, and love. Finney rejects the old-style doctrine of regeneration because he rejects the old Reformed doctrine of human depravity and the bondage of the will to sin. He denies the Calvinist position that the total depravity of the human soul necessitates a wholly supernatural act of regeneration. He explains:

> To be born again is the same thing, in the Bible use of the term, as to have a new heart, to be a new creature, to pass from death unto life. In other words, to be born again is to have a new moral character, to become holy. To regenerate is to make holy. . . .
>
> Both conversion and regeneration are sometimes in the Bible ascribed to God, sometimes to man, and sometimes to the subject; which shows clearly that the distinction under examination is arbitrary and theological rather than biblical.
>
> The fact is that both terms imply the simultaneous exercise of both human and divine agency. The fact that a new heart is the thing done, demonstrates the activity of the subject; and the word regeneration or the expression "born of the Holy Spirit" asserts the divine agency. The same is true of conversion, or the turning of the sinner to God. God is said to turn him and he is said to turn himself. God draws him and he follows. In both alike God and man are both active, and their activity is simultaneous. God works or draws, and the sinner yields or turns, or which is the same thing, changes his heart, or, in other words, is born again. [pp. 283–84]

The identification of conversion with regeneration was to become a common presupposition within popular evangelism throughout the nineteenth and into the twentieth century.

With respect to the reception of truth presented by the Holy Spirit via the preached word of the Bible, Finney held that the subject is passive. However, when responding to this word the subject is active:

> He is passive in the perception of the truth presented by the Holy Spirit. I know that this perception is no part of regeneration. But it is simultaneous with regeneration. It induces regeneration. It is the condition and the occasion of regeneration. Therefore the subject of regeneration must be a passive recipient or percipient of the truth presented by the Holy Spirit, at the moment and during the act of regeneration. The Spirit acts upon him through or by the truth: thus far he is passive. He closes with truth: thus far he is active. What a mistake those theologians have fallen into who represent the subject as altogether passive in regeneration! This rids the sinner at once of the conviction of any duty or responsibility about it. It is amazing that such an absurdity should have been so long maintained in the church. But while it is maintained, it is no wonder that sinners are not converted to God. While the sinner believes this, it is impossible, if he has

it in mind, that he should be regenerated. He stands and waits for God to do what God requires him to do and which no one can do for him. Neither God, nor any other being, can regenerate him, if he will not turn. [p. 290]

Finney was able to lecture in this manner because he believed that the human will is free to choose God. He held that "God cannot do the sinner's duty, and regenerate him without the right exercise of the sinner's own agency." Concerning the duty of ministers he observed, "Ministers should lay themselves out and press every consideration upon sinners, just as heartily and as freely as if they expected to convert them themselves. They should aim at, and expect the regeneration of sinners, upon the spot, and before they leave the house of God" (p. 299). Since he put such stress on the moral government of God, it is not surprising that Finney also laid the duty of sanctification and holiness upon converts and insisted that they be concerned with social righteousness as well as personal holiness.

Post–Civil War Urban Evangelism

By far the most important and influential evangelist in the last quarter of the nineteenth century was Dwight Lyman Moody (1837–1899), a Congregational layman.[9] He appealed to a wide spectrum of people, especially the business classes, and he employed business techniques in publicizing and organizing his meetings. He was not a sophisticated theologian; his message revolved around the "three R's"—"ruin by sin, redemption by Christ, and regeneration by the Holy Spirit."

According to records kept by Moody he preached his sermon on "The New Birth" some 184 times between October 23, 1881, and November 2, 1899.[10] He never conducted a mission without preaching on the new birth or at least incorporating the substance of this celebrated message into another sermon. The sermon on regeneration appears in nearly every book of sermons by Moody,[11] and it appears frequently in paraphrase in newspaper reports of his campaigns.

Moody often began the sermon by stating what inward regeneration is not. It is not to be identified with going to church, being baptized, being confirmed, saying one's prayers, regularly reading the Bible, or

---

9. For Moody see Stanley N. Gundry, *Love Them In: The Life and Theology of D. L. Moody.*

10. Ibid., p. 122.

11. In, e.g., *The Best of D. L. Moody: Sixteen Sermons by the Great Evangelist,* ed. Wilbur M. Smith, pp. 90–95.

being the best one can be. These things are good in themselves, but they do not constitute regeneration. God alone, insisted Moody, can bring about the new birth, just as he alone created the universe.

> In the first chapter of Genesis we find God working alone; he went on creating the world all alone. Then we find Christ coming to Calvary alone. And when we get to the third chapter of John we find that the work of regeneration is the work of God alone. The Ethiopian cannot change his skin, nor the leopard his spots; we are born in sin, and the change of heart must come from God. We believe in the good old Gospel.

Here Moody sounds like an old New England Calvinist (he was born in Massachusetts). However, he did not believe in the necessity of a long preparation of the heart for regeneration. As an evangelist preaching to the thousands, he called for immediate acceptance of Christ as Savior and Lord.

Moody was not a systematic thinker but a practical man and an evangelist whose aim was to convert people at the moment they heard him, not the next day or week. Thus, while teaching that regeneration is the work of God alone, he also insisted that those who responded to the gospel he preached would by God's help and intervention be regenerated and converted. Accordingly, he would typically say to the crowds:

> If you would be saved, call upon God first, and then God will give you help, and by His power you can turn away from sin, and from your evil thoughts, and will get pardon. But you haven't power to give up your evil courses until you call upon God, and until He gives you strength. After you have called upon the Lord, you must receive Him when he comes; you must make room for Him.[12]

Moody's sense of human responsibility before God caused him to use aggressive evangelistic methods; however, his keen awareness that regeneration is the giving of a new heart and nature by the Holy Spirit restrained him from employing excessive tactics.

Moody certainly believed in instantaneous conversion and regeneration (words he never carefully distinguished and often used as synonyms). He was criticized for holding such a view by a variety of people from Unitarians through Disciples of Christ to high Calvinists. In response he insisted that the act of conversion and regeneration is like Noah's walking through the doorway of the ark and into safety, or a slave's crossing a national border into safety. He admitted, however, that

---

12. Cited by Gundry, *Love Them In,* p. 126.

some people—especially children—will not know the precise time of their regeneration. But they will certainly be able to affirm with joy, "Once I was blind, but now I see."

Following in the steps of Moody were such evangelists as Rodney (Gipsy) Smith (1860–1947), Sam (Samuel Porter) Jones (1847–1906), John Wilbur Chapman (1859–1918), and Billy (William Ashley) Sunday (1862–1935).[13] Sunday was known for his flamboyant style and sensational tactics, but what he said about regeneration was much the same as Moody had said. For example:

> Multitudes are in the church visibly but they have never been born again. They are members of the physical church but not members of the body of Christ, although the members of the visible church and of the body of Christ ought to be synonymous. But everybody that is a member of the visible church is not a member of the body of Christ. One of the first evidences, if not the very first evidence, of the divine Spirit in a man or woman is the fact that that man or woman is reaching out after those that are not Christians and trying to help them become Christians. Now, that being true, you can see that mighty few in the church have ever been born again.
>
> You have got to have a spiritual birth, and a spiritual birth is to come through the shed blood of Jesus Christ. You were born of the flesh—there you are—but you've not been born of the Spirit. So there are two births, the flesh and the Spirit. But being born again isn't by money or culture but by faith in Jesus Christ.[14]

Sunday's sermons are typical of the popular—sometimes vulgar—presentations of the gospel that have often embarrassed the faithful in the traditional denominations. However, since his day there have been many evangelists with a similar message.

We turn now to consider the message of Reuben Archer Torrey (1856–1928), who, in many ways, is considered the natural successor of Moody.[15] He came from a well-to-do New York family and attended Yale, where he professed evangelical conversion just before his graduation in 1875. He then entered Yale Divinity School, where, towards the end of his course, he heard Moody, who challenged him to work for the Lord by winning converts. Before being ordained to the Congregational ministry Torrey studied the writings of Charles Finney. While not agreeing

---

13. For Sunday see William G. McLoughlin, *Billy Sunday Was His Real Name*, and William T. Ellis, *"Billy" Sunday: The Man and His Message*.

14. From a sermon preached on April 28, 1917, in New York and found among the papers of William and Helen Sunday in the Billy Graham Center Archives, Wheaton, Illinois.

15. There is useful material in Roger Martin, *R. A. Torrey, Apostle of Certainty*.

with all he read therein, he did come to the conclusion that the church of
God ought to be perpetually revived by the Holy Spirit. A period of study
in Germany led him to value his Bible the more, and during a pastoral
and evangelistic ministry in Minneapolis he came to believe that the
baptism with the Holy Spirit is not identical with initial regeneration
and conversion. Thus he helped prepare the way for the distinction
which the charismatic movement draws between regeneration and baptism in the Spirit. From Minneapolis he moved to Chicago to work with
Moody, and from that point began his career as a much-traveled and
successful evangelist, Bible teacher, and educator.

Torrey stated his theological views clearly in many books. In his
frequently reprinted *What the Bible Teaches* we find that his doctrine of
regeneration is in essence much the same as that of Moody. (However, as
we have noted, Torrey did distinguish the initial act of God in regeneration from a further act of God which he called the baptism of the Spirit.
This latter event could occur immediately after conversion, or it could
occur later in response to a heartfelt desire for it.)

At the end of the chapter on new birth Torrey writes:

> In the new birth the Word of God is the seed; the human heart is the soil;
> the preacher of the Word is the sower, and drops the seed into the soil; God
> by his Spirit opens the heart to receive the seed (Acts 16:14); the hearer
> believes; the Spirit quickens the seed into life in the receptive heart; the
> new divine nature springs up out of the divine Word; the believer is born
> again, created anew, made alive, passed out of death into life. [p. 335]

Earlier he had insisted that baptism is not the new birth and that the
"water" of John 3:5 does not refer to the physical water of baptism, but to
the cleansing effects of the Word of God. Also he emphasized that regeneration means both the arrival of the Spirit to indwell the soul and
the beginnings of a changed life of holiness and righteousness.

We should also note Torrey's involvement in the editing of *The Fundamentals,* a twelve-volume series of articles (1910–1915) defending
Protestant orthodoxy. Essay 39, entitled "Regeneration–Conversion–
Reformation," was written by George W. Lasher, a friend of Torrey. The
teaching is similar to that of Torrey himself. There is a definite rejection
of the concept of baptismal regeneration, and conversion is presented as
the visible expression of inward spiritual regeneration. Likewise a genuine reformation of life is seen as proceeding from true inward regeneration.

Torrey asserted that regeneration ought to be followed as soon as
possible by the baptism with the Spirit: this is "a definite experience of
which one may and ought to know whether he has received it or not"

(p. 270). It is given by God for the purpose of strengthening the believer to serve the kingdom of Christ. With the baptism of the Spirit come gifts of the Spirit, power for service, boldness in testimony, and deeper love of the truth, God, and needy sinners. Torrey taught that baptism with the Spirit is bestowed upon those who fulfil certain fundamental conditions: these are repentance, faith in Jesus Christ as an all-sufficient Savior, and baptism in the name of Jesus Christ for the remission of sins. Often the gift is bestowed only after earnest prayer has been offered. (It is interesting that Torrey, citing texts like Acts 19:2–6, made baptism in water a condition for baptism with the Spirit, whereas, as we have noted, he saw no necessary connection between baptism in water and inward regeneration.) Torrey obviously held that there is no effective Christian living and witnessing unless one is filled with the Spirit, that is, has been baptized with the Spirit. In regeneration, life is imparted, while in the baptism with the Spirit, power for service is given.

Billy Graham and Modern Evangelism

Billy (William Franklin) Graham was born in 1918 in North Carolina. He was ordained as a Southern Baptist pastor and then became the first evangelist of the Youth for Christ movement.[16] Since 1954 he has enjoyed a world reputation as an evangelist and ambassador of peace. At the time of writing he is still engaged in holding crusades in various countries.

Graham often speaks of "being born again," using the expression as if it is virtually synonymous with "receiving Christ," "making a decision for Christ," and "being converted." In fact he has a book entitled *How to Be Born Again*. This is an odd title when judged by either classical Reformed or Arminian theology because both view the how of regeneration as known only to God himself. Graham's theme might more correctly be stated as "how to become a Christian who can humbly claim to have been born again by the Holy Spirit." The book has three sections: the first deals with "man's problem" (sin and self-centeredness), the second with "God's answer" in the person and work of Jesus Christ, and the third with "man's response" in terms of the new birth. The third part has but three chapters entitled "The New Birth Is for Now," "The New Birth Is Not Just a 'Feeling,'" and "Alive and Growing." In the first of

---

16. In *Campus Life: Operations Manual* (1984) the Youth for Christ movement still characterizes itself as a "soul-winning" organization, asserting in its statement of faith, "We believe that, for the salvation of lost and sinful man, regeneration by the Holy Spirit is absolutely essential." The contents of the manual suggest that regeneration is equivalent to making a decision for Christ.

these Graham insists, "Jesus said that God can change men and women from the inside out. It was a challenge—a command. He didn't say, 'It might be nice if you were born again,' or, 'If it looks good to you, you might be born again.' Jesus said, 'You *must be* born again' (John 3:7)" (p. 131). Here we encounter the common mistake made by so many evangelists who take the words of Jesus in John 3 concerning the necessity of new birth as though they were a command to us to do something about it.[17]

But *How to Be Born Again* is a popular book and to look for theological precision in it is perhaps unfair. So let us turn instead to "The New Birth," an essay Graham contributed to a serious volume entitled *Fundamentals of the Faith*.[18] In contrast to the rest of the essays (which are basically academic statements), "The New Birth" moves from what seems to be fairly serious theology to sermonic style. Toward the beginning, for example, there is a theological description of the person who has been born again: "The Bible teaches that his will is changed, his objectives for living are changed, his disposition is changed, his affections are changed, and he now has purpose and meaning in his life. In the new birth, a new life has been born in his soul" (p. 192). Then a little later the evangelist comes out of the skin of the theologian: "Any person who is willing to trust Jesus as his personal Saviour can receive the new birth now. The early Methodist preachers were called the 'now preachers' because they offered salvation on the spot" (p. 193). The evangelist is further revealed in a section entitled "How to Become a New Man," which includes a couple of stories; an explanation of conversion, repentance, and faith; some comments on emotion, the will, and assurance; and a step-by-step account of how to receive Christ. In this section Graham appears to assume that the new birth encompasses conversion, for he recognizes that there are some fine Christians (including his own wife) who know they have received Christ but who cannot remember a specific time of conversion.

Graham explains that those who have made a decision for Christ and received him have become children of God. He moves on to deal with "the dynamics of the new man." When we are converted, he explains, our sin is forgiven and we are justified by faith. Further, we are adopted by God and receive the gift of the indwelling Spirit and through his power the possibility of victory over sin and temptation. All this happens in direct

---

17. This mistake is made, for example, by another Southern Baptist evangelist, Clifton Woodrow Brannon (b. 1912), whose papers in the Billy Graham Center Archives equate conversion (turning from sin to Christ) with regeneration.

18. Billy Graham, "The New Birth," in *Fundamentals of the Faith*, ed. Carl F. H. Henry, pp. 189–208. The material in the essay originally appeared in Graham's *World Aflame* (Garden City, N.Y.: Doubleday, 1965).

connection with being born again and converted. To make his position clearer, Graham adds:

> Let it be said at once that the new man is not the old man improved or made over. He is not even the old man reformed or remodeled, for God does not make the new out of the old nor put new wine in old bottles. The new man is Christ formed in us. As in the creation, we were created in the image of God. In the new creation, we are re-created in the image of Christ. . . .
>
> The new man is actually Christ in the heart, and Christ in the heart means that He is in the center of our being. The Biblical use of the word "heart" symbolizes the whole realm of the affections. Into this area Christ comes to transform our affections, with the result that the things for which we formerly had affection pass away, and the things for which we now have affection are new and of God. If Christ dwells in the heart, it means that He dwells also in the mind with its varied function of thinking and self-determination. In the process of change into a new creature when Christ indwells the heart, the human personality is neither absorbed nor destroyed. Instead it is enriched and empowered by this union with Christ. [p. 203]

In this careful statement we encounter Graham the theologian again.

In the rest of his essay, Graham works on the assumption that a Christian believer has two natures, the new and the old. The new cannot sin but the old wants to sin. Thus there is spiritual conflict, and the new nature, in order to be victorious, has to be regularly fed while the old nature is starved. The feeding consists of Bible reading, prayer, and Christian fellowship.

It would appear, then, that Graham holds that the act of regeneration and conversion signifies the entry of Christ (in and through the Holy Spirit) into the heart of a believer to provide a new center, motivation, and power so that a life of faith, hope, love, and obedience is possible. This new birth, conversion, or coming of Christ into the heart normally occurs when a person in faith and repentance makes a conscious decision for Christ; however, it may occur without one's being aware of a specific moment of decision and of inner change. In such a case, the person will know afterwards that he or she is a child of God. Like other evangelists Graham insists that the onus is upon everyone who hears the gospel message to accept it there and then. Though he holds to a doctrine of original sin, he believes that the will is sufficiently free to choose Christ and in choosing him to be transformed by him.

Further information concerning Graham's view of new birth is available in the literature used in training the people who counsel those who come forward at the end of his services. At the London crusade of 1954 a leaflet entitled "Lead Them to Christ! A Talk to Inquiry Room Workers" was distributed to the counselors. After discussing the skill needed to lead a person to Christ, this well-written British publication describes the moment of new birth:

> The actual moment of the new birth is the point at which the soul *sees* Christ crucified as his own Saviour; when the Saviour becomes *real* to him; it is a moment of vision. It is variously described in the Bible. It is believing, in the sense of a conviction which inevitably will mould conduct. It is trusting, as a child relaxes into the arms of a rescuing parent. It is receiving, as a wife opens the door to her husband when he comes home. It is calling, as a patient calls for his nurse. It is coming, as a guest to a feast. It is repenting, as a would-be murderer drops his weapon ere he is reconciled to his victim. It is obeying, as a casting obeys a mould before it sets. But the one who is alongside to help as the soul is born of God is responsible to bring the Scriptures to bear, so that Christ is kept to the forefront of the mind. When anyone is born again, it is by believing, trusting, receiving, obeying Christ; calling upon him, repenting towards him, coming to him. It is always to Christ that we must lead them.

Here inward regeneration and conversion are seen as basically the same, and the final decision is wholly that of the individual being counseled.

Apart from conducting crusades, Graham also has been responsible for convening important conferences. One of these was the World Congress on Evangelism, held in Berlin in 1966. Here different views of regeneration emerged as papers were delivered and discussion was pursued. Basically there were those who are commonly called Arminian and those commonly called Calvinist, along with a few Lutherans who did not fit into either bracket. Harold J. Ockenga, then minister of Park Street Church in Boston, presented the Arminian view: on hearing the gospel a person is free to choose Christ, to repent and believe; on actually doing so, one is born again by the Spirit. Ockenga was supported by Bishop Maurice A. P. Wood of England. In contrast, various American Presbyterians distinguished between regeneration as a secret act of God and conversion as a human activity arising from the new presence and power within the soul. They insisted that new birth implies total inability and passivity.

Interesting differences arose in the discussion of baptism. Out on a wing was the Lutheran doctrine of baptismal regeneration, a view commonly condemned by popular evangelists from Finney to Graham, but defended by Richard Møller Petersen of Copenhagen. George R. Beasley-Murray pointed out that in the apostolic age the first and most important way to confess that one belonged to Christ was in the rite of baptism. His definition of regeneration is also of interest: "Regeneration signifies entry into the 'regeneration' which is the new age or the new world (Matt. 19:28). It takes place when the Holy Spirit unites a man with the Lord, who by his resurrection initiated the new creation. Paul expressed the thought without the word when he spoke about a man becoming a new creation in Christ (2 Cor. 5:17)." Similar references to the new age and order, the regeneration of the cosmos, are rare in evangelistic sermons and literature.

The Berlin congress revealed that while evangelism is a priority for all evangelicals, there is no basic agreement among them on whether original sin affects a person's ability to choose the gospel, whether regeneration is the cause of conversion or a synonym of conversion, and whether regeneration once having occurred can be taken away or lost. The majority of those involved in evangelistic enterprises do, however, like Graham, appear to equate regeneration and conversion and to believe that, in essence, every person, in his or her own power as God's creature, is free to choose or reject Christ.

Six months before the congress in Berlin, there had been a congress in Wheaton, Illinois, on a similar theme—"The Church's Worldwide Mission." It was attended by delegates of the Interdenominational Foreign Mission Association and the Evangelical Foreign Missions Association, societies very sympathetic to the work and message of Graham. In the resultant document, entitled the Wheaton Declaration, the delegates stated a theology much like that of Graham, including the view that regeneration is something we have to set in motion by our believing:

In Christ has been made possible a new type of life, a Christ-centered, Christ-controlled life. Through the crucified and risen Lord Jesus Christ, we call every man, wherever he may be, to a change of heart toward God (repentance), personal faith in Jesus Christ as Savior, and surrender to that Lordship. The proclamation of this "good news" has at its heart the *explicit imperative,* "Ye must be born again" (John 3:7). God says he will judge the world by his crucified, risen Son. We believe that if men are not born again, they will be subject to eternal separation from a righteous, holy God. "Except ye repent, ye shall all likewise perish" (Luke 13:3).

The emphasis upon the explicit imperative[19] is to be interpreted as a reaction against the doctrines of universalism and liberalism favored by

---

19. Compare the title of an Inter-Varsity booklet of the same period—"Regeneration: The Inescapable Imperative." See also Charles H. Troutman, *Seven Pillars: Distinctives of Evangelical Student Witness*. This book and Troutman's papers as general director of the Inter-Varsity Christian Fellowship, which are housed at the Billy Graham Center Archives, show that he clearly saw "Ye must be born again" as a command to make a decision for Christ.

leaders within the missionary societies of certain mainline denominations. The evangelicals wanted to make it known that they held to the absolute necessity of new birth. In emphasizing this point they often made the mistake of treating regeneration as if it were something human beings are commanded to bring about in their lives. They made it (functionally at least) the equivalent of a decision for Christ.

Graham gave the opening address at the International Congress on World Evangelization at Lausanne, Switzerland, in 1974. This congress produced what has become known as the Lausanne Covenant, which must rank as one of the best (if not the best) modern statements of the nature and task of evangelism. Regrettably for our purposes, it does not have a specific section on regeneration and conversion. It does, however, state:

> To evangelize is to spread the good news that Jesus Christ died for our sins and was raised from the dead according to the Scriptures and that as the reigning Lord he now offers the forgiveness of sins and the liberating gift of the Spirit to all who repent and believe. . . . Evangelism is the proclamation of the historical, biblical Christ as Savior and Lord with a view to persuading people to come to him personally and so be reconciled to God.

Despite Christ's command in Matthew 28:19, no mention is made of baptism as the outward and visible sign of the inward spiritual change and gift of the indwelling Spirit. In fact, though much is said about the church and its task of evangelism, nothing at all is said about the sacraments of the church. The only use of the verb "to be born again" occurs in the section on Christian social responsibility where we read that "when people receive Christ they are born again into his kingdom and must seek not only to exhibit but also to spread its righteousness in the midst of an unrighteous world." The truth is that Lausanne had the same mix of theological views concerning regeneration as had the earlier Berlin congress.

Epilogue

14

Born from Above

I t is now the moment to look back over the sacred text of Scripture and the teaching within the church in order to come up with some guidelines for a contemporary doctrine of regeneration. How these guidelines are used will in part be determined by the context in which the doctrine is being expressed, whether in baptismal liturgy, in preaching, or in teaching.

1. Regeneration occurs and will occur because Jesus Christ, risen from the dead, is exalted at the right hand of the Father in heaven as the Lord and as the Head of the church.

Here regeneration is understood both as inward spiritual renewal today and as cosmic renewal in the future.[1] There are the washing of regeneration (Titus 3:5) and universal regeneration (Matt. 19:28). By his death and resurrection, Jesus became the Head of a new creation and order. Spiritual birth from above (where Christ is exalted) within a human soul causes an addition to the new creation which will replace the present creation after the last judgment. By inward regeneration a person is united to Jesus Christ in and around whom the new creation exists and is growing.

Thus we agree with George R. Beasley-Murray, who told the Berlin World Congress on Evangelism (1966) that "regeneration signifies entry

---

1. On the subject of cosmic regeneration see Peter Toon, *Heaven and Hell: A Biblical and Theological Overview.*

into the regeneration which is the new age or the new world (Matt. 19:28). It takes place when the Holy Spirit unites a man with the Lord, who by his resurrection initiated the new creation." We also agree with the following explanation of the Anglo-Catholic theologian E. L. Mascall:

> Becoming a Christian means being incorporated into the human nature of Christ, the very human nature which he united to his divine Person in the womb of the Blessed Virgin and which he offered on the Cross as "a full, perfect and sufficient sacrifice, oblation and satisfaction for the sins of the whole world," the human nature which in his Resurrection and Ascension has been glorified and set free from the spatial limitations of ordinary human existence. This adoptive union with the triumphant Christ is altogether unique in its kind: it involves a real participation in Christ's human nature on the part of the believer and a real communication of it to him. By it the believer's own human nature is not destroyed but is strengthened and perfected by its grafting into the archetypal human nature of the Ascended Lord. There is no destruction of the created person, nor in being supernaturalized is he removed from the natural order. His life as a citizen of Earth continues, but he has a new and greater citizenship in Heaven. He is a new man, because he has been re-created in the New Adam. And because the Christ is both God and man, the Christian, by his incorporation into Christ, has received a share in the life of God himself. He has been made a partaker of the divine nature, the nature of God who is Trinity. His life is hid with Christ in God.[2]

2. Regeneration of an individual person occurs when the Holy Spirit enters the soul.

Being omnipresent, the Holy Spirit is present in and throughout the whole of the created order. Sent by God the Father in the name of Jesus Christ, the Holy Spirit secretly and invisibly works upon and in the hearts of those who hear and know the gospel of God, convincing them of sin, righteousness, and judgment (John 16:7–11). And as the Spirit of the exalted Lord Jesus, he actually enters the soul of those who believe the Good News.

The arrival of the Holy Spirit, as the Spirit of Christ, to dwell in the soul constitutes the essence of regeneration. He comes both as the Holy Spirit, the Third Person of the Holy Trinity, and as the Spirit of sanctification, that is, the Paraclete of Christ. As a member of the Holy Trinity, the eternal bond of love uniting the Father and Son, the Spirit brings into the soul nothing less than true love, *agapē,* God's own love. And as the Paraclete of Christ he brings the mind, virtue, character, and gifts of the exalted Head of the church.

---

2. E. L. Mascall, *Christ, the Christian and the Church,* p. 109.

Understood in this way, it is difficult to see how regeneration could be improved upon by a decisive second experience of the Spirit (as many Christians insist is necessary). On the other hand, the testimony of those who claim to have been baptized in or filled with the Spirit cannot be set aside or discounted. Many sincere Christians have had a decisive second experience of the presence and power of the Spirit of God, an experience which has transformed their lives. Perhaps the best expression for this additional experience is "release of the Spirit," for such an expression safeguards a full doctrine of inner regeneration as well as accepts the reality of a second decisive experience.[3]

Of course, we must not think of the indwelling Holy Spirit as if he were like a new organ implanted in the soul. His dwelling in believers is not to be thought of in materialist categories but rather as a spiritual presence who can make himself felt and known as he pleases. We talk of his entering in and his coming in power for this is how his visitation seems to us; but we must remember that all these expressions are merely attempts to describe something which, being supernatural, is beyond words. The Spirit's presence is known primarily through the fruit that he causes to appear (Gal. 5:22–23).

3. Inward regeneration may be said to be paradoxical in that it can be regarded as both (a) the internal cause of true faith and genuine repentance and (b) God's gift to those who repent and believe the gospel.

If we begin from an Augustinian doctrine of original sin, human depravity, and the bondage of the will, we must conclude that there can be no authentic response to the gospel unless the Holy Spirit, working within the soul, enables or causes its faculties of understanding, will, and affections to move towards God and holiness. Also, if we believe that an infant who dies can enter into God's holy presence in heaven but must be regenerate in order to do so, then we must similarly conclude that regeneration is (at least in this case) an act of God in which the human subject is passive.

On the other hand, the New Testament often represents the gift of the indwelling Spirit of regeneration as following the exercise of faith and repentance. In John's Gospel, coming to Christ, believing on him, and drinking his life-giving water precede the arrival of the Spirit (John 4:10–14; 6:35; 7:37–39). In the Acts of the Apostles those who repent and believe receive the Spirit (2:38; 3:19; 5:32; 10:43–44; 11:14–17). Like-

---

3. Theologians who espouse the charismatic movement and also belong to churches which practice both infant baptism and confirmation (Roman Catholic, Lutheran, and Anglican) are often much exercised to define the relationship between the release of (baptism in, filling with) the Spirit and these rites, especially confirmation, which traditional Roman Catholic theology sees as the sacramental giving of the Holy Spirit to strengthen the Christian.

wise Paul speaks of receiving the Spirit in faith (Gal. 3:2, 14; Eph. 1:13). It would seem that in the case of adults the Spirit first empowers the soul to engage in faith and repentance, and then enters that soul with re-generating grace, his own presence.

4. *Conversion may be understood either as a synonym for internal regeneration or as the immediate result of regeneration.*

A converted person is one who freely trusts, serves, and loves God in the name of Jesus Christ. While there are those who from their child-hood have genuinely loved God and desired to serve him, the majority who are now Christians have had an explicit experience of conversion (the duration of the experience varies from one individual to the next). They are conscious that their attitude, aims, and actions have·changed from what they were; and further, they realize they ought to change more in the direction of God and his will in Jesus Christ.

The understanding of conversion as equivalent to regeneration is characteristic primarily of those who firmly believe that God himself must actually redirect the human will to choose the gospel. However, it is probably best to use the word *conversion* to point to a change in attitude and behavior, thinking and lifestyle, created by the gospel of Christ.

5. *Regeneration is certainly a personal experience, but it is not meant to be an individualistic experience.*

The Spirit who comes to dwell in the soul and who unites the soul to the exalted Lord Jesus also unites the soul to others who likewise are temples of the Holy Spirit. Regeneration certainly establishes a rela-tionship with God the Father so that the regenerated become the adopted children of God; it also necessarily gives to the regenerated individual a membership in God's family. To use a different image: the regenerate person becomes a member of the body of Christ and functions along with its other members—what is a toe without a foot without a leg. . . ? Thus regeneration is the beginning of both a personal pil-grimage of holiness and a membership amongst a people who are in-volved with God in his mission in the world as well as with one another, encouraging and building each other up in the faith.

6. *The rite of baptism is not only God's appointed way of his either bestowing or confirming the gift of the Holy Spirit (i.e., the grace of regeneration) and of our entering into the church of Christ, but it is also the means by which the new Christian testifies to having been born from above and converted to the Lord Jesus Christ.*

To speak of baptism as the new Christian's testimony to rebirth is of course to refer to adult baptism, which is the form of baptism described in the New Testament. In the growing secularism of Western society this form of baptism will become more common, and thus the church will be given the chance to recover that approach to baptism which was known in the early centuries. If baptism were once again to be scheduled for Easter Day or some other festival, and if converts were schooled in Christian faith and morals, and then if the actual baptism were set in an appropriate rich ritual and liturgy, the dynamic relationship between regeneration and baptism, so obvious in the New Testament and patristic literature, would perhaps be recovered. Ritual is very important in human society (witness the extent of ritual at American political rallies and football games);[4] thus the early church showed profound insight in developing the rite of baptism in such a way as to reflect (a) the turning of the soul from the devil and sin to God and (b) the baptized individual's entry into the church and the service of Jesus Christ. A further incentive for reestablishing certain elements of the ancient ritual is that an appropriate policy for the baptism of the infant children of committed church members cannot truly be worked out until a deep understanding of the relationship of baptism and regeneration is recovered by the Western churches.

When all our studies are over, the questions that each of us must face are: Am I begotten of God the Father? Am I born from above where Christ is exalted? Am I born again by the Holy Spirit? Am I a new creation in Christ Jesus?

To know (in the full sense of the word) the doctrine of new birth means to have experienced the new birth and to be living as a new creature. Regrettably, it is possible (in fact too easy) to know much about the doctrine and not have had the experience of birth from above.

> Heavenly Father,
> by the power of your Holy Spirit
> you give to your faithful people
> new life in the water of baptism.
> Guide and strengthen us by that same
>   Spirit,
> that we who are born again
> may serve you in faith and love,
> and grow into the full stature of your Son
>   Jesus Christ,
> who is alive and reigns with you and the
>   Holy Spirit,
> one God now and forever. Amen.

---

4. No longer do anthropologists look upon ritual as belonging exclusively to primitive societies and cultures, but they see it as a fundamental expression of human rationality. The Christian church has lost much by failing to develop an appropriate ritual for Christian initiation, a ritual to symbolize inner regeneration and outward conversion to God. This failure is particularly obvious in evangelical circles.

Bibliography

Abbott, Byrdine Akers. *The Disciples: An Interpretation*. St. Louis: Bethany, 1964.

Adamson, James B. *The Epistle of James*. Grand Rapids: Eerdmans, 1976.

Althaus, Paul. *The Theology of Martin Luther*. Translated by Robert C. Schultz. Philadelphia: Fortress, 1966.

Anderson, Bernhard W. *The Old Testament and Christian Faith*. New York: Harper, 1963.

Armstrong, Brian G. *Calvinism and the Amyraut Heresy*. Madison: University of Wisconsin, 1969.

Augustine. "St. Augustine on the Creed: A Sermon to the Catechumens." Translated by C. L. Cornish. In *A Select Library of the Nicene and Post-Nicene Fathers of the Christian Church*, edited by Philip Schaff. Vol. 3. Grand Rapids: Eerdmans, 1956.

──────. *Confessions*. Edited by E. M. Blaiklock. Nashville: Thomas Nelson, 1983.

──────. "Enchiridion." Translated by J. F. Shaw. In *A Select Library of the Nicene and Post-Nicene Fathers of the Christian Church*, edited by Philip Schaff. Vol. 3. Grand Rapids: Eerdmans, 1956.

──────. Epistle 98. In *Patrologiae cursus completus*, edited by J. P. Migne. Series latina. Vol. 33. Paris: Garnier, 1845.

──────. "On Baptism, Against the Donatists." Translated by J. R. King. In *A Select Library of the Nicene and Post-Nicene Fathers of the Christian Church*, edited by Philip Schaff. Vol. 4. Grand Rapids: Eerdmans, 1956.

──────. "A Treatise on the Merits and Forgiveness of Sins, and on the Baptism of Infants." Translated by Benjamin B. Warfield. In *A Select Library of the Ni-*

cene and Post-Nicene Fathers of the Christian Church, edited by Philip Schaff. Vol. 5. Grand Rapids: Eerdmans, 1956.

Bacon, Leonard Woolsey. *A History of American Christianity.* New York: Scribner, 1900.

Bangs, Carl. *Arminius: A Study in the Dutch Reformation.* 2d ed. Grand Rapids: Francis Asbury, 1985.

Barrett, C. K. *A Commentary on the Epistle to the Romans.* Harper's New Testament Commentary. New York: Harper, 1958.

_____. *The Gospel According to St. John.* London: SPCK, 1955.

_____. *The Holy Spirit and the Gospel Tradition.* London: SPCK, 1947.

Bauckham, Richard J. *Jude, 2 Peter.* Word Biblical Commentary. Waco, Tex.: Word, 1983.

Bauer, Walter. *Griechisch-deutsches Wörterbuch zu den Schriften des Neuen Testaments und der übrigen urchristlichen Literatur.* 4 vols. Berlin: Topelmann, 1952.

Beasley-Murray, George R. *The Book of Revelation.* New Century Bible. Greenwood, S.C.: Attic; London: Oliphants, 1974.

Bedell, George C., Leo Sandon, Jr., and Charles T. Wellborn. *Religion in America.* New York: Macmillan, 1975.

Best, Ernest, ed. *I Peter.* New Century Bible. London: Oliphants, 1971.

Beyreuther, Erich. *Der junge Zinzendorf.* Marburg: Francke, 1957.

_____. *Zinzendorf und die sich allhier beisammen finden.* Marburg: Francke, 1959.

_____. *Zinzendorf und die Christenheit, 1732–1760.* Marburg: Francke, 1961.

Black, Matthew. *Romans.* New Century Bible. Greenwood, S.C.: Attic; London: Oliphants, 1973.

Book of Common Prayer. Everyman edition. London: J. H. Dent, 1952.

Book of Common Prayer, with the Additions and Deviations Proposed in 1928. London: Oxford University Press, 1928.

Brannon, Clifton Woodrow. Papers. Billy Graham Center Archives, Wheaton, Illinois.

Bright, John. *Jeremiah.* The Anchor Bible. Garden City, N.Y.: Doubleday, 1965.

Bromiley, Geoffrey W. *Baptism and the Anglican Reformers.* London: Lutterworth, 1953.

Brown, Colin, ed. *The New International Dictionary of New Testament Theology.* 3 vols. Grand Rapids: Zondervan; Exeter: Paternoster, 1975–1978.

Brown, Peter. *Augustine of Hippo.* Berkeley: University of California; London: Faber, 1967.

Brown, Raymond E. *The Epistles of John.* The Anchor Bible. Garden City, N.Y.: Doubleday, 1982.

_____. *The Gospel According to John.* 2 vols. The Anchor Bible. Garden City, N.Y.: Doubleday, 1966, 1970.

Bruce, F. F. *Commentary on the Book of Acts.* New International Commentary on the New Testament. Grand Rapids: Eerdmans, 1954.

_____. *The Epistle of Paul to the Romans.* Tyndale New Testament Commentary. Grand Rapids: Eerdmans; Leicester: Inter-Varsity, 1983.

Brunner, Heinrich Emil. *Dogmatics*. Vol. 3. *The Christian Doctrine of the Church, Faith, and the Consummation*. Translated by David Cairns. London: Lutterworth, 1962.

Calvin, John. *Acts of the Council of Trent with the Antidote*. In *Tracts and Treatises: In Defense of the Reformed Faith,* translated by Henry Beveridge. Vol. 3. Grand Rapids: Eerdmans, 1958.

————. "Calvin and Baptism." In *Christian Initiation: The Reformation Period,* by J. D. C. Fisher. London: SPCK, 1970.

————. *Consensus Tigurinus*. In *Collectio Confessionum in Ecclesiis Reformatis Publicatarum,* edited by H. A. Niemeyer. Leipzig: Julius Klinkhardt, 1840.

————. *Institutes of the Christian Religion*. Edited by John T. McNeill. Translated by Ford Lewis Battles. Philadelphia: Westminster, 1960.

Campbell, Alexander. *The Christian System*. New York: Arno, 1969.

Cartwright, Peter. *The Autobiography of Peter Cartwright*. Nashville: Abingdon, 1956.

Chadwick, Owen. *The Reformation*. Harmondsworth, England: Penguin, 1964.

Cherry, Conrad. *The Theology of Jonathan Edwards: A Reappraisal*. Garden City, N.Y.: Anchor, 1966.

Chrysostom, John. *Baptismal Instructions*. Edited and translated by P. W. Harkins. Westminster, Md.: Newman, 1963.

Citron, Bernhard. *New Birth: A Study of the Evangelical Doctrine of Conversion in the Protestant Fathers*. Edinburgh: University Press, 1951.

Cochrane, Arthur C., ed. *Reformed Confessions of the Sixteenth Century*. Philadelphia: Westminster, 1966.

The Confession of Faith. Edinburgh: Free Presbyterian Church of Scotland, 1967.

Copleston, F. C. *Aquinas*. Harmondsworth, England: Penguin, 1955.

Cranfield, C. E. B. *The Gospel According to St. Mark*. Cambridge Greek Testament Commentary. Cambridge: University Press, 1959.

Cyprian. "Epistle to Donatus." In *Receiving the Promise,* edited by Thomas Weinandy. Washington, D.C.: The Word Among Us, 1985.

————. "Epistle to Donatus." Translated by Ernest Wallis. In *Ante-Nicene Fathers,* edited by Alexander Roberts and James Donaldson. Vol. 5. Grand Rapids: Eerdmans, 1951.

Cyril of Jerusalem. *The Works of Saint Cyril of Jerusalem*. Translated by Anthony A. Stephenson and Leo P. McCauley. 2 vols. Washington, D.C.: Catholic University of America, 1969–1970.

Dallimore, Arnold. *George Whitefield*. 2 vols. Westchester, Ill.: Cornerstone; Edinburgh: Banner of Truth, 1984.

Daniélou, Jean. *Bible et liturgie*. Paris: Cerf, 1958.

Davids, Peter H. *The Epistle of James*. New International Greek Testament Commentary. Grand Rapids: Eerdmans, 1982.

Davidson, A. B. *The Book of the Prophet Ezekiel*. Cambridge: University Press, 1916.

Deeter, Allan C. "An Historical and Theological Introduction to P. J. Spener's *Pia Desideria:* A Study in German Pietism." Ph.D. diss., Princeton University, 1963.

de Rys, John, and Lubbert Gerrits. "A Brief Confession of the Principal Articles of the Christian Faith." In *Baptist Confessions of Faith,* edited by William Joseph McGlothlin. Philadelphia: American Baptist Publication Society, 1911.

de Schweinitz, Edmund A., ed. *The Moravian Manual.* Philadelphia: Lindsay & Blakiston, 1859.

Dunn, J. D. G. *Jesus and the Spirit.* London: SCM, 1975.

Edwards, Jonathan. *A Faithful Narrative of the Surprising Work of God in the Conversion of Many Hundred Souls in Northampton, . . . New England.* 1737. In *Works of Jonathan Edwards,* edited by Edward Hickman. Edinburgh: Banner of Truth, 1974.

_____. *Treatise on Grace.* Edited by Paul Helm. Cambridge: James Clarke, 1971.

Ellis, William T. *"Billy" Sunday: The Man and His Message.* Philadelphia: John C. Winston, 1914.

Fenton, J. C. *The Gospel of St. Matthew.* Pelican Gospel Commentary. Baltimore: Penguin, 1964.

Finney, Charles Grandison. *An Autobiography of Charles G. Finney.* Edited by Helen Wessel. Minneapolis: Bethany Fellowship, 1977.

_____. *Lectures on Systematic Theology.* Edited by J. H. Fairchild. Oberlin, Ohio: E. J. Goodrich, 1878; Grand Rapids: Eerdmans, 1964.

Fisher, J. D. C. *Christian Initiation: Baptism in the Medieval West.* London: SPCK, 1965.

_____. *Christian Initiation: The Reformation Period.* London: SPCK, 1970.

Flannery, Austin, ed. *Vatican Council II: The Conciliar and Post Conciliar Documents.* Wilmington, Del.: Scholarly Resources, 1975; Leominster, England: Fowler Wright, 1981.

_____. *Vatican Council II: More Postconciliar Documents.* Grand Rapids: Eerdmans, 1982.

Flemington, W. F. *The New Testament Doctrine of Baptism.* London: SPCK, 1953.

Freeman, A. J. "The Hermeneutics of Count Nicholas Ludwig von Zinzendorf." Ph.D. diss., Princeton Theological Seminary, 1962.

Furnish, Raymond. *The Meaning of Baptism: A Comparison of the Teaching and Practice of the Fourth Century with the Present Day.* London: SPCK, 1985.

Garden, Alexander. *Six Letters to the Rev. George Whitefield.* Boston, 1740.

Garrison, W. E., and A. T. DeGroot. *The Disciples of Christ.* St. Louis: Christian Board of Publication, 1948.

Gaustad, Edwin S. *A Religious History of America.* New York: Harper & Row, 1966.

Gerrard, W. A. "Walter Scott, Frontier Disciples' Evangelist." Ph.D. diss., Emory University, 1982.

Gerstner, John H. *Steps to Salvation: The Evangelistic Message of Jonathan Edwards.* Philadelphia: Westminster, 1960.

Gillies, John. *Memoirs of George Whitefield . . . and an Extensive Collection of His Sermons and Other Writings.* Middletown, Conn.: Hunt and Noyes, 1837.

Goode, William. *The Doctrine of the Church of England as to the Effects of Baptism in the Case of Infants.* London: J. Hatchard, 1850.

Goppelt, Leonhard. *New Testament Theology.* 2 vols. Edited by Jürgen Roloff. Translated by John E. Alsup. Grand Rapids: Eerdmans, 1981–1982.

Graham, Billy. *How to Be Born Again.* Waco, Tex.: Word, 1977.

———. "The New Birth." In *Fundamentals of the Faith,* edited by Carl F. H. Henry. Grand Rapids: Zondervan, 1969.

Gray, John. *The Biblical Doctrine of the Reign of God.* Edinburgh: T. & T. Clark, 1979.

Grayston, Kenneth. *The Johannine Epistles.* Grand Rapids: Eerdmans, 1984.

Green, Michael. *I Believe in the Holy Spirit.* Grand Rapids: Eerdmans; London: Hodder and Stoughton, 1975.

———. *The Second Epistle General of Peter and the General Epistle of Jude.* Tyndale New Testament Commentary. Grand Rapids: Eerdmans; Leicester: Inter-Varsity, 1968.

Gritsch, Eric W., and Robert W. Jenson. *Lutheranism: The Theological Movement and Its Confessional Writing.* Philadelphia: Fortress, 1976.

Gundry, Stanley N. *Love Them In: The Life and Theology of D. L. Moody.* Chicago: Moody, 1976.

Guthrie, Donald. *New Testament Theology.* Downers Grove, Ill.: Inter-Varsity; Leicester: Inter-Varsity, 1981.

———. *The Pastoral Epistles.* Tyndale New Testament Commentary. Grand Rapids: Eerdmans; London: Tyndale, 1957.

Guthrie, William. *The Christian's Great Interest.* London: Banner of Truth, 1969.

Harrisville, Roy A. *The Concept of Newness in the New Testament.* Minneapolis: Augsburg, 1960.

Hendriksen, William. *The Gospel of John.* Grand Rapids: Baker, 1953.

Heppe, Heinrich. *Reformed Dogmatics Set Out and Illustrated from the Sources.* Edited by Ernst Bizer. Translated by G. T. Thomas. London: Allen & Unwin, 1950.

Heron, Alasdair I. C. *The Holy Spirit.* Philadelphia: Westminster, 1983.

Hill, David, ed. *The Gospel of Matthew.* New Century Bible. London: Oliphants, 1972.

Hodge, A. A. *Outlines of Theology.* New York: R. Carter, 1879.

Hoekema, Anthony A. "A New English Translation of the Canons of Dort." *Calvin Theological Journal* 3 (1968): 133–61.

Hull, J. H. E. *The Holy Spirit in the Acts of the Apostles.* London: Lutterworth, 1967.

Hunter, A. M. *Christ and the Kingdom.* Ann Arbor, Mich.: Servant, 1980.

International Congress on World Evangelism at Lausanne, Switzerland (1974). Papers and booklets. Billy Graham Center Archives, Wheaton, Illinois.

Jeremias, Joachim. *New Testament Theology.* Translated by John Bowden. New York: Scribner; London: SCM, 1971.

Johnson, Charles A. *The Frontier Camp Meeting.* Dallas: Southern Methodist University, 1955.

Käsemann, Ernst. *Commentary on Romans*. Edited and translated by Geoffrey W. Bromiley. Grand Rapids: Eerdmans, 1980.

Kelly, J. N. D. *A Commentary on the Epistles of Peter and Jude*. New York: Harper and Row; London: A. & C. Black, 1969.

———. *A Commentary on the Pastoral Epistles*. New York: Harper and Row; London: A. & C. Black, 1963.

———. *Early Christian Doctrine*. 4th ed. London: A. & C. Black, 1968.

Kohl, M. W. "*Wiedergeburt* as the Central Theme in Pietism." *Covenant Quarterly* 32 (Nov. 1974).

Lampe, G. W. H. *The Seal of the Spirit*. 2d ed. London: SPCK, 1967.

Lane, William L. *The Gospel According to Mark*. Grand Rapids: Eerdmans, 1974.

Laurence, David. "Jonathan Edwards, Solomon Stoddard, and the Preparationist Model of Conversion." *Harvard Theological Review* 72 (1979): 267–83.

"Lead Them to Christ! A Talk to Inquiry Room Workers." Papers. Billy Graham Center Archives, Wheaton, Illinois.

Leith, John H., ed. *Creeds of the Churches*. Rev. ed. Richmond, Va.: John Knox, 1973.

Leonard, Emile G. *A History of Protestantism*. Edited by H. H. Rowley. Translated by Joyce M. H. Reid. London: Thomas Nelson, 1965.

Lewis, A. J. *Zinzendorf: The Ecumenical Pioneer*. London: SCM, 1962.

Linder, Robert D. "Brunner, Heinrich Emil." In *Evangelical Dictionary of Theology*, edited by Walter A. Elwell. Grand Rapids: Baker, 1984.

Lovelace, Richard. *The American Pietism of Cotton Mather*. Grand Rapids: Eerdmans, 1979.

Lumpkin, William L., ed. *Baptist Confessions of Faith*. Chicago: Judson, 1959.

Luther, Martin. "Luther's First Taufbüchlein." In J. D. C. Fisher, *Christian Initiation: The Reformation Period*. London: SPCK, 1970.

———. "Preface to the Romans." In *The Reformation Writings of Martin Luther*, edited by Bertram Lee Woolf. New York: Philosophical Library, 1953–.

———. *Works*. Vol. 53. Edited by Ulrich S. Leupold. Philadelphia: Fortress, 1965.

McGlothlin, William Joseph, ed. *Baptist Confessions of Faith*. Philadelphia: American Baptist Publication Society, 1911.

McLoughlin, William G. *Billy Sunday Was His Real Name*. Chicago: University of Chicago, 1955.

Marsden, George M. *The Evangelical Mind and the New School Presbyterian Experience: A Case Study of Thought and Theology in Nineteenth-Century America*. New Haven: Yale University, 1970.

Marshall, I. Howard. *The Acts of the Apostles*. Tyndale New Testament Commentary. Grand Rapids: Eerdmans; Leicester: Inter-Varsity, 1980.

Martin, Roger. *R. A. Torrey, Apostle of Certainty*. Murfreesboro, Tenn.: Sword of the Lord, 1970.

Mascall, E. L. *Christ, the Christian and the Church*. London: Longmans & Green, 1956.

Matthews, Arnold G., ed. *The Savoy Declaration of Faith and Order, 1658.* London: Independent, 1958.

Moody, D. L. "The New Birth." In *The Best of D. L. Moody: Sixteen Sermons by the Great Evangelist,* edited by Wilbur M. Smith. Chicago: Moody, 1971.

Morris, Leon. *The Gospel According to John.* New International Commentary on the New Testament. Grand Rapids: Eerdmans, 1971.

Nash, Gary B., and Thomas Frazier, eds. *The Private Side of American History: Readings in Everyday Life.* 3d ed. 2 vols. New York: Harcourt Brace, 1983.

Neil, William. *The Acts of the Apostles.* New Century Bible. London: Oliphants, 1973.

Noll, Mark A. "Edwards, Jonathan." In *Evangelical Dictionary of Theology,* edited by Walter A. Elwell. Grand Rapids: Baker, 1984.

———. "Pietism." In *Evangelical Dictionary of Theology,* edited by Walter A. Elwell. Grand Rapids: Baker, 1984.

———. "Puritanism." In *Evangelical Dictionary of Theology,* edited by Walter A. Elwell. Grand Rapids: Baker, 1984.

Occasional Service Book. Philadelphia: Fortress, 1962.

Odeberg, Hugo. *The Fourth Gospel: Interpreted in Its Relation to Contemporaneous Religious Currents in Palestine and the Hellenistic-Oriental World.* Uppsala, 1929; Chicago: Argonaut, 1968.

Owen, John. *Pneumatologia: A Discourse Concerning the Holy Spirit.* In *The Works of John Owen,* edited by William H. Goold. Vol. 3. Edinburgh: Banner of Truth, 1966.

Perkins, William. *The Work of William Perkins.* Edited by Ian Breward. Appleford, England: Sutton Courtenay, 1970.

Pettit, Norman. *The Heart Prepared: Grace and Conversion in Puritan Spiritual Life.* New Haven: Yale University, 1966.

Philip, Dietrich. *Enchiridion.* Translated by A. B. Kolb. Elkhart, Ind.: Mennonite, 1910.

Piepkorn, Arthur C. "The Lutheran Understanding of Baptism." In *Lutherans and Catholics in Dialogue I–III,* edited by Paul C. Empie and T. Austin Murphy. Minneapolis: Augsburg, 1974.

Pierce, R. H. "George Whitefield and His Critics." Ph.D. diss., Princeton University, 1961.

Ridderbos, Herman. *The Coming of the Kingdom.* Edited by Raymond O. Zorn. Translated by H. de Jongste. Philadelphia: Presbyterian and Reformed, 1962.

———. *Paul: An Outline of His Theology.* Translated by John Richard DeWitt. Grand Rapids: Eerdmans, 1975.

Sattler, Gary R. *God's Glory, Neighbor's Good: A Brief Introduction to the Life and Writings of August Hermann Francke.* Chicago: Covenant, 1982.

Schaff, Philip. *Creeds of Christendom.* 3 vols. New York: Harper; London: Hodder & Stoughton, 1877.

Schmid, Heinrich. *The Doctrinal Theology of the Evangelical Lutheran Church.* 3d ed. rev. Translated by Charles A. Hay and Henry E. Jacobs. Minneapolis: Augsburg, 1961.

Schmidt, Martin. *John Wesley: A Theological Biography*. 2 vols. Translated by Norman P. Goldhawk. New York: Abingdon, 1962–1963.

Schrotenboer, Paul G. "Emil Brunner." In *Creative Minds in Contemporary Theology*, edited by Philip E. Hughes. Grand Rapids: Eerdmans, 1969.

Schweizer, Eduard. *The Good News According to Matthew*. Translated by David E. Green. Atlanta: John Knox, 1975.

Smeaton, George. *The Doctrine of the Holy Spirit*. Edinburgh: T. & T. Clark, 1882; London: Banner of Truth, 1958.

Smith, Henry Boynton. *System of Christian Theology*. 4th ed. Edited by William S. Karr. New York: A. C. Armstrong, 1890.

Snyder, Howard. "Pietism, Moravianism and Methodism as Renewal Movements: A Comparative and Thematic Study." Ph.D. diss., University of Notre Dame, 1983.

Spener, Philipp Jakob. *Pia desideria*. Translated by Theodore G. Tappert. Philadelphia: Fortress, 1964.

Spurgeon, Charles Haddon. *The Full Harvest*. Rev. ed. Edinburgh: Banner of Truth, 1973.

Stott, John R. W. *The Epistles of John*. Tyndale New Testament Commentary. Grand Rapids: Eerdmans; Leicester: Inter-Varsity, 1983.

Strong, Augustus Hopkins. *Systematic Theology*. Rochester: E. R. Andrews, 1886; Philadelphia: Judson, 1960.

Sunday, William, and Helen Sunday. Papers. Billy Graham Center Archives, Wheaton, Illinois.

Tappert, Theodore G., ed. *The Book of Concord: The Confessions of the Evangelical Lutheran Church*. Philadelphia: Fortress, 1959.

Theodore of Mopsuestia. *Commentary of Theodore of Mopsuestia on the Lord's Prayer and on the Sacraments of Baptism and the Eucharist*. Edited by A. Mingana. Cambridge: W. Heffer, 1933.

Thomas Aquinas. *Summa theologiae*. New York: McGraw-Hill; Cambridge: Blackfriars, 1964–.

Thompson, J. A. *The Book of Jeremiah*. New International Commentary on the Old Testament. Grand Rapids: Eerdmans, 1980.

Toon, Peter. *The Development of Doctrine in the Church*. Grand Rapids: Eerdmans, 1978.

———. *Evangelical Theology 1833–1856: A Response to Tractarianism*. Atlanta: John Knox; London: Marshall, Morgan and Scott, 1979.

———. *God's Statesman: The Life and Work of Dr. John Owen*. Exeter: Paternoster, 1971.

———. *Heaven and Hell: A Biblical and Theological Overview*. Nashville: Thomas Nelson, 1986.

———. *Justification and Sanctification*. Westchester, Ill.: Crossways, 1983.

———. *Puritans and Calvinism*. Swengel, Pa.: Reiner, 1973.

Torrey, R. A. *What the Bible Teaches*. Chicago: Revell, 1898.

Troutman, Charles H. *Seven Pillars: Distinctives of Evangelical Student Witness*. Downers Grove, Ill.: Inter-Varsity Christian Fellowship, 1962.

———. Papers. Billy Graham Center Archives, Wheaton, Illinois.

Wacker, Grant. *Augustus H. Strong and the Dilemma of Historical Consciousness*. Macon, Ga.: Mercer University Press, 1985.

Walker, Williston, ed. *The Creeds and Platforms of Congregationalism*. Philadelphia: Pilgrim, 1960.

Weddle, David L. *The Law as Gospel: Revival and Reform in the Theology of Charles G. Finney*. Metuchen, N.J.: Scarecrow, 1985.

Wendel, François. *Calvin: The Origins and Development of His Religious Thought*. Translated by Philip Mairet. London: Collins, 1965.

Wesley, John. *The Journal of the Rev. John Wesley*. Edited by Nehemiah Curnock. London: Epworth, 1938.

———. *A Plain Account of Christian Perfection*. London: Epworth, 1968.

———. *Sermons on Several Occasions*. London: Epworth, 1954.

"The Wheaton Declaration." Papers and booklets. Billy Graham Center Archives, Wheaton, Illinois.

Whitaker, E. C., ed. *Documents of the Baptismal Liturgy*. London: SPCK, 1960.

Whitefield, George. *George Whitefield's Journals*. Rev. ed. London: Banner of Truth, 1960.

———. *Sermons on Important Subjects*. New ed. Edited by Joseph Smith. London: W. Baynes, 1825.

———. *Sermons on Important Subjects*. . . . London, 1828.

Williams, George Huntston. *The Radical Reformation*. London: Secker & Warburg, 1962.

———, ed. *Spiritual and Anabaptist Writers*. Philadelphia: Westminster; London: SCM, 1957.

Wolff, Hans Walter. *Anthropology of the Old Testament*. Translated by Margaret Kohl. Philadelphia: Fortress; London: SCM, 1974.

Wood, Arthur Skevington. *The Inextinguishable Blaze: Spiritual Renewal and Advance in the Eighteenth Century*. Grand Rapids: Eerdmans; London: Paternoster, 1960.

World Congress on Evangelism at Berlin (1966). Papers and booklets. Billy Graham Center Archives, Wheaton, Illinois.

Zimmerli, Walther. *Ezekiel: A Commentary on the Book of the Prophet Ezekiel*. Edited by Frank Moore Cross and Klaus Baltzer. Translated by Ronald E. Clements. Philadelphia: Fortress, 1983.

Scripture Index

Genesis

1:3–5—44
1:26–27—44
1:27—55
2:7—19, 55

Judges

3:9–10—61
6:34—61
11:29—61
16:20—61

1 Samuel

16:13—22

Psalms

2:7—22, 29, 56
32:1—74, 75
51:10—56
89:20–21—22

Isaiah

1:16—74
1:16–20—72
2:1–5—54
9:2–7—51

11:1–5—17
11:1–9—51
11:2—22
42:1—22
42:1–4—17
44:3—107
49:5–13—51
49:14–26—54
53:11—22
54—54
60:16—41
61:1—17, 22
63:11–12—22
65:17—51, 52
65:17–25—53
66:13—40
66:22—51, 52

Jeremiah

31:31–34—56–57, 58
31:33—107
32:37–41—57–58

Ezekiel

11:14–21—58
11:19–20—58
36:22–32—58

36:25–26—45
36:25–27—22, 58
36:26—107
36:27—21, 47, 107
37—14
37:1–14—58–59
37:9—19
37:14—17, 21
39:29—47
47:1–12—22

Daniel

7:13—50

Joel

2:28—107
2:28–29—47, 61
2:28–32—20
3:18—41

Zechariah

13:1—22

Matthew

1:18–20—17
3:11—18, 45, 107

199

3:13–17—21
3:15—22
3:16—17
4:1—17
5:13—86
8:11—51
10:20—18
10:34–39—112
12:24–32—18
19:16–30—49
19:28—52, 181, 185, 186
19:28–29—50
22:1–14—51
22:14—43
24:29—52
24:35—52
25:31–46—50
26:28—63
28:19—182

Mark

1:8—18, 45
1:9–11—21
1:10—17, 22
1:12—17
1:14–15—37–38
2:5–12—63
3:20–30—18
10:13–16—38, 93, 95
10:15—41
10:38—22
10:45—63
13:11—18
13:28—38
16:15—97
16:16—99, 102, 112, 113, 169

Luke

1:15—17
1:35—17
1:41—17
1:67—17
2:25–27—17
2:34—112
3:16—18, 45
3:21–22—21
3:22—17
4:1—18
4:14—18
11:13—18, 48

11:14–23—18
12:12—18
12:50—22
13:3—181
13:29—51
14:16–24—51
19:10—73
21:25—52
22:28–30—50
24:49—18, 19

John

1:1–18—24
1:4—31
1:11–13—24
1:12—26, 107
1:13—68, 107
1:29—34
1:32–33—18
1:33—19, 45, 107
2—17
3—72
3:1–8—26
3:1–15—13–15
3:3—27, 31, 68, 107
3:3–6—127
3:5—27–28, 31, 45, 68, 107, 112, 176
3:5–6—107
3:5–8—19, 59
3:7—28, 59, 68, 162, 178, 181
3:8—164
3:11–12—59
3:13—22
3:14—28
3:14–15—16
3:15–16—31
3:34–35—19
4:10–14—31, 187
4:14—32
5:21—32
5:24—32
5:26—31
6:27—46
6:35—31, 187
6:48—31
6:62—22
6:63—19, 31, 32, 127
6:68—31
7:37–38—31

7:37–39—19, 187
7:38—32
7:38–39—107
8:12—31, 32
8:31–32—32
8:32—106
8:47—107
8:51—32
10:10—32
10:28—120
11:25—31
12:34—28
12:35—32
12:46—32
13:34—32
14–16—19, 20, 30
14:6—31
14:15—32
14:16—19
14:16–18—19
14:21—32
14:25–26—19
15:5—119
15:9–10—32
15:26—19
16:7–11—19, 30, 186
16:8–11—26, 127, 128
16:12–15—19
17—31
17:19—32
17:23—32
20:17—22
20:22—19, 48

Acts

1—20
1:4–5—19
1:5—45
2—19, 20, 48
2:4—67
2:32–33—20
2:38—23, 40, 161, 169, 187
2:38–39—21
2:38b–39—48
2:39—104
3:19—161, 187
3:19–21—51
4:8—67
4:31—67
5:32—161, 187

Subject Index

Adoption, reception of the Spirit of, 45
Alexander of Hales, 81
Alive, being made, 43
Amyraldus (Moise Amyraut), 130, 148
Anabaptists, 106–07
Anglican service of baptism, 95–96, 114–17
Apocalyptic literature, 50
Aquinas, Thomas, 81, 84–86
Arminianism, 118–20
Athanasius, 73
Atonement, universal, 119
Augsburg Confession, 96–97
Augustine, 81–83, 96, 113
Awakening: First, 144; Second, 167–73

Baptism: by immersion (Disciples of Christ), 169; of Jesus, 17, 21–23; Pauline view of the Spirit and, 46–47; and regeneration, 124–25; ritual of, 188–89. *See also* Baptismal regeneration; Infant baptism
Baptismal regeneration, 78, 79, 81–82, 84, 85, 87–88, 91, 103, 108–17, 176, 180
Baptism in water. *See* Water, baptism in

Baptism with the Spirit. *See* Spirit: baptism in (with) the
Barnes, Albert, 130
Barrett, C. K., 25–26
Bath of regeneration, 76
Beasley-Murray, George R., 180, 185
Belief in Jesus and new birth, 25–26
Berlin congress, 180–81
Beza, Theodore, 118
Birth from God, concept of, 24–42
Book of Common Prayer, 95
"Born of God," 24–42
Brunner, Heinrich Emil, 133–35
Bucer, Martin, 91–92

Calling, effectual, 42–43, 118–35, 140
Calvin, John, 92, 94–95, 97–98, 103–05, 123
Cambridge Platform, 143
Campbell, Alexander, 168–70
Camp meetings, 167
Cartwright, Peter, 167
Chalmers, Thomas, 127
Change of state, regeneration as a, 170
Charismatic movement, 47. *See also* Spirit: baptism in (with) the

Lampe, G. W. H., 46–47
Lasher, George W., 176
Latin West, 78–88
Lausanne Covenant, 182
Law, William, 164
Life, new, 32
Light, 31–32
Love, 32, 35, 164; divine, 147–48; of God, 45
Luther, Martin, 86, 90–91, 93, 101–03
Lutheran service of baptism, 114–17

McGready, James, 167
Magdeburg rite, 86–87
Mascall, E. L., 186
Medieval interpretations, 84–88
Melanchthon, Philipp, 96
Mennonite Confession, 106–07
Moody, Dwight Lyman, 173–75
Moral ability, 130, 148
Moravians. See Zinzendorf, Nicholas Ludwig von

Natural ability, 130, 148
New covenant, 56–61
New creation, 44, 51, 52–53, 61
New Hampshire Confession, 133
New heavens. See Cosmic regeneration
New man, 179
New School theology, 130–33

Ockenga, Harold J., 180
Odeberg, Hugo, 28
Old covenant, regeneration under the, 59–61
Old School Presbyterians, 131
Old Testament roots of the doctrine of regeneration, 55–61
One-time nature of baptism, 46, 65
Orange, Council of, 83–84
Original sin, 82, 96–97, 98–99, 100, 103, 108–09, 141, 161, 187
Owen, John, 126, 141–43

Pajonism, 129
Patristic interpretations, 71–84
Pelagians, 82–83, 96–97
Pentecost, 20
Perfection, 34, 164–65
Perkins, William, 119, 137–41
Perseverance of the saints, 122
Personal renewal, 37–48, 56–58, 67

Petersen, Richard Møller, 180
Philips, Obbe, 106
Pietism, 136, 137, 148–56, 168
Pouring of the love of God, 45
Predestination, 81, 118–21, 124. See also Election
Preparationism, 141
Princeton divines, 131
Puritanism, 136–48

Radicals. See Anabaptists
Rebirth, concept of, 24–42
Reductionism, 168
Reformation, 89–107
Reformed theology, 118–35. See also Calvin, John
Regeneration, 85; cosmic, 49–54, 58, 67–68, 141, 181, 185
Release of the Spirit, 187
Remonstrance, 119–20
Renewal, individual, 37–48, 56–58, 67
Renewing grace, 138
Repentance, 62–63, 104
Restraining grace, 138
Resurrection, 32, 43–44, 51
Revivalists, 130, 156–82
Righteousness, 33
Ritual, 189
Roman Catholic teaching, 108–14

Sacraments, 85, 86, 88, 97, 98, 99, 111
Sanctification, 66–67, 98
Saumur, 129–30, 148
Saving grace, 146, 148
Savoy Declaration, 126, 143
Scots Confession, 98–99
Scottish divinity, 127–31
Sealing by the Holy Spirit, 46
Second Awakening, 167–73
Second work of grace, 165
Self-reliance, 168
Servant, Suffering, 22
Sin, 34, 36; original. See Original sin
Smeaton, George, 127–30
Smith, Henry Boynton, 131–33
Sons of God, 25
Special grace, 146
Spener, Philipp Jakob, 148–51
Spirit: baptism in (with) the, 21, 23, 45, 47–48, 176–77, 187; as divine love, 147–48; fillings with the, 67; indwelling of the, 21, 46–48, 67; Jesus